HOLLYWOOD'S
CANADA

Pierre Berton

★

HOLLYWOOD'S CANADA

★

The Americanization of Our National Image

★

McClelland and Stewart Limited

ISBN: 0-7710-1223-3

The Canadian Publishers
McClelland and Stewart Limited
25 Hollinger Road, Toronto

Endpapers by John Richmond

Printed and bound in Canada by
T. H. Best Printing Company Limited,
Don Mills, Ontario

Contents

INTRODUCTION: **The Movies and the Image**   11

PART ONE: **The Great Woods and the Big Snows**   13
1. From Rin-Tin-Tin to Rose Marie   15
2. God's Country and other euphemisms   19
3. I left my heart in the Saskatchewan Arctic   30
4. Hot-blooded romance in the land of snows   47
5. "Safe from the evils of civilization . . ."   52

PART TWO: **Primitive Passions in the Untamed North**   73
1. The old-fashioned, red-blooded look   75
2. Happy-go-lucky rogues in tuques   79
3. "The volatile blood of the French and the crafty daring of the Indians . . ."   86
4. "Savage tribes . . . ready to explode . . ."   101

PART THREE: **Perils of the Royal Mounted**   109
1. "Broken hearted, he carries out orders . . ."   111
2. "Fights, thrills, fast riding, gunplay . . ."   119
3. Louis B. Mayer always gets his man   123
4. Trials of a technical director   139
5. The gospel according to DeMille   146

PART FOUR: **Canadian Co-operation, Hollywood Style**   167
1. The seduction of Donald Gordon   169
2. The tribulations of Constable Pedley   175
3. Red-wing orioles from Canada   186

PART FIVE: **It Wasn't Like That At All**   201
   1.   The blurring of the image   203
   2.   How Randolph Scott saved the Northwest   207
   3.   "Love and Lynch Law where it's 'Five Shirts Cold'"   215
   4.   "Too many deeds of Yankee valor"   230
   5.   Peace and fishing, billions of pine trees, frozen waste   236

ACKNOWLEDGEMENTS   241
PHOTO CREDITS   243
APPENDIX   245
NOTES   271
INDEX   289

Illustrations

This Is Canada?   33-40
Passionate French-Canadians   57 61
Hollywood Indians   65-72
The Wicked Half-Breed   89-96
Movie Mounties   129-136
Myth and Reality   153-160
The Blurred Image   193-200
Transplanted Westerns   217-224

Books by Pierre Berton

The Royal Family
The Mysterious North
Klondike
Just Add Water and Stir
Adventures of a Columnist
Fast, Fast, Fast Relief
The Big Sell
The Comfortable Pew
The Cool, Crazy, Committed World of the Sixties
The Smug Minority
The National Dream
The Last Spike
Drifting Home
Hollywood's Canada

PICTURE BOOKS
The New City (with Henri Rossier)
Remember Yesterday
The Great Railway

ANTHOLOGIES
Great Canadians
The Centennial Food Guide (with Janet Berton)
Historic Headlines

FOR YOUNGER READERS
The Golden Trail
The Secret World of Og

In memory of
GEORGE FEYER
Budapest, 1921 – Hollywood, 1907

Introduction: The Movies and the Image

The first movie that ever made me really mad was a picture about the Klondike gold rush, *The Far Country*, starring James Stewart. I saw it in 1954, when I was working on a book about the same subject, and it made me mad because it was so *wrong*. It had very little to do with the real Klondike and even less to do with the real Canada, although it was supposed to be about both. It was a shoot-'em-up American western, which helped perpetuate the easy assumption that there is no essential difference between Canadians and Americans. As a student of the Klondike I knew differently and I wrote a long letter of complaint to the director – something I'd never done in my life before and have never done since. He didn't reply.

I assumed that this movie was in a class by itself, a bad picture by a scriptwriter and a director who hadn't done their homework. It didn't occur to me then that it might be part of a long tradition of moviemaking that stretches back to the dawn of the silent era, in which Canadians on the screen have been made to look and act like Americans – even to the extent of electing a US marshal to bring the law to British territory, as was done in *The Far Country*.

Many years later when I was working on another book – this one about the building of our first transcontinental railway – I screened another movie, *Canadian Pacific*. This, too, turned out to be an American western, which had nothing whatsoever to do with the history it was supposed to portray. You couldn't get mad at that picture; it was just too far-fetched: two-gun Randolph Scott, single-handedly building the CPR. A million laughs!

Not long after that I happened to catch *North West Mounted Police* on television. This time I got mad at myself because I realized I'd seen it before at the age of twenty and had enjoyed it. Those were the days when, as a product of the Canadian educational system, I didn't know much about our own past. I was even stupid enough to believe that the Métis had the Gatling gun in the Saskatchewan Rebellion of 1885, because Mr. Cecil B. DeMille said they did.

So I got to wondering about the movies: if a university graduate had accepted the DeMille version of our history, how many others had? And how many Hollywood pictures had blurred our national identity to the point where we didn't seem to have any? How many movies had Hollywood made about Canada, anyway? Were they all like these? Do the pictures about Canada that millions still see on television have a common ancestry? What kind of image do they project?

The results of my inquiry are to be found in this book. It covers more than half a century, during which time Hollywood made close to six hundred movies about Canada, before the fashion for this kind of picture died a natural death. It covers big movies and it covers little movies. It covers thirteen-part serials, one-reel silents, Technicolor epics, and B-grade quickies designed for the bottom half of double bills in small-town picture palaces.

It looks not at quality but at content. It's not concerned with intent but with effect. If Hollywood brain-washed its audiences into accepting its own version of Canada, it doesn't really matter that the process was accidental. Nor does the end result have anything to do with whether or not the movies in question were frivolous, cheaply produced, melo-dramatic, badly written, or masterpieces of the moviemakers' art.

What does matter is the kind of image Hollywood was showing to the world and to Canadians. What impression of the Canadian character, the Canadian heritage, and the Canadian environment would a moviegoer in Liverpool, Little Rock, or even Langley Prairie have, after seeing a number of these pictures? Were they in any sense "distinctively Canadian" – to use that most wistful of nationalistic phrases?

For the *only* consistent impression of us that outsiders have received in this century has come from the motion picture. Books, newspapers, magazines, radio, and television have made scarcely any impact beyond our own borders. It is the movies that have projected our image to the world and also, to a considerable extent, to ourselves. And by "movies" I don't mean the earnest and often brilliant documentaries of the National Film Board. I mean the commercial pictures that Hollywood made, scores of which are still being seen on smaller screens.

If tourists arrive at the border on a hot summer's day loaded down with furs and skis – and they have – it is because of what the movies told them about Canada. If Americans keep telling us "you're the same as we are" – and they do – it is because the movies have convinced them of that fact. If Europeans are baffled when they reach our shores to find that most of us live in cities – and they are – it is because the movies have misled them. And if Canadians continue to hold the belief that there is no such thing as a national identity – and who can deny that many hold it? – it is because the movies have frequently blurred, distorted, and hidden that identity under a celluloid mountain of misconceptions.

12

PART ONE

The Great Woods and the Big Snows

1: From Rin-Tin-Tin to Rose Marie

The year is 1907 and the month is September. In the cramped Nickelodeon – its name might have been Bijou Dream, Nickolette, Pictorium, or Jewel (8,000 such moving picture houses had already opened in North America) – about one hundred patrons are squirming on hard chairs awaiting the newest production of the American Mutoscope and Biograph Company. Urchins scramble about the aisles hawking popcorn, horehound drops, and bottles of sarsaparilla. The ladies, obeying the command of the hand-coloured slides, have deferentially unpinned their hats. The projector has been repaired at last, the piano begins to tinkle, and now the whistling and stamping dies away as the little square screen flickers into life and the main title appears: *An Acadian Elopement.*

That naïve one-reeler was the first story-film made about life north of the border as seen through foreign eyes. But for the next half-century, American motion picture companies, which we lump together under the generic title "Hollywood," would make hundreds more. Some of the greatest stars of the era would play in them, some of the best directors would direct them, and millions of moviegoers, still munching popcorn and often stamping their feet, would enjoy them and passively accept the view the movies projected of a country most of them would never visit.

The most popular names of the silent era appeared above and below the titles of many of these pictures. Lon Chaney, Victor McLaglen, H. B. Warner, Lewis Stone, Jack Holt, Dustin Farnum, Wallace Beery, Ben Lyon, Ed Wynn, John Gilbert, Warner Baxter, and Lionel Barrymore, together with leading ladies of the calibre of Joan Crawford, Dolores del Rio, Lupe Velez, Clara Bow, Colleen Moore, Renée Adorée, Mae Busch, Billie Dove, and Mae Marsh, all portrayed Canadians in Canadian settings or pseudo-Canadian settings.

The four great cowboy stars of the silents, William S. Hart, Tom Mix, Hoot Gibson, and Ken Maynard, played leading roles in about a dozen Canadian westerns. They were followed in the sound era by their singing counterparts, Gene Autry and Roy Rogers. The talkies brought a roster of new names to Hollywood's Canada: Clark Gable, Robert Montgomery,

James Stewart, George Brent, William Boyd, Randolph Scott, Dennis Morgan, Ray Milland, James Cagney, Errol Flynn, Dick Powell, Gary Cooper, Paul Muni, Charles Boyer, Rock Hudson, Montgomery Clift, Tyrone Power, Alan Ladd, and another bevy of leading ladies: Shelley Winters, Madeleine Carroll, Greer Garson, Anne Baxter, Claire Trevor, Loretta Young, Ann Sheridan, Myrna Loy, Shirley Temple, Paulette Goddard, and Linda Darnell.

Sandow the Strong Man appeared in a movie with a Canadian setting. So did Rin-Tin-Tin, Rex the Wonder Horse, Bela Lugosi, and Mrs. Vernon Castle, the finest ballroom dancer of her day. Directors whose names are enshrined in the Hollywood pantheon had a hand in many of these pictures – men of the calibre of D. W. Griffith, John Ford, King Vidor, Frank Borzage, Raoul Walsh, W. S. Van Dyke, William Wyler, Michael Curtiz, William Wellman, Cecil B. DeMille, Otto Preminger, Mervyn LeRoy, and Alfred Hitchcock.

Then why are these movies so unmemorable? If you ask the average Canadian to name a Hollywood film about his country, he'll automatically come up with *Rose Marie* – the one in which Jeanette MacDonald keeps calling for Nelson Eddy. If you press him, he'll scratch his head and mention *Saskatchewan* with Alan Ladd, a long-standing Canadian joke because the movie's all about Alberta. He might recall a few others he's seen on television but not very many.

Try this test on a friend: ask him how many movies he thinks Hollywood has made about Canada. I'll bet he says twenty, because that's the answer I generally get when I ask the question. The actual number astonishes almost everybody: since 1907, American film companies have produced 575 motion pictures in which the plot has been set entirely or mainly in Canada. That figure does not include documentary films, foreign-produced films, international co-productions, or films made by Canadian companies.

Then why have we forgotten all but a handful? You'd think we'd be more likely to remember films about our own country than those about Africa, India, Mexico, or the American wild west. But I don't think there's much argument that *Stagecoach, Gunga Din, The Lives of a Bengal Lancer, Beau Geste, The African Queen, Lawrence of Arabia, Casablanca, The Treasure of the Sierra Madre, Union Pacific, Shane, High Noon,* and *The Wild Bunch,* to choose only a dozen, are greener in the minds of Canadians than all but three or four movies having to do with their own land.

One of the reasons is that most of the movies made about Canada have been pretty awful. There is a sameness to them – a monotony of background, of character, and of style, unrelieved by comedy or commitment. The classic studies of the American cinema fail to list any films with Canadian subject matter, except *Nanook of the North,* a documentary beyond the scope of this study. Of 575 movies, not a single one deserves to be called great, and I doubt if you'd need the fingers of both hands to list those that might be labelled good, for late-night television viewers.

Hollywood, blinded no doubt by its own view of Canada as a land of snow, mountains, and pine trees, has treated almost every picture with deadly seriousness. All the early silent movies were melodramatic, but the ones made with a Canadian setting seem to me to be more melodramatic than most – the villains more villainous, the heroines purer, and the heroes (Mounties, of course) nobler. This great outpouring of melodrama was unrelieved by the kind of comedy that Mack Sennett and Hal Roach were turning out in urban American settings, or by the multiplicity of landscapes and plots that screenwriters were able to find in movies about their own and other countries.

No one can argue that the movies have not introduced Americans to their own land in all its infinite variety. American movie audiences have been able to share a common heritage because so many pictures have been set in Monument Valley, the high Sierras, the painted desert, the Maine coastline, the Mississippi valley, the Florida Everglades, the Tennessee hill country, the redwood forests, and the deep south, not to mention the great cities and the small midwestern towns. But the great majority of movies about Canada, as we are going to see, have had only two backdrops – the Rocky Mountains or an anonymous wilderness. And the plots, for the most part, like the "Canadian" characterizations, have been just as consistently predictable. There was a sameness to the melodramas of the silent years and to the B pictures of the thirties, forties, and fifties that made many of them almost interchangeable.

Even the so-called big pictures, with a few exceptions, are easily forgettable. Something seemed to happen to American directors and actors when they set out to make a picture about Canada. One of Shirley Temple's movies, *Susannah of the Mounties,* was "Canadian" through and through but the critics agreed that its pedestrian plot and its hackneyed situations made it her worst. The last of several pictures that Greer Garson made with Walter Pidgeon, *Scandal at Scourie,* was set in turn-of-the-century Ontario. It was a weak movie – the poorest of the cycle – and Pidgeon felt that it should never have been made.

Something happened to Paul Muni when he attempted the role of the explorer, Pierre Radisson, in a picture about the founding of the Hudson's Bay Company. He could play Émile Zola, the Frenchman, with ease and with distinction but the stock role of the happy-go-lucky French-Canadian was too much for him. He could not rise above the clichéd characterization which had been the hallmark of Canadian outdoor movies since the beginning. He always regretted that he had accepted the part.

Two of Hollywood's most memorable epics have been *The Iron Horse* and *Union Pacific*, both dealing with the building of the first transcontinental railroad across the United States. One of the *least* memorable was Hollywood's version of the building of the Canadian Pacific. But then no American director could be expected to feel for this country the commitment that John Ford, for example, felt for the American west or that D. W. Griffith felt for the American south. When *Canadian Pacific* was made, the director's heart wasn't in it: to him it was just another western.

Obviously, Hollywood felt that Canada was somehow different from the United States – otherwise why move cameras into Canadian or pseudo-Canadian settings? The moviemakers wanted to give a different perspective to an otherwise routine story. But the differences that Hollywood showed were always superficial ones: instead of desert sands, the movie audiences got snowy wastes; instead of typhoons, thundering avalanches. Jungles became pine forests; American sheriffs were transformed into mounted policemen; Mexican villains switched accents and became French-Canadian bad guys. I don't think Hollywood had any particular duty to show the real Canada any more than it had a duty to show the real Himalayan frontier or the real Sahara. It didn't take Canada seriously, but then why should it? Its business was fantasy, not education, and its Canadian fantasies made money just as the others did.

That kind of fantasy is no longer acceptable to a new kind of film audience. Hollywood movies about America and the rest of the world began to grow up in the late 1950's when television stole the mass market. But Hollywood movies about Canada simply dried up. In the so-called Golden Age of the motion picture, from 1931 to 1951, American producers made 108 movies with Canadian settings. In the twenty years that followed they made only thirty-one. Now they don't make any. Hollywood's Canada continues on television but not on the wide screen. The task of making films about Canada has been left at last to the people best able to make them – ourselves.

2: God's Country and other euphemisms

Canada was never Hollywood's favourite word. In fact the moviemakers went out of their way *not* to use it. In scores of cases, the only way you knew a movie was about Canada was when a Mountie or a French-Canadian trapper hove into view.

Take a look at the titles: the words Canada and Canadian scarcely ever appeared. Instead, every possible euphemism was used to get around those dreadful words. But everybody knew, when a picture came out using code words like Northwest or Big Snows or Great Woods, that the setting was north of the border. More than 170 movies bore that kind of code in their titles; only eight dared to use Canada or Canadian.

Code Word	Number of Titles
North, Northwest Northern, Northwoods	79
Wild, Wilderness, or Trail	50
Mounties or Mounted	37
Klondike or Yukon	18
Snow	11

Even best-selling Canadian classics were carefully de-Canadianized by the moviemakers. It's been largely forgotten that there was a period in Canadian literary history when certain Canadian novels were in furious demand by an international audience and therefore by the movies. Of the five best-selling Canadian authors of all time, four have had their classic novels transferred to the screen by Hollywood. They are: Ralph Connor, Mazo de la Roche, L. M. Montgomery, and Robert W. Service. Only the work of Stephen Leacock, perhaps the biggest seller of them all, has never been given feature film treatment.

These best sellers were all unmistakably Canadian – a fact that in no sense conspired against their popularity. The first American printing of Ralph Connor's novel The Sky Pilot, for instance, was 250,000 copies. The novel's eventual sales exceeded one million copies.* Hollywood bought it, of course, but then proceeded to de-Canadianize it. The only Canadian reference in the entire picture is to the fact that the Sky Pilot comes from Montreal. Presumably the setting is the Canadian Rockies; but the movie was shot on location at Truckee, California, and the saloons, gun-fights, and even the costumes are those of the American wild west. The major trade reviews didn't even mention the story's Canadian origin but praised

---

*A later Connor novel, The Man from Glengarry, sold five million copies.

the picture as "an exceedingly good western"[1] with a "collection of thrilling punches."[2]

The other big best sellers were given a similar laundering. Service's novel, The Trail of '98, is all about the Klondike gold rush but the only evidence of any Canadian location in the movie is a fleeting shot of a British flag at the summit of the Chilkoot Pass.

The picture made from Mazo de la Roche's prize-winning novel, Jalna, had only three direct references to Canada and a few indirect ones. The characters were shown speaking with English accents, living in a panelled English manor, dressed in English tweeds, indulging in English upper-class slang (meself, old gel) and being waited on by jovial Cockney servants, all of whom knew their place.

The movie version of L. M. Montgomery's classic novel, Anne of Green Gables, did have a few references to Prince Edward Island and an opening scene or two showing the gentle island landscape, but its sequel, Anne of Windy Poplars, was not identifiably Canadian. Except for a single reference to Charlottetown it could just as easily have been made in the American midwest, and there were undoubtedly thousands of movie-goers who thought it was.

The situation has not changed. When Margaret Laurence's important Canadian novel, A Jest of God, was made into the film Rachel, Rachel, the location was changed, for no very good reason, from Manitoba to Maine.

It's a curious kind of attitude, when you think about it: make use of the Canadian classic novels; make use of the Canadian background; make use of the mounted police; but try not to mention Canada. As far as I can tell, ours is the only country that Hollywood treated in this fashion. But then it wasn't as easy to take a novel set in the African jungle or the China seas or the English countryside or a Graustarkian palace and camouflage it to the point where it might have taken place somewhere in America.

Actually, in the very beginning, some pioneer moviemakers exploited the name of Canada in their advertising. There was a kind of vogue for Canadian pictures before the Great War. The country, to most Americans, was almost unknown and therefore exotic.[3] With an entrepreneurial zeal unmatched in later generations, the Canadian Pacific Railway, through its subsidiary, the Canadian Pacific Irrigation Colonization Company, seized on this curiosity about Canada to commission the Edison Company to cross the nation and make a series of movies calculated to encourage immigration. To this end, a special train was placed at the company's disposal to carry the entire cast and technical crew across Canada from Montreal to Victoria, with a side trip on the Sault line. The purpose was:

. . . to show to the struggling farmer through the medium of the moving picture the premium that western Canada offers for home-making and independence to the man of energy, ambition and small capital; to picture the range cattle, fat and happy, roaming the foothills of the mighty Rockies; to tell the piscatorial enthusiast of cool retreats beside rushing streams where the salmon and trout lurk beneath the rock's overhanging shade; to whisper to the sportsman and the hunter of the big and little game skulking the plains or roaming the mountainsides, waiting his coming; to depict to the tourist and traveller the beauties of mountain, wood and valley, prairie, crag and torrent, and the comfort and luxury of modern hotel, train, boat and steamer; to tempt the Alpine climber to further prowess on the great glaciers of central British Columbia . . .[4]

It was the kind of crazy scheme that could either be an unqualified success or a magnificent bust. This one was a success. The Edison Company ground out thirteen one-reel movies about Canada, using locations that ran the gamut from the open prairie to a CPR Princess boat in the Gulf of Georgia. Although the stories are farcical by today's standards, these films, two of which still exist, were among the most authentic made about the Canadian west. The Canadian prairie, for instance, was scarcely ever again shown in a Hollywood movie. The Columbia valley was never to be seen again, either, because Oregon with its big trees was closer to the border. And who has ever bothered to go on location in Strathmore, Alberta, since 1910?

Strathmore was the setting of *An Unselfish Love,* the first CPR film the Edison Company shot. It was a picture designed to boost, not too subtly, the irrigated farmland of the far west. John, the hero, cannot marry the girl he loves because her tyrant of a father prefers a wealthier suitor. Dejected, John boards the CPR train for Strathmore, where after a good deal of ploughing and harrowing he proceeds to grow incredibly rich, building for himself a prairie mansion complete with a handsome library and a marble bust of Beethoven, the status symbol of the period. A Strathmore spinster of uncertain years falls for the handsome Toronto-nian and demonstrates her affection by forcing bunches of flowers on him at every opportunity, a gesture which he accepts with ill concealed distaste. Meanwhile, back in the east his erstwhile sweetheart, Mabel, is the subject of a cunningly wicked deception by her father, who obviously doesn't believe that *anybody* can get rich in Strathmore. He destroys Mabel's letters to the west and even goes so far as to insert in the local paper a notice to the effect that John is marrying a prairie girl. The camera registers pique on Mabel's face at the news of this betrayal, whereupon the old man, who has been hiding behind the staircase, produces with a flourish an alternate suitor, pudgy and top-hatted: an obvious member of the Toronto stock exchange.

In Strathmore, John, framed by his valuable bust of Beethoven, is shown gazing at the wedding invitation, stunned. Heartbroken, he begins to compose a letter to Mabel when in comes the love-sick spinster with more flowers. John, who can't stand her or the flowers, beats a hasty retreat. In his absence she reads the letter and, grasping the situation in a trice, rushes to the station and boards a speeding CPR special for the east. There she shakes some sense into Mabel, who escapes from her father's home by a ladder and, again thanks to the CPR, heads west as fast as the train will carry her.

Into John's palatial prairie home once more comes the unselfish spinster, clutching this time a bouquet of roses. John, his success turned to ashes, dashes the posies angrily from her grasp. Struggling with her emotions – for her heart is broken – she nonetheless summons his true love from behind the door. Again he feels the touch of a woman's hand on his shoulder. What! *More* flowers? He brushes the hand aside and then, turning, realizes it is Mabel. Rapture, joy, and gratitude are registered as the old maid, brushing a tear from her eye, slowly turns away and the picture fades to black.

The movies have changed since those days, but it is important to know – especially in the light of what follows – that this was exactly the kind of picture the audience loved. It's safe to say that when *An Unselfish Love* was shown there wasn't a dry eye in the local Bijou. Moving Picture World reserved its strongest praise for this movie, declaring that its dramatic qualities had "seldom been surpassed." The review called it "an extraordinary production, deserving of an indefinite run."[5]

The same review made another point: "The educational value of the picture must not be overlooked." The scenes at Strathmore "afford a clear impression of . . . the manner of living and the marvellous agricultural development now in progress there." *An Unselfish Love* was followed by a dozen more CPR films, all of them photographed by Edison's prize-winning pioneer cameraman, Henry Cronjager, then considered the ablest technician in the field. Since later American productions confined themselves for Canadian locations almost exclusively to the Banff-Jasper area, the audiences of 1910 were probably given a more varied view of Canada in this baker's dozen of one-reelers than in any movies since.

After 1914 the moviemakers' view of Canada became more cynical. When the Kalem Company went on location to the Island of Orleans in the St. Lawrence River that year to make an historical movie about Wolfe's conquest of French Canada, some Canadian newspapers claimed that it

This 1921 advertisement doesn't mention Canada, but the code word Northwest, not to mention the Mountie and the villain with the tuque, identify the locale.

James Oliver CURWOOD'S

Drama of the Hudson Bay Country

JAN
OF THE
BIG SNOWS

Directed by Charles M. Seay

All the force of Curwood is dramatically revealed in this "snow picture" of the lonely wastes; a band of strong men protecting a beautiful girl from the tempter from the city. Blizzard-swept settlements; troopers and traders; a woman hovering on the brink of eternity; a husband lost among snows, with a single grave amid the frozen plains.

The well-beloved Curwood stuff; told with power and filled with woesome passion. Ably directed and with a cast that includes Louise Prussing, Warner Richmond, and Richard Neill.

American
RELEASING CORPORATION
In Canada: Canadian Releasing Corporation, Limited

Once again the moviemakers declined to mention Canada in this advertisement, preferring more exotic phrases like "Hudson Bay Country" and "Big Snows."

was actually a German company, using the device of a movie production to establish a secret store of arms and build concealed gunpits. Whether or not that helped to discourage production in Canada I don't know, but the filming of authentic Canadian themes dried up.[6]

Hollywood preferred to stick to that vast, mythical region, never geographically defined, which it invented and called the Northwoods. That was the leading euphemism for Canada in the advertisements, the press sheets, and the reviews of the silent pictures.[7] It wasn't necessary to mention Canada at all if you talked about the Woods, the Northwoods, the Northwest Woods, or the Great Woods. In *The Confession,* the bearded villain who enters a Montana saloon is easily tagged as a Canadian because he says: "I come from the Northwoods." In *God's Country and the Law,* the subtitle tells us "a hunted man came out of the night into the bar of McQueen's Tavern on the edge of the Great Woods."

The phrase instantly conjures up a vision of a vast and virtually impenetrable forest, mysterious and almost enchanted, stretching back forever into the mists of the Unknown. The phrase didn't die with the silent pictures but kept turning up again and again. When Nelson Eddy reported for duty in *Rose Marie,* his superior officer knew what to do with him. "I'm sending you back to the woods," he said.

It was always the woods and never the plains that formed the setting for Hollywood's Mountie movies. The woods were wild; the plains had been tamed by the plough. The plains were American; it was the woods and the forests that related to Canada. One reviewer wrote about "that paradise of the storyteller – the Northwoods"[8] almost as if the Northwoods was a nation unto itself, inhabited by what one piece of promotional literature called "forest people" and "the simple people of the woods."[9] One gets an impression of strange, elfin creatures, flitting among the trees and never emerging into the sunlight.

The "woods story," as it was called, became a distinctive Hollywood genre just after the Great War – "a Canadian woods story . . . the kind that never fails to take well with the public,"[10] as one writer remarked of a 1919 feature. The name stuck. In 1934 one of the first fan letters to reach the mother of the Dionne Quintuplets was addressed simply: "Mrs. Oliva Dionne . . . Northwoods, Canada."

Two other code words for Canada were Northwest and Big Snows. The Northwest could be anywhere in Canada – ranching country in one picture, the St. Lawrence lowlands in another.[11] The Big Snows formed an equally vague geographical entity. The principal characters in *The Courage of Marge O'Doone,* for instance, were described as "people who live up in the big snows."[12] In the eyes of the moviegoing public, Canada seemed to be covered by a kind of perpetual blanket of white – an unbelievably vast drift that began almost at the border and through which the Big Snow People plodded about like the denizens of Lower Slobbovia. A typical plot, from a picture called *From Out of the Big Snows*, gives an idea of the way Canada was seen by the scriptwriters:

> Harris, a young adventurer into the big snows of the Northwest, through an accident becomes a friend of Dr. Brandon, who warns him against his fascination for Marie, woman of the dance hall. He tells him of Jean, her half-breed lover, and that he is a bad man. Harris disregards this and Jean, returning from a trapping expedition, finds Marie in his arms. Concealing his hatred, he contrives a fiendish plan, and in pursuance of this, wins the friendship of Harris. They go on a hunting expedition together and in the dense forest, Jean overpowers his unsuspecting victim and ties him to a tree, leaving him to be devoured by the wolves. Brandon becomes worried over his friend and after a long search finds Harris, just in time to save his life. After recovering from his experience, Harris goes looking for Jean, prepared to shoot on sight. They meet and Harris kills him. Dr. Brandon hides him from the Mounted Police, then sees him safely over the boundary line.[13]

Far-fetched though this early three-reeler sounds, it contains all the elements of the standard Hollywood movie about Canada, elements which would return again and again, not only in the formative period of the black-and-white melodrama but also in later years, when motion pictures dealing with other subjects began to take on a measure of sophistication. Hollywood's Canada has always been a country where man-eating wolves stalked their victims through the Big Snows.

The snow country was also God's Country – another euphemism for Canada. In fact this phrase has appeared just as often in movie titles as the words Canada or Canadian. It was invented by history's most prolific screen contributor, James Oliver Curwood, to describe the unsullied north, an environment held by both Curwood and Hollywood to be untainted by the crass influences of civilization, although rape, murder, theft, lust, greed, passion, violence, and torture seem to have been exploited to the full in almost every reel of every film made about the northland.

Curwood was one of the most remarkable and intriguing figures to dance on the periphery of the Hollywood stage. He was born in 1878 in Owosso, Michigan, and died there forty-nine years later in a log castle he built with profits from his books and films. In that relatively short life he produced an awesome volume of work, most of it about the Canadian north. He laboured twelve hours a day to turn out twenty-six novels. His screen credits were even more prodigious: no fewer than 122 motion pictures have been based on Curwood novels or short stories. A good number were scripted by Curwood himself and some of the films were produced by him. Like his contemporary, the writer Edgar Wallace, he operated with machine-like efficiency, employing three assistants – a reader, a stenographer, and a professional advisor. His reader spent six hours a day soaking up ancient and modern history and another hour telling Curwood what he had read, thus saving the author a lifetime of original reading. Curwood also had a young woman poring through all screenplay announcements and reviews; her job was to keep him in touch with current and past ideas. She checked every one of his plots, and if they bore a resemblance to an idea previously or currently in use Curwood made changes or scrapped the project. His stories, one gathers, were dictated directly to a stenographer at a breakneck pace. No wonder one literary magazine called him "the prize literary hustler on the continent."[14]

For half a century scarcely a year went by without one or more Curwood tales reaching the screen; and yet – and this is the remarkable aspect of Curwood's character – there is not so much as a single phrase in his autobiography, Son of the Forests, touching on these films. He doesn't mention them; it is as if they did not exist; and this in spite of the fact that he himself took crews into the Canadian wilderness to make such movies as *Nomads of the North*. It's small wonder that Ray Long, the editor of Cosmopolitan, described him as "a vastly peculiar man; a personality that invited misunderstanding."[15]

Obviously it was the Canadian north that fascinated Curwood, not the movies made about it. His love affair with it was unique and in no sense accidental, since it was the Canadian government that acted as matchmaker. Curwood is the only American and, as far as I know, the only writer of any nationality to be employed by the Canadian government as an exploratory and descriptive writer. About the same time that the CPR was luring an American motion picture company into the burgeoning west, Ottawa decided to pay Curwood to venture into the north and to write novels about the frontier. He was hired for $1,800 a year plus expenses "to explore the picturesque prairie provinces of the west and then go up into the North to gather material for articles and stories intended to induce settlers into that country."[16] He spent two or three months each year for ten years at this task, during which time he made God's Country a household word.

Whether the Canadian government got value for its money is arguable. Curwood's special vision of Canada coincided with Hollywood's and,

Curwood's name on a movie had box-office appeal. This one was designed for release in the midsummer of 1922 when snow pictures were all the rage.

in fact, had a good deal to do with inspiring Hollywood. When Curwood's *The Alaskan* was filmed in 1924, Hector Charlesworth, the dean of Canadian critics, breathed a sigh of relief in print over the change in locale:

> For one I am glad that Curwood has gone to Alaska . . . and is leaving this Canada of ours alone. Some time ago I was told that the Canadian Pacific Railway and the Canadian National Railways would give a good deal if they could induce Mr. Curwood to leave the name of Canada out of his film dramas or at any rate limit their circulation to this continent. The immense popularity of Curwood films in Great Britain and European countries is one of the gravest handicaps that Canadian emigration agents abroad have had to deal with. Overseas the teaching of geography is an even more perfunctory business than it is with us, and millions of Europeans who have seen the Curwood films imagine that they revealed the general conditions in Canada . . . [17]

Charlesworth spoke too soon. The Curwood mania had only begun. Scores of movies based on Curwood stories were yet to be produced about Canada; pictures about God's Country were still being made in the late 1950's.

The idea that there was a distant and exotic corner of the continent that was the special property of the deity was an appealing one. Variations of the phrase kept turning up in non-Curwood pictures. A good example is the opening subtitle of William S. Hart's *Blue Blazes Rawden* (which borrows liberally from Longfellow):

> This is the forest primeval. . . . The murmuring pines and the hemlocks.
> . . . Into the silence of God's great cathedral. . . .

At this point the audience is treated to a vision of God's great cathedral: the Great Woods of the northwest in a long shot. Then a huge tree topples toward the camera as the title concludes with:

> . . . Man – the despoiler!

But where was this God's Country? A study of the eight God's Country movies leads only to confusion. The original *God's Country and the Woman* was filmed in Bear Valley in the San Fernando Mountains, 9,000 feet above sea level. The scenery was pseudo-Canadian, to say the least, but Moving Picture World's reviewer, Marion Howard, didn't think so: "It did not seem credible that the scenery was not truly Canadian," he wrote, "but actually done in California, which is truly God's Country."[18] The producers did not seem too clear about where God's Country was. The trade synopsis placed it vaguely "away in the timber lands of the North where the purity of women is placed above all else,"[19] wherever that may be.

A second version of the same story, filmed twenty-one years later, managed to confuse everyone. The National Council of Jewish Women, who reported on the suitability of current movies, described it as "a dramatic, interesting story of the Alaskan lumber industry."[20] Daily Variety placed it in "the Canadian wilds."[21] The Hollywood Reporter indicated it was set in "the big timber country of Washington [State]."[22] A viewing of the film, however, makes it clear that the locale is logging country not far from Vancouver.

A 1953 re-make of *Back to God's Country,* starring Rock Hudson, only added to the confusion. The story was set somewhere on the Mackenzie River between the delta and Fort Simpson, but it was not until late in the film that the audience was made to understand that this was *not* God's Country. The wind was shrieking across the snowy wastes. Potential avalanches were poised atop precipices. Ships were trapped in the ice. Wicked men with guns were weaving intricate and evil plots. Rock Hudson was shown desperately trying to get *back* to God's Country, which turned out to be the United States in general and Seattle, Washington, in particular.

It should come as no surprise, then, to learn that when *The Man from God's Country* was made in 1958, it wasn't set in Canada at all but in the American southwest in the bad old days of the railroad, the gunmen, the cowboys, and the tin-horn gamblers, a situation not calculated to make James Oliver Curwood rest easily in his Michigan grave.

3: I left my heart in the Saskatchewan Arctic

At the opening of a film called *Fort Vengeance,* the hero, played by James Craig (a kind of wartime replacement for Clark Gable) is seen fleeing with his brother across the Alberta-Montana border, pursued by a hard-riding posse. The two fugitives make it into the dense forests of Canada in the nick of time. "Notice how big and friendly the trees are," Craig remarks as the two men gallop to freedom.

In Hollywood's eyes Canada was all forest. The Northwoods began at the boundary line and stretched on to the Arctic's rim. As far as the moviemakers were concerned the breadbasket of the world never existed. The golden prairie, rolling off to the big sky, was shown in one motion picture and one only. This was *The Canadian,* the only Hollywood feature-length picture that ever attempted to portray Canadian farming conditions.*

The serious daily newspaper reviewers liked the picture, but the realistic trade paper critics made no bones about the fact that "the story of drab Canadian farm life makes for a rather dull atmosphere."[23] The Prime Minister, Mackenzie King, didn't help either; he protested that it should be re-entitled *The Canadian Pioneer* because the conditions depicted dealt only with the pioneering phase of Canadian life and might easily mislead prospective newcomers.[24]

That marked the beginning and the end of prairie dramas. There would be plenty of cowboys seen in the future pictures but the plains would never again be shown. Even in *Pierre of the Plains,* which was made twice under that title, the plains were never seen. The most recent version, starring John Carroll as Pierre, was filmed in Hollywood's favourite Canadian setting, the Rockies. A small obeisance, however, was made to the prairie country at the opening of the film by having Carroll warble "I left my heart in Saskatchewan" as he rode his horse in the shadow of the towering peaks, accompanied by his drunken Indian guide, Crying Loon.

Saskatchewan has always been one of Hollywood's favourite words, along with Athabasca and Blackfoot. The movie people, however, never seemed sure exactly where Saskatchewan was. Vitagraph made a film in 1911 called *In The Arctic Night,* which was set in "the Saskatchewan country." In this story, a missionary received a call to take up his duties among the Indians and *Eskimos* of Saskatchewan. He is forced to choose between what the trade synopsis called "the Saskatchewan Arctic" and the woman he loves, since her father refuses to allow her to make her home "in such a God forsaken place."[25] The missionary chooses the Arctic which, in this movie, is apparently only a few miles north of Prince Albert.

In 1954 Universal chose the title "Saskatchewan" before it had a story to go with it. As everybody knows, this too was a mountain picture set in what was termed "the Saskatchewan river country," a phrase no Canadian would apply to the Rockies. In the movie, Sergeant O'Rourke, played by Alan Ladd, is forced with other Mounties to evacuate Fort Saskatchewan for Fort Walsh. Although Fort Walsh is in the present province of Saskatchewan, the producer plunked it down in the heart of the Alberta foothills. Thus, instead of cantering across the open prairie, Ladd and his followers were shown riding up and down the sides of mountains until they finally made their way to their destination in a brigade of birchbark canoes.

---

*There is a farming sequence in the British movie, *The Forty-Ninth Parallel.*

31

It seems to have been a Hollywood axiom that the famous riders of the plains should never be shown *on* the plains; they were always portrayed galloping through forests of varying density, barely missing the gigantic sequoias, redwoods, and Ponderosa pines that barred their way, or trotting up the flanks of spectacular peaks in Jasper Park, Lake Tahoe, or Yosemite. The opening subtitle of William S. Hart's *O'Malley of the Mounted* promised, but did not deliver, the prairies: "In the sweeping cattle lands of Canada, grim, scarlet-coated riders carry the Queen's law." Those words, however, were superimposed on a painting of the usual snow-capped mountain. The sweeping cattle lands turned out to be rocky promontories, cliffs, and boulder-strewn mesquite bush country, which bore a remarkable resemblance to the American desert. Thirty-two years later, 20th Century-Fox made *Pony Soldier* with Tyrone Power, also set in the sweeping cattle lands of the Canadian west. The picture was shot in Arizona, which explains why Canadian border country was positively littered with flat-topped mesas.

In Hollywood's Canada the mountains could be anywhere.[26] In *Northern Pursuit*, an Errol Flynn vehicle made in 1943, the west coast of Hudson Bay, which is actually low, drowned land, was shown ringed with snow-capped mountains so treacherous that an avalanche destroyed several of the Nazis who landed there. That mountain range, at least 6,000 feet high, apparently extended across most of Manitoba and Saskatchewan. And the first shot of Nelson Eddy in *Rose Marie*, supposedly in the woods of northern Quebec, showed him at the head of a body of singing Mounties, limned against a range of white-capped peaks.

In the last version of *Rose Marie*, made in 1954, Howard Keel led *his* singing Mounties through a forest of Ponderosa pines. The pine has always been Hollywood's favourite Canadian tree – in fact very nearly its only Canadian tree. The Ponderosa was its favourite pine tree, a massive, straight-trunked conifer with distinctively mottled yellow-orange bark that photographed beautifully in Technicolor. The Ponderosa is handy to Hollywood, but unfortunately it does not grow in Canada except in a small enclave that juts into southern British Columbia in the Okanagan country. Hollywood has never set a movie in the Okanagan but it has planted Ponderosa pines the length and breadth of the land.

Without the mighty Ponderosa, *Heart of the North*, a 1938 production starring that bulwark of the B movies, Dick Foran, could hardly have been made. In this picture the action takes place at Fort Endurance, a mounted police post on the Mackenzie River, deep in Ponderosa pine country. A steamboat is heading for Edmonton, unfamiliar black smoke pouring from its funnel. Birch, the traditional hardwood fuel of the river, which produces white smoke, is not in evidence but woodsmen are seen hacking

This typically Canadian scene may puzzle geographers, and with good reason.
The mountain background is clearly that of Yosemite National Park in California.
The picture is Tiger Rose, *made in 1929. The movie Mountie is Monte Blue.*

This Is Canada?

Arizona, Idaho, Lake Tahoe, and Yosemite Park
turn up time and again as stand-ins for
Canadian scenery; and God's Country can be
just about anywhere.

33

Here's another typical Canadian scene—supposedly southern Saskatchewan. However, the director couldn't wait for spring to make Pony Soldier *in Canada, so he shot it in Arizona, which helps to explain the curiously un-Canadian background.*

And this is supposed to be a scene taken among the gigantic sugar pines of central Manitoba. The tree is indigenous to the west coast, not the prairies. The movie is Mantrap, *made in 1926, with Clara Bow and Ernest Torrence.*

This is Hollywood's version of what it called "The White Horse Pass" in
The Far Country, *"two miles straight up"* according to the script, but pretty
tame here for an ersatz Chilkoot. The picture was actually shot not far from
Alan Ladd's country, just off the Banff-Jasper highway.
Below: How the real pass actually looked.

Opposite is Hollywood's Saskatchewan, from the picture of the
same name. Alan Ladd is leading his
Mounties towards Fort Walsh,
which as every schoolchild knows
was in the Cypress Hills. Hollywood
moved the Fort 300 miles west in
order to make use of the mountain
scenery and to make Ladd's trip
more arduous.

God's Country could be anywhere in Canada. In Back to God's Country, *above, made in 1927, it was a Hollywood backlot with gypsum snow. The 1953 version with Rock Hudson (below, in the sled) featured one of the worst totem poles ever carved for the movies. In this picture, set on the Mackenzie River, Hudson is trying to get back to what he calls God's Country—the United States.*

God's Country and the Woman *(1937)*, *starring Beverly Roberts and George Brent,* *was supposedly set in British Columbia but was filmed in the state of Washington.*

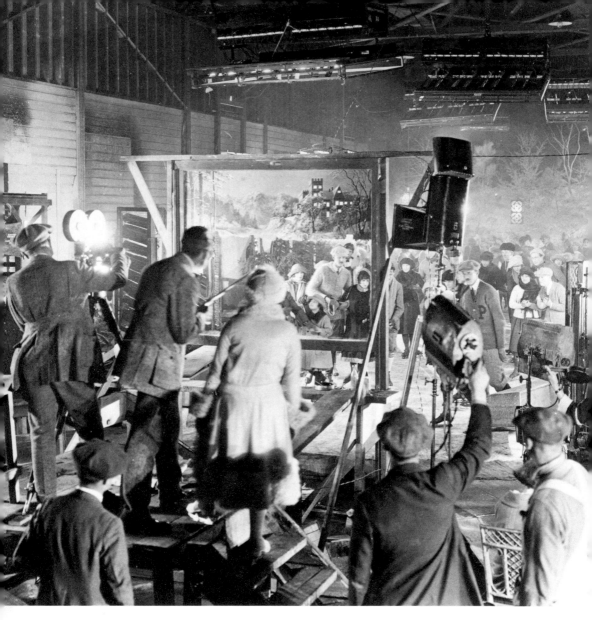

On the set with **Slander the Woman**, *a "snow picture" made in 1923. The New York Times praised the picture because it was shown during a hot spell: "In these warm days it is an unexpected relief to see a photoplay . . . begin with an ice-skating rink, and to have the whole story take place in the frigid temperature of a Canadian winter. It seems to exude coolness." Only the actors perspired.*

down huge Ponderosas and chopping them into cordwood for the furnace. A hijacking follows and Foran gives chase; to locate his quarry he scales a handy Ponderosa. Meanwhile back at the trading post, the unruly miners decide to lynch a suspect. They advance on the jail carrying torches of Ponderosa pine.* Having subdued Foran's superior, they smash down the jail with a Ponderosa pine log and then prepare to hang their innocent victim to the branch of a nearby Ponderosa tree, just as Foran arrives back with information on the real killer.

The distinctive trees of the north, of course, are not pines at all but birches, spruce, and aspen poplars. There are no pines, for example, in most of the Yukon Territory. Ironically, when a British film company wanted to approximate the look of the Russian forests along the Trans-Siberian railway for *Dr Zhivago*, it sent a crew to Canada to photograph the birches. But I have never seen a birch tree in a Hollywood movie about Canada. There are plenty of birchbark *canoes;* on the screen these have been the only means of locomotion on the rivers and lakes of the Northwoods. But where are the long reaches of skeletal trunks, ghost-white in the twilight of the sunless noons? Where are the shivering aspens, pale olive against the black smudge of the spruce? Where are the larches, choking the valleys with a chartreuse mist in the springtime? Hollywood has never shown them.

In the fall, when the deciduous leaves of the north turn flaming yellow and the buckbrush on the hilltops changes to deep maroon, the land glows; but Hollywood has never captured it in Technicolor. Even its pines are not our pines – those windblown giants of the Thomson and Jackson paintings, perched like tattered sentinels above the ribbed inland seas.

And whatever became of the flaming maples of the east? Ever since the talkies were invented, The Maple Leaf Forever has been Hollywood's favourite Canadian background music, played behind the opening credits of movie after movie.[27] In *The Country Doctor* the lumbermen of northern Quebec, heading back to Montreal by paddlewheel steamer (yes, paddlewheel steamer) for the winter, actually break into a jovial chorus of The Maple Leaf Forever, just as if it were number one on the Quebec hit parade. But I have never seen a maple tree or even a maple leaf in Hollywood's Canada – just acres of monotonous pines.

The only Canada that Hollywood ever showed, with a handful of notable exceptions, was the ersatz Canada of the American location or the studio backlot, or else the tourist Canada of the Banff-Jasper highway. I would estimate that at least three-quarters of all the pictures filmed in Canada were shot in the Canadian Rockies, and not without reason:

---

*All lynching scenes in Hollywood movies take place at night and flashlights or lanterns are never used – only pine torches.

almost every one was praised, if not for its plot, at least for its mountain background, which has always dazzled foreign reviewers.[28]

The 1936 version of *Rose Marie* drew raves for its scenery. Kine Weekly reported that the picture was "played straight against some of the most impressive Canadian wild country ever seen on the screen," while The New York Herald Tribune praised the background of "lakes and mountains of the Canadian Northwest." Actually most of the picture was photographed at Lake Tahoe on the California-Nevada border, where the scenery bears about as much relation to the country north of Montreal as Okotoks, Alberta, does to Sudbury.

But who can blame the American reviewers, whose knowledge of Canadian geography comes only from the movies? Lake Tahoe, Bear Mountain, the San Fernando valley, Mount Shasta, and Truckee, California, have all stood in for the Northwoods. So have the mountains of Idaho, Yosemite and Yellowstone National Parks, the woods of Maine, and the mesquite of Flagstaff, Arizona.[29]

Except for a small corner of the Rockies the world has rarely been shown the real Canada on the commercial screen and, perhaps more important, neither have Canadians been shown it. Nationalism has many roots, but one of them certainly is the common sharing of a unique environment. Ours is more varied than most because of the country's size; but also because of the country's size not all Canadians have been able to experience it. I suspect that some of the insularity that conspires against a unified national feeling comes from the fact that many Canadians don't really feel a kinship with distant parts of the country. For the United States, the movies have helped establish that kinship. Every American who has seen a John Ford western feels a sense of ownership in the natural obelisks of Monument Valley. But in Canada, the mass audience hasn't had a similar opportunity.

As far as I can discover, the great Laurentian Precambrian Shield, which covers two-fifths of the country, has never been used as a background for a movie. This vast expanse of ancient rock, pitted by myriad lakes and chewed by glacial action, is part of the distinctive Canadian mien, giving the nation a common landscape from Great Bear Lake to Sudbury, from North Bay to the Gatineau, from the cottage country of Muskoka to the ravelled coast of Labrador. Visually there is nothing more Canadian than this rumpled landscape; it is unique; no other corner of the world resembles it. Many a Canadian, dropped onto any portion of the Shield between Artillery Lake and Ungava, would surely realize that he was in his homeland. The painters of the Group of Seven understood this; but the moviemakers never did.

Where are the great Canadian rivers, the Yukon, Mackenzie, Sask-

Mountains exist north of Hudson Bay only in the movies. The geography was so mixed-up that the title was easily changed to *North of the Yukon* in England.

atchewan, St. Lawrence, and Fraser, flowing majestically through their immense, mile-wide valleys, carved out over the ages? Not in Hollywood's Canada. When they have been seen in the movies they have been shown as scrawny streams, easily forded. Where is the tundra, lonely and forbidding, flecked each spring by a Persian carpet of lichens and wild flowers, mantled each winter in a desert of snow? Where are the vast lakes, so immense that the shoreline is lost to view and the savage waters stretch off to the misty horizons? Where are the serpentine fiords, winding back between the wet cliffs and the dark forests of the west coast? Not in the movies.

The prairies, stretching for almost a thousand miles across the midriff of the nation, are capable of providing some stunning special effects. But Hollywood never used them. Every settler has known the horror of a whiteout, that uniquely Canadian blizzard that has made men lose their way and die within yards of their front doors. The prairie fires of the past – great walls of flame stretching across the horizon – are the stuff of which big pictures are made. But Hollywood has ignored them along with all the other prairie phenomena: the waves of grasshoppers blotting out the sun, and the horrifying hailstorms – millions of white cannonballs ravaging the fields, decimating the livestock and even hammering their way through the thin roofs of the homesteaders. All these manifestations of nature have gone unrecorded. The moviemakers have contented themselves with more familiar disasters: the mandatory avalanche, the predictable race through the rapids, the obligatory tumble over the cataract, and the ski-chase down the dizzy mountain slopes of Saskatchewan.

There is something else missing from the movies about Canada. It was only after viewing several score of them and after reading the story lines of several hundred more that I came to a startling realization: *There were no cities shown.* In fact there weren't even many small towns. Well over 90 per cent of the pictures made about this country were set either out of doors or inside log cabins or saloons. Anybody introduced to Canada entirely through motion pictures – and that includes hundreds of thousands of people around the world – would find it impossible to believe that since the mid-1920's this has been predominantly an urban country. The physical symbols of a sophisticated society – skyscrapers, bridges, neon signs, traffic lights, university campuses, football fields, suburban streetscapes, department stores – simply did not exist in the movies about Canada.

Only one city was mentioned in any consistent fashion and that was Montreal. In one of the Curwood movies, for instance, "God's Great Wilderness" was situated "1,500 miles northwest of Montreal,"[30] although Vancouver, Edmonton, Calgary, and Winnipeg were all much closer. As far as the moviemakers were concerned, Toronto scarcely existed. In fact, when 20th Century-Fox made *The Country Doctor* it moved North Bay to Quebec so that Montreal and not Toronto could be the closest city. No Toronto critic seemed to be bothered by that slight, although a Montreal reviewer, in praising the picture, did note that the screenplay conveyed "some strange ideas concerning Canada and Canadians."[31] It certainly did: it connected North Bay to Montreal by an unnamed river, complete with paddlewheel steamer. The terrain was made to appear suitably rugged by the insertion of a stock piece of footage into the middle of the movie: The Whitehorse, my favourite sternwheeler, puffing its way through the famous Five Finger Rapids of the Yukon.

Hollywood thought nothing of moving Canadian scenery and geography around the map to suit its purpose.[32] This was especially true of stories about the Klondike and the Yukon Territory. I can still remember, during my boyhood in the north, my father's real annoyance when letters arrived addressed to Dawson City, Yukon, *Alaska*. "Don't they know this is British territory?" he used to say. But they didn't know because the movies rarely made it clear.

They still don't know. I've lost count of the times I've been introduced to Americans and Europeans as a Canadian born in the Klondike. I know in advance what the reaction is going to be: "But surely the Klondike's in Alaska!" And so it is – in the movies. In the earliest picture I've been able to find that mentions the word Klondike, a picture called *The Ace of Spades* made in 1912, the gold-fields are actually set on the edge of the southwest American desert! That movie was advertised as a Klondike picture.

Shortly after that Hollywood moved my home town, Dawson City, to Alaska and there it has remained. When Robert Service wrote The Spell of the Yukon during his days as a Canadian Bank of Commerce teller in Whitehorse, there was no mistaking his Canadian locale. But when Hollywood bought the poem even the reviewers thought it was set in Alaska. ("The Alaskan scenes are impressive,"[33] the British trade paper, The Bioscope, reported.) Service's most memorable poem, as everyone knows, was set in the Malamute Saloon in Dawson City, but *The Shooting of Dan McGrew* does not mention Canada. "Vast Alaskan snows!" reads a subtitle, "Land of hope and promise. Where new faith is born and ugly pasts lie buried." Moving Picture World thought Service was an American: "The Shooting of Dan McGrew is arousing great interest in Alaska, where Robert Service lived when he wrote the poem," it reported in 1924. "The cottage in which it was written is being preserved by Alaskan authorities."[34]

So appealing were words like Klondike and Yukon that movie producers stole them for pictures that had nothing to do with Canada:[35] *Klondike Annie,* starring Mae West, was set in Nome, Alaska. In spite of the title, the word Klondike was never mentioned in that film and Mae was never called Klondike Annie. All the same, one knowledgeable critic, Graham Greene, was taken in. His geography went askew when he described the movie in his review in The Spectator, reporting that Mae "brings prosperity to a Klondike settlement house."[36]

In the dying days of the B picture Monogram made a series of second features, all with the same setting (boulders and pine trees) and with interchangeable titles like *Fangs of the Arctic* and *Yukon Vengeance.* The locale was never the Yukon and never the Arctic. In the opening scene of *Yukon Manhunt,* for instance, the Mountie superintendent at district headquarters stabs his finger at a map of Canada and hits the middle of Manitoba: the train from Fort Henry to the mines at Big Creek has suffered a payroll snatch and it is Corporal Rod Webb's job to nab the miscreants. Off Webb trots to board the train and do battle with the thieves. Rocks and pine trees vanish; fenced cattle land springs into view. This is a *Yukon* film? Webb rolls about in the pay car, tussling with the marauders and tossing them off the train one by one into the California landscape. We wait patiently for the manhunt to spread to the Yukon and justify the title, but it never does.

The same landscape – rolling farmland, deciduous trees (a change, admittedly, from the endless stands of Ponderosa pines) – turns up in *Dangers of the Canadian Mounted,* an interminable serial set in the town of "Alcana," allegedly situated on the border between Alaska and the Canadian Yukon. The name was a happy choice for it allowed the scriptwriters to have the best of both countries, an idea no doubt filched from another serial called *The Royal Mounted Rides Again.* In that offering, Universal solved the mix-up between the two countries by inventing a new international region which it called "Canaska." The press sheet made the most of the union:

A brave girl is tossed from her canoe into the whirling rapids of a Canaskan river in the amazing climax of Chapter 3.

Silhouetted against a Canaskan skyline, a courageous Royal Mounted Captain is marked for death in the spine-tingling climax of Chapter 4.

A runaway buckboard dooms a beautiful Canaskan heroine when it careens over a cliff in Chapter 7. . . .

This ingenious solution to an irritating geographical problem requires only a few minor changes in our literary heritage to become acceptable – nothing more serious than, say, the switch from Fahrenheit to Celsius. Klondike Kate becomes Canaskan Kate without disturbing the ailiteration. Edmonton, Alberta, which is after all no more distant from Dawson than Nome, transforms its Klondike Days into Canaskan Days and scores another beat over the Calgary Stampede. And Robert Service's poem is slightly revised for the schoolchildren:

"This is the law of Canaska," it now must read, "and ever she makes it plain. . . ."

1: Hot blooded romance in the land of snows

Another startling discovery about the Hollywood attitude to Canada – to me, at any rate – was the realization that, over a period of more than half a century, the moviemakers produced only six comedies with a Canadian setting. Almost six hundred pictures and only six of them purposely funny! In the vintage days of the Hollywood movie, when Howard Hawks, Frank Capra, Preston Sturges and many others were making sophisticated and witty films about their own country, Canadians were still shown chasing each other endlessly over vast, snow-clad wastes.

It's no accident that four of those six comedies based their humour on the idea of snow and cold. The earliest of all was a curiosity titled *Her Nephews From Labrador,* a one-reeler that exploited the universally held impression that Canadians are creatures of the cold. In the story, two youths from far-off Labrador are sent to visit their American aunt on a farm. When they arrive at the railway station a blizzard is in progress but the Canadians are shown in their shirt sleeves, vigorously fanning themselves. Then, rather than bundle up, they take off for the nearest lake where they don bathing suits, whirl about on the ice, dive cheerfully into the snow to cool off and splash about in the frigid waters. Hilarious! "Really the funniest picture ever," as the advertisements put it.

From then on the movies perpetuated the concept of Canada as a frozen wasteland. In early August, when the temperature at Fort Smith in the Northwest Territories has been known to rise as high as 106°F., Rock Hudson in *Back to God's Country* is shown up to his hips in snow. And yet the Hollywood snow is not Canadian snow and the Hollywood version of the cold is not the Canadian version. The Mackenzie River is freezing up, but Rock Hudson's breath does not freeze. Cabins groan under the weight of a white blanket, but no icicles drip from the eaves. A blizzard

47

howls across Hollywood's Northland, but no frost appears on Rock Hudson's eyebrows or on the fur of his parka.

In the real north, when the temperature drops below −40°F. the whole world takes on a spectral guise. The wind is stilled and the smoke from the cabins pillars vertically into the pale sky. A creeping fog rises from the chili land, turning the trees to shadows, and through this ghostly mist move the blurred figures of men, muffled to the eyebrows, creeping carefully from door to door to avoid the exertion that can draw freezing air into the lungs and cripple the unwary for life. When the temperature plunges past −60°F., human beings, like jet aircraft, leave vapour trails behind them. Nothing moves, for exposure means death. The land itself is a tomb. This is part of the Canadian heritage and the Canadian experience but it has no place in any Hollywood drama.

I've been waiting, vainly, for a movie that will help me re-create my childhood winters among the birches and spruces of the Yukon hills. There is nothing quite as serene as the silence of the December forest. The light is flat, for the days are sunless, and the hills cannot echo because the snow itself acts as a soundproof blanket. The dark conifers are shrouded in white, their branches bending to the ground under the weight of the snow, which undulates back like the ocean swell into the shadowy depths of the mysterious woods. Here, the softest whisper will carry for half a mile, the snap of a twig will resound like a pistol shot through the cold air. But nothing moves; no breeze rustles the branches; no birds flit between the trees; no animal cries shatter the stillness. The silence crowds in upon you, as unnerving in its own way as a shriek in the night. This is the true Canadian north, uncanny, bewitching, and deadly, captured occasionally on canvas by the best of our painters but never on film by the men who make the movies.

Hollywood snow was necessarily fake snow, except in those rare cases where movies were shot in the mountains. The famous scene in *The Call of the Wild* when the dog, Buck, pulls a sled with a load of a thousand pounds and wins a wager for his master, was filmed in the San Fernando valley in temperatures that bordered on 100°F. In the picture the snow looks like white sand; actually it was gypsum.

For years, Hollywood's Canada was shown to be covered with this gypsum snow, summer and winter. Hollywood's "snow pictures," as they came to be called, had such a vogue that the world became convinced that Canada was a "land of measureless snows,"[37] to lift a phrase from the description of a Tom Mix picture. An English reviewer referred to "the eternal snows of Northern Canada,"[38] apparently in the belief that nothing ever melted north of '53, and the purple prose of the silent subtitles perpetuated the myth:

PLAY THIS AND BEAT THE HEAT !

GRAB IT—BOOST IT!

Don't be licked by summer slumps when you can play such attractions as this—

Fight the competition of ball parks, carnivals, beaches and other outdoor amusements—

Wade right in with this rattling big show and jam it across with our ROUSING EXPLOITATION—our roaring posters—our virile accessories—and our RED-BLOODED AND INTENSELY PRACTICAL METHODS OF SHOWMANSHIP—

There's a certain SCOOP awaiting every showman who plays this splendid summer attraction and uses our big ideas to drive it over!

RC PICTURES PRESENTS

The Incomparable Jane Novak
in a gripping drama of self sacrifice

"Colleen of the Pines"

A CHESTER BENNETT PRODUCTION

DISTRIBUTED BY FILM BOOKING OFFICES OF AMERICA

NOTE
To all exhibitors

We give you not only the show, but a great, big, powerful exploitation campaign to put it over FOR BIG MONEY. We get right behind you with a brand of showmanship that outclasses anything in the film business today.

Try it and see!

A typical advertisement for a snow picture in the days before air conditioning. Audiences didn't need to be told the locale was Canada. The snow said it all.

49

This design for a snow lobby contrasted the climate on both sides of the border.

A Seattle theatre delayed this picture in order to play it during a hot spell.

Where the snow tyrant rules the great white wastes and the dominant spirit of nature throbs throughout the heart of the vast domain, man is but an atom amidst the turbulent roar of crashing ice and blinding snow. In every fleck of snow lurks death. . . .

(from *The Heart of the North*)

The advertisements could not resist the obvious:

HOT-BLOODED ROMANCE IN THE LAND OF SNOWS
(for *Out of the Snows*)

WHERE THE AURORA BOREALIS PLAYS ITS CHANGING LIGHTS ON THE HOT PASSIONS THE ETERNAL SNOWS CAN NEVER COOL
(for *Under Northern Lights*)

But the real value of the Canadian snow pictures was that they acted as coolants to the sweating audiences who crammed themselves into the airless theatres in those summer dog-days before air conditioning.

"The scorching days have come, the saddest of all the year," a 1916 trade advertisement read. "But to make all Universal photo fans '20 degrees cooler than the street outside,' there will be released on July 22nd a Bison two-reel northwestern picture entitled A MIDWINTER MADNESS, all the action of which takes place in the snow country."

"*Snowblind* will cool your house and make your patrons happy," a similar advertisement read in 1921. "Towering mountain peaks crowned with white – mile upon mile of banked-up snow – ice-encrusted pine trees – Arctic winds whistling through the valleys!"

And Universal recommended the following catch line for its *Wolves of the North* in the summer of 1921: "If You Are Hot And Tired From Working In The Sweltering Weather, The Gorgeous Snow Scenes Will Refresh You."

Exhibitors were quick to exploit snow pictures for the summer trade, even refusing to play some of them until a hot spell hit town, as the owner of a Seattle theatre did with *The Love Master*. And the snow lobby became a standard feature with theatre owners, especially in southern United States, whenever a Canadian feature came along.

The snow lobby took various forms: cut-out icicles hanging from the marquee, or blue lights flickering over painted backdrops portraying blizzards; white paint on the box office, sprinkled with mica to glitter like snow; theatre façades draped with pine boughs or covered with false logs. One promoter even built a frozen lake in his lobby.

Some of the larger theatres introduced snow pictures with specially staged live prologues, such as the "real frosted, way-below-zero, rim-of-the-Arctic appetizer," served up at the Brooklyn Theatre when Curwood's *The Golden Snare* played there in 1921 at the height of an August hot spell. "Everything that modern theatrical genius could contrive to develop an atmosphere of cold went into the prologue,"[39] a trade reporter told his readers. There was an aurora borealis effect on the stage and also a snowstorm. There were icicles, snowdrifts, and a background of hills covered in snow. Through the electric imagery a "Canadian snow-trekker" was observed plodding along with a pack on his back and "to cap this cool appetizer, two noted dancers in snow white ballet costumes with silver snowflakes illuminating them danced in the guise of snow sprites." The report added that "those who enjoyed this prologue and were made cool by it were swept into the film story at once, thus continuing the wintery atmosphere."

Another theatre owner, capitalizing on a movie called *Over the Border,* made it clear to his patrons exactly how frigid conditions were over the border. He divided his lobby into two sections. The left side, representing the United States, was garlanded in green foliage and bathed in hot lights. The right side, representing Canada, was framed by cotton-topped fir boughs and lit by frigid blue.

It remained for the manager of the Casino Theatre in Lakeland, Florida, to anticipate the coming of air-conditioning and the eventual demise of the snow lobby. Just before *I Am the Law* was projected, the house lights turned to green and he dumped a load of ice into the fan duct and a bushel of finely cut snow into the blowers. That, doubtless, was the beginning of the end. When theatres were able to advertise that they really *were* twenty degrees cooler inside, the Canadian snow picture had to make it on gypsum alone.

5: "Safe from the evils of civilization . . ."

"From the land of snows comes this story, where only two occupations seem to be open to a woman – the delirious uncertainty of a cabaret dancer's life or monotonous marriage, isolated from any human inter-course but that of the husband, by miles and miles of untrodden snow."[40]

That's how The Bioscope in 1918 described a picture called *Her Fighting Chance,* by the ubiquitous James Oliver Curwood. No reader needed to be told that the land was Canada. Where else would a woman be separated from all human intercourse by miles and miles of untrodden snow?

52

This theme of isolation was very strong in the Hollywood view of Canada. Again and again moviegoers throughout the world were introduced to men who lived totally alone, cut off from civilization, stranded as on a desert island from any contact with their fellows. Women were rare and "pure" women even rarer. Joan Gray, heroine of *Paid in Advance,* was "the one pure woman in a winterbound palace of pleasure."[41] In *Tyrant Fear* Allaine Grandet lived in the "barren land of the north where women are nothing more than mere chattels."[42] And in several silent movies, audiences were invited to believe that there were men living in the Canadian woods who had never *seen* a woman.[43]

The entire plot of *Petticoat Fever* hinges on the assumption that there were no white women in Labrador in the 1930's. Robert Montgomery, playing a telegraph operator at the lonely outpost of Eskimo Point, keeps announcing that he hasn't seen a woman of any kind in five months, hasn't seen a white woman in twelve months, and hasn't seen a pretty woman in two years.

The theme of isolation was also the pivot on which the plot of *The Country Doctor* turned. Here an entire Quebec village was supposedly cut off from all communication with civilization for five months of the year. The main title made it clear that life was pretty grim: "North of Montreal are the timber lands where seven months of the year the green hills ring with activity. Then the Arctic winter closes in, sub-zero in its cold, and the country is emptied of all but those whom duty holds to their posts." One man whom duty holds to his post is the kindly country doctor who tells an injured lumberjack: "There'll be no Montreal for you. The country's frozen out. You're going to be here all winter." The last boat (!) has already left for civilization.

Preposterous though this was (the year of the story was 1935), the movie was widely accepted at the time as an authentic portrait of actual Canadian conditions. Graham Greene in The Spectator called the movie "an honest film." He wrote: "The picture of the small Canadian timber station, cut off in winter from the outside world . . . is admirably genuine: the camera – rare instance in the cinema – doesn't lie. . . ."[44]

To Hollywood this Canadian isolation meant that the north could be a sanctuary for hunted men. How many desperate criminals, one wonders, have attempted to elude justice by fleeing to the Northwoods, only to discover that there is no place to hide? In the real Canadian north, the stranger stands out like a fox in a barnyard. Within minutes of his arrival, his presence is known to all. The mounted police, whose job it is to check on newcomers, begin to make enquiries, as the so-called Mad Trapper of Rat River discovered when he turned up in Fort McPherson in 1931. In the north, there is no concealment. The most isolated cabin, the most obscure valley, the tallest peak, provide no security. Everybody in the north knows everybody else and tells everybody else. The legend, expressed in the opening subtitle of *The Law of the North* (1917), that "North of '53 a man is a man and his past is his own" is straight hokum. The concept of a northern breed who keep their mouths shut and never ask a man his business is a Hollywood illusion, suitable perhaps for westerns but not for real life, at least not in Canada.

Yet, throughout the history of the movies, Canada has been tagged as a place to which men and women escape. It has rarely been depicted as a place one sets out for voluntarily (as America has). In the movies, Americans are shown *fleeing* to Canada, most often because they are being pursued by the police.

In the days when the silent film was in full flower, the Great Canadian Theme was that of an American accused of a crime, almost always wrongly, who escapes to the Northwest. Between 1918 and 1925 Hollywood made at least two dozen features with this same general plot.[45]

By 1925, with Hollywood's Northwoods jammed with wanted men all loudly protesting their innocence, the genre began to fade but the idea that a man can flee across the supposedly empty wastes of the Canadian north continued to crop up in such later pictures as the wartime *Northern Pursuit* in which a group of Nazi spies, having captured Errol Flynn, manage to cross two provinces without encountering a single soul.

Men also escaped to Canada in the silent era to Forget – the past, an unfaithful wife, or a dead sweetheart. The mounted police were seen as a kind of local Foreign Legion – a lot handier than the one across the waters – where a man could bury the past.[46] Women, small children, and household pets were shown escaping successfully across the boundary line into the anonymity and peace of the Great Woods. Even zoo animals made it. In *Soul of the Beast* Ruth Lorrimor, abused by her wicked stepfather, a circus owner, escaped to the Canadian woods along with the circus's prize performer, Oscar the Elephant.

Alcoholics and compulsive gamblers were shown escaping from their obsessions by fleeing to Canada where they were miraculously cured of their weaknesses. In spite of the fact that boozing, gambling, lust, and murder formed the themes of most of the pictures about the Northwest, Hollywood's faith in the restorative powers of the Canadian wilds remained unshaken. The woods were seen to be spiritually rejuvenating. They cured illnesses; they made weak men strong; they turned pampered women into loving wives.

Take Major John Gordon, the hero of *In The Shadow of the Pines*. He's been shot through the lung at Waterloo and left for dead. Then his doctor orders him into "the balsamic airs of the Canadian pine forests."[47] A few

54

sniffs of the evergreens and he's a new man. Or how about Arnold Hammon, the New York businessman in *The Best Man,* who "having disposed of a great deal more than his share of highballs and brought on a bad case of the shakes goes up north and puts himself under the care of a skillful old physician in a Nova Scotia village?"[48] These old themes did not die out. A quarter of a century later Ray Milland, in *Untamed,* was cured of a nervous breakdown by a swift trip to the same healing airs of the Canadian forest country.

Moral recuperation was an even stronger theme. The bracing air of Canada, the absence of any cities, the stark simplicity of life in the raw, the cleansing effect of the eternal snows – all these elements were seen by Hollywood as an antidote to the corruption of an urban society. As Richard Winthrop puts it in *For Another Woman.* "I came here to escape the grind and greed of commerce." Winthrop, of course, has it made. He's installed himself as overlord of a simple French-Canadian village "in the Adirondacks [sic]." Winthrop, the American businessman, is king; the simple people of the village are his lackeys.

The Escape from a Corrupt Society theme is even stronger in *The Lure of the Wild.* Jim Belmont, a wealthy Los Angeles tycoon partially estranged from his wife because of a series of business absences, returns home to find her in the arms of his best friend, Daniels. Not realizing that she has actually been resisting the bounder, Belmont decides to leave her forever.

"I'm going to take her away from this rotten civilization!" he cries, snatching little Cuddles from his wife's arms, and off he goes with the child in his chauffeur-driven Dusenberg accompanied by his faithful dog. Everybody in the audience realizes where he's heading. Where else would a cuckolded husband go to escape this kind of moral corruption? Soon we see the familiar vista of Hollywood pine trees, snow-capped mountains, and sunlit waters accompanied by a subtitle which tells us that father, daughter, and household pet are "Far away in Canada – safe from the evils of civilization." And there, ensconced in a log cabin, is Jim Belmont in breeches, an open shirt, and the Tom Mix ten gallon hat that was all the rage in the Canadian woods in the 1920's. There is a good deal more to the plot; but the theme that a jaded dilettante can find happiness in the Canadian woods is constant throughout.

Like Old Doc Kelly's Tiger Balm, Canada was seen in movie after movie as a kind of cure-all for the ills of big city life:

"Shocked by his daughter's flirtatious behaviour, Robert Endicott takes her on a trip to the Canadian Northwest."[49]

"Bored with her friends and her life as a society leader, Nina Le Comte goes north to Hudson Bay."[50]

Overworked to exhaustion, John Benton, a New York artist, "resolves to seek inspiration in a country where the conventionalities of city life have not penetrated."[51]

There was, to note one movie slogan, "no room for a weakling in the great Northwest."[52] A man (or a woman) shaped up or went under. As the hero of *Silent Jim* declared: "I came here from England to become a man!"[53] In picture after picture, wayward boys were banished from the city and given "a taste of rugged life in the Canadian woods"[54] in the hope of turning them into men.

And then there is Lois, the spoiled American society girl of *The Snow Bird,* who goes to "the heart of the Canadian woods" where she meets a brutal and primitive French-Canadian, Jean Corteau, who – although he admits he's a bit of a beast – turns out to be a real man, quite different from the insipid, tennis-playing, country-club youths shown at the picture's opening. She marries the beast and brings him back to the potted palms, marble fountains, tennis clubs, and classical statuary of her father's New York estate. But after her sojourn at Great Whale River, County of Chalet, Province of Ungava, Canada, these luxuries seem sterile. "Are you happy here?" the ex-beast inquires. She shakes her head sadly. "I want to go back to the land of the whispering pines – to the great Northland with you," she murmurs. And so we leave them, muffled in furs, surrounded by sled dogs, up to their waists in gypsum snow, heading for their log paradise in the pine-covered hills.

Paul Muni in the clichéd role of the ebullient French-Canadian woodsman in Hudson's Bay.

Renée Adorée in The Eternal Struggle *(1923).*

Passionate French-Canadians

Hollywood sprinkled them all over Canada, dressing them in tuques and fur hats and making them either villains or happy-go-lucky bon vivants. The women were passionate spitfires.

57

J. Carroll Naish, an Irishman, plays a comic French-Canadian guide, using what he considers appropriate gestures. The motion picture is Saskatchewan *(1954).*

In Slander the Woman, *made in 1923, Geno Corrado slipped easily into the role of Tetreau (below), the happy-go-lucky French-Canadian guide.*

More happy-go-lucky French-Canadians, this time in a rare urban setting: Ottawa. The picture is The Happy Time *(1952). From left to right: Kurt Kaszner, Bobby Driscoll, Marcel Dalio and Louis Jordan—an unlikely mix of accents.*

Below, happy-go-lucky French-Canadian trapper Jean Dubois (Mitchell Lewis) and his daughter, Renée (Renée Adorée), arrive at Carbeau's trading post in the 1927 version of Back to God's Country. *Note that the Hollywood French-Canadian stance is exactly the same in all these movie stills—feet planted firmly apart.*

French-Canadian villains were generally unkempt, like Black Bastien, above, menacing Joan Crawford in the first released version of Rose-Marie *in 1928.*

The baddie with the gun is obviously a French-Canadian because he's wearing a tuque. Gene Autry will best him, however, in this movie which is called, naturally, Gene Autry and the Mounties.

Noah Beery, wearing his enviable Hollywood French-Canadian trapper suit, attempts the seduction of Madge Bellamy in Soul of the Beast *(1923).*

Tuques were mandatory for movie French-Canadians; the one at the top was never shown because the picture was scrapped. That's John Carroll below with Ruth Hussey in Pierre of the Plains *(1942).*

Jules of the Strongheart, *perfectly got-up in the tuque-sash-and-pipe costume.*

Pierre the trapper in Baree, Son of Kazan. *No pipe—but the pants make up for that.*

Margery Wilson as Lois LeMoyne in The Primal Lure *was never without her tuque.*

Typical French-Canadian poses are struck by typical Hollywood French-Canadians in two movies, sixteen years apart. At the left, William Garwood "takes his terrible oath of vengeance" in The Oath of Pierre, *a silent film made in 1914. On the right, Gilbert Roland adopts a similar stance in* Men of the North, *made in 1930. You can tell that both these men are <u>good</u> French-Canadians because they're clean-shaven <u>except</u> for the mandatory pencil moustache.*

The Blackfoot, who never burned anybody at the stake, were maligned as early as 1916 in The Primal Lure, *starring William S. Hart. Everything about this picture is wrong, including the costumes and the locale.*

Hollywood Indians

Canadian Indians acted just like American Indians
in Hollywood movies, battling the white man every inch of the way
with bow and arrow and trusty tomahawk.

The 1936 version of Rose Marie, *supposedly set in Quebec, featured a dance sequence complete with Hollywood totem poles and dancing Indians, including several who looked more Mexican than Montagnais.*

In the 1954 version of Rose Marie *the great Busby Berkeley directed the Indian dance sequence. The setting is supposedly the Canadian Rockies but the costumes and fake rocks are more reminiscent of the American southwest. The totem pole at the left was the largest in movie history and, as usual, in the wrong place.*

67

In this still from Susannah of the Mounties *(1939), Hollywood's favourite predatory Indians, the Blackfoot, are about to burn Randolph Scott at the stake. They would have, too, if it hadn't been for Shirley Temple.*

These Hollywood Indians are supposed to be Canadian Cree, and, as usual, they're on the
warpath in Pony Soldier. Who can stop them? Tyrone Power can, that's who.

More Indians menace J. Carroll Naish in Canadian Pacific. They want to stop the
railway from going through. Naish blows them all up with dynamite sticks.

*Above: The Indian as faithful servant.
Numa stands by his master, who is berating
the woman he loves because her father has
murdered his father and kidnapped his sister.
The movie is* The Law of the North *(1918).*

*Left: The Indian as wicked henchman.
In* Murder on the Yukon *(1940) Renfrew of
the Mounted subdues Monti, a minor heavy
played by Chief Thundercloud. Indians
rarely got leading roles in the movies.*

Indian women were useful in the movies. They confessed to murders, thus saving the white heroine from disgrace or execution, as in Slander the Woman *(above)*, a 1923 silent. Or they gave their lives so the heroine might marry the white hero, as did Tanaka *(played by Laska Winters, far right)* in Fashion Madness *(1928)*.

The Hollywood Instant Indian kit is evident here in The Wild North *(1951).*
This is how the moviemakers thought Chipewyan Indians dressed. Actually, the
beaded headband was a Hollywood invention designed to hold on the wigs.

PART TWO

Primitive Passions in the Untamed North

1: The old-fashioned, red-blooded look

If one were restricted to a single word to describe Hollywood's image of
Canada that word would be "primitive." The movie geography, as we
have seen, was positively primordial: mountains older than time, forests
more ancient than man, snows that could never melt. Against that paleo-
crystic backdrop Hollywood's stock company of stereotypes worked out
their passions. Trappers, lumberjacks, prospectors, saloonkeepers, Hudson's Bay factors, quaint fishermen, quainter habitants, half-breeds, and
Indians – these were the people of the shadow plays. Even the Mounties,
clean-cut and semi-sophisticated, were forced to act like primitives.[1]

Hollywood divided these primitive Canadians into two species: the
wild, passionate, lawless kind and the simple, unworldly, picturesque
kind. "Picturesque," like "primitive," was a well-worn movie adjective.
Silent Years, for example, was described as being set "in the picturesque
region of the St. Lawrence Valley, where dwell the French-Canadians.
Their primitive ways of living in the open forest country combine in a
picturesque background."[2]

The moviemakers undoubtedly viewed Canadians as simpler, less
complicated versions of Americans. In the silent era especially, the contrast was sharply etched. In *The Barbarian,* to note one example, members
of a wealthy American family are depicted as predators invading the
unspoiled forest north of Winnipeg. They arrive with monstrous striped
marquees and a flitch of servants, intent on swindling the primitive hero
out of his land. In the movies it was always the Americans who were the
sophisticates.

Here is Mary Kelly, an American reviewer, describing *The Valley of
Doubt,* a movie about a young American girl in the Canadian Northwoods:

> In casting, a successful effort had been made to select a variety of racial
> types such as would naturally be found in surroundings as remote and
> sparsely settled as these. There's a certain crudeness of feature and
> manner that belongs to such characters and this the director has not lost
> sight of. The presence of conventional folk from the city only further
> emphasizes this quality.[3]

One of the oddest juxtapositions of primitive forest and sophisticated high life appeared in *The Country Beyond,* filmed at Jasper Park in 1926. The opening subtitle suggested the remoteness of the setting: "Land and mountains drowsed in the July sun – not a sound broke the silence – save for the coming of Roger McKay." Enter Roger McKay, an American, fleeing from the madding crowd in his birchbark canoe. Soon another birchbark canoe turns up, this one paddled by a child of the forest, one Valencia. She speaks: "I thought I had this corner of Canada all to myself." How she could think that is incomprehensible since the movie shortly reveals that there is a luxurious hotel at the other end of the lake, crammed with American tourists, all dressed in formal evening clothes and dancing to a jazz band. The plot revolves around the attempts of one of these Americans, identified as "a jaded New Yorker," to seduce Valencia and make her a Broadway star. Jaded Americans regularly seduced unspoiled Canadian girls in the movies – or tried to.[4]

This portrayal of Canada as a picturesque, unsophisticated, and rather old-fashioned country was consistent throughout the Hollywood era. The very first movie ever made about Canada, *An Acadian Elopement,* carried that theme and so did the last really good one, *Johnny Belinda.*

An Acadian Elopement, which the Biograph Company kept calling "An Arcadian Elopement," was made before Hollywood existed, when the American story-picture was less than five years old. Happily, a print still exists and can be seen at the National Film Archives in Ottawa. The press handout described it at the time as "without doubt one of the most picturesque films ever made," and exclaimed about "the Normandie of the New World with its blossomy fields and lanes shaded with masses of pendulous foliage, colored with ephemeral clusters of wild flowers." The modern viewer, accustomed to wide screen Technicolor, may miss these delicate shadings but there is no denying the rustic quality of the story. A pretty Quaker maiden and her affianced are shown setting off to be married "in a neolithic buggy" with "a meditative horse." There follows a series of pastoral adventures, including a "novel scene" of natives opening clams for the market and an "Arcadian sight-seeing equipage – an ox-wain heaped high with rusting salt hay."[5]

Forty-one years later Warner Brothers made *Johnny Belinda,* also set in Nova Scotia and starring Jane Wyman in an Academy Award performance as the deaf mute. This picture managed to gather to itself all the stereotyped concepts about Canada that Hollywood nurtured through the years. When I first viewed it I assumed it was set in the 1890's until, in several brief city shots – presumably Halifax – I spotted some 1947 automobiles among the buggies in the streets and some contemporary

Hollywood persevered with these primitive pictures for half a century.[10] Elsewhere, the movies began to change but Hollywood's version of Canada remained frozen in its mould. As late as 1959 20th Century-Fox Studio made *Woman Obsessed,* a film set in contemporary northeastern Canada, in which Stephen Boyd plays an inarticulate roughneck who beats his wife and small son. Variety made the point: "The film is a throwback, in a way, to the days of the motion picture drama when stories were told in bold strokes, filled in with deep hued colors."[11]

After fifty years, *Woman Obsessed* was the last of its genre.

2: Happy-go-lucky rogues in tuques

The impression still persists in some parts of the world and, indeed, in some parts of neighbouring United States, that almost every Canadian speaks French. I have even met, in the course of various travels, some people – again including Americans – who assume that French, and *only* French, is the mother tongue of Canada. (Others, equally misinformed, believe that Canada is actually a part of the United States. That view is especially prevalent in eastern Europe, where little distinction is made between the two countries.)

That idea could come from one medium only: the movies. In Hollywood's Canada the forest people were almost always French-Canadians, although they weren't confined to Quebec. Actually there appear to have been more French-Canadians *outside* of Quebec than in the ancient province. As we'll see, Hollywood made several pictures set in Quebec which are remarkable for the absence of French-speaking Canadians. But elsewhere, from southern British Columbia to northern Manitoba, from the Yukon border to the Cypress Hills, they turned up in picture after picture, speaking a kind of pidgin tongue ("Dees Canada, she's lak beeg woo-*man!*"), sporting their colourful tuques and sashes, smoking their clay pipes, indulging in broad gestures, grimacing and capering, seducing willing women, raping unwilling ones, filching deeds for lost gold mines or simply sitting around in the virgin wilderness scraping away on fiddles.

There were only four classes of forest dwellers who were *not* French-Canadians: prospectors, mounted policemen, lumbermen, and Hudson's Bay Company factors.

The prospectors were usually Americans, invading Canada in order to strike it rich before retreating to warmer climes. Most were amateurs, such as Clark Gable in *The Call of the Wild,* while others were really cowboys, like Randolph Scott in *The Cariboo Trail* or James Stewart in *The Far Country.*

The mounted policemen tended to be Irish, with names like Moran, Callaghan, O'Rourke, and Shaughnessy. Eleven of the twenty names of policemen which appear in motion-picture titles, for instance, are Irish. O'Malley of the Mounted turns up three times.

The lumbermen were mostly Anglo-Saxons and they came in two models: the Roistering Lumberjack and the Villainous Timber Magnate. The roistering image was indelibly established in 1918 by William S. Hart, the pioneer western star, in the title role of *Blue Blazes Rawden,* a man with an apparently hollow leg and a legendary reputation ("The boss one time he keel a bear weeth hees hands!").

"Going to hit that Hell hole, Timber Cove, like a blaze of glory!" Rawden shouts at the beginning of the picture as he and his men, firing their pistols into the air, advance upon the little lumber town for an evening of sport. In the saloon Rawden swallows his liquor neat, smashes the empty glasses on the floor, beats up the bartender, one La Barge ("the best rough and tumble fighter in the Cove"), calls for more booze ("Whisky, you frog-eater or I'll swab your own bar with you"), guzzles it straight from the bottle, plucks a half-breed girl, Babette DuFresne, from the arms of the monocled proprietor, Ladyfingers Hilgard, and finally in a *mano a mano* gun-fight shoots Hilgard dead.

It is an exhausting movie – almost as exhausting for the audience as it must have been for Hart, who appears to be engaged in calisthenics to the very end of the picture when, stricken by remorse (and also by a bullet), he stumbles off into the storm to Die Alone. No one, certainly not George Brent or even Barton MacLane, who were pitted against each other two decades later in another hard-fisted lumbering yarn, *God's Country and the Woman,* equalled Hart's portrayal.

I suspect that Hollywood preferred the Villainous Timber Magnate – men like J. Van Dyke Parker, millionaire lumberman, whose plotting and dynamite drive his partner into bankruptcy in *The Knockout;* or Hurd, the powerful lumber baron of *The Ancient Highway,* who has sworn to ruin his beautiful Canadian rival, Antoinette St. Ives, unless she marries him (more dynamite); or Garne, general manager of a Rocky Mountain timber firm who in *Forest Havoc* treacherously diverts valuable logs into a secret pond for his own use. Such tycoons outnumbered the logger heroes in the movies.

The Scots were given one role only in Hollywood's Canada. They were, naturally enough, factors of Hudson's Bay trading posts and they were almost all cruel or at the very least domineering.[12] These fur-trading pictures were set mostly in the twentieth century but, as in other Holly-

80

wood offerings about Canada, the mores were those of the eighteenth. There were undoubtedly tens of thousands of moviegoers who believed that in the Canadian north, factors held "absolute sway"[13] over their underlings, like The Eagle in *The Law of the North* or Hal Sinclair, "whose word was Law"[14] in *The Law of the Great Northwest*. And why wouldn't they believe it when the critics themselves appeared to? An American reviewer, Matthew A. Taylor, reporting on a re-make of *The Call of the North* in 1921, told his readers of "the tyranny of the Factors of the Hudson Bay Company . . . who even today in the more remote sections are practically absolute."[15] Three years later The Bioscope, reviewing Tom Mix's *North of the Yukon* (as it was titled in England), explained that "apparently there is a law in the North that, if a man commits murder, or helps one who has committed murder, the guilty party shall be driven off into the snow and deprived of food, fuel or weapons until he dies."[16]

This hardy Hollywood myth of La Longue Traverse or Journey of Death had its genesis in the original version of *The Call of the North,* an early DeMille opus. It kept turning up in later films and was apparently swallowed whole by a generation of moviegoers. In the Mix version the wicked factor, Cameron MacDonald, is shown to be The Law, even though in one shot the director apparently couldn't resist showing a mounted policeman in full-dress uniform. The redcoat is produced like a rabbit out of a hat and then conveniently vanishes, leaving MacDonald to run the court according to his personal whim. Since he wants to get his hands on the rich ore that Mix's dead brother has discovered, he swiftly sends the cowboy hero off on the Journey of Death. There is a nice touch at this point: before Tom Mix takes the long walk, the ever-present Roman Catholic priest blesses him.

When *The Call of the North* was re-made in 1921 the Hudson's Bay Company decided that enough was enough. The movie showed HBC factors attacking free-traders, burning down their shacks and generally breaking the law in a twentieth-century setting. The company filed a damage suit in London against the Famous Players-Lasky Corporation and won.[17] The court held that the movie distorted conditions in Canada as they existed after 1870 and ordered that the objectionable portions of the picture be revised. After that Hollywood was more careful about identifying its factors as Hudson's Bay men.[18]

By the mid-twenties, with the Mountie craze at its height, the all-powerful factor was obsolete. The French-Canadian trapper/guide farmer/habitant, however, was a key figure from the very beginning to the very end of the cycle of Canadian-content movies. The French-Canadian was to the northerns what the Mexican was to the westerns – an exotic primitive, adaptable as a chameleon to play a hero or a heavy.

In the early pictures there were two distinct French-Canadian stereotypes. On the one hand there was the Diabolical French-Canadian, a fiendish and often lecherous killer and thief. On the other there was the Happy-Go-Lucky French-Canadian, so cheerful, so humane, so fond of his fellow men that he was too good to be true. In the silent days, the devils outnumbered the saints by about two to one. Then, when the talkies arrived and screenwriters started putting some shading into their characters, the stereotypes began to blend and a kind of mutant appeared on the screen – the happy-go-lucky rogue, who couldn't be all bad. Gilbert Roland, John Carroll, Fernando Lamas, Paul Muni, and Stewart Granger all took a turn at playing this role which, with its Gallic shrugs, broad gestures, and eye-rolling, was easily adaptable and had been so ever since Lon Chaney first created it in 1920.

Good or bad, almost all of these French-Canadians were presented as untutored children of the forest. One child of the forest who had some tutoring was Jean Courteau, the beast-hero of *The Snowbird*. A character in the story clearly had Courteau's number when he described him as "the type of bold French-Canadian with a good education, *which makes him shrewd and cunning* [my italics]."

The first French-Canadian characters to appear in a Hollywood movie turned up in 1908 in Griffith's *A Woman's Way,* a print of which has been preserved in the Library of Congress in Washington. The heavy is easily identified as a French-Canadian because he wears a tuque and a sash, sports a shaggy Louis-Napoleon moustache and beard, and is clearly a sex maniac. The hero is easily recognizable, too. He wears pure white buckskins and a coon cap. Other French-Canadians in the background wear tuques and sashes and smoke clay pipes. There is little time for plot development: the gesturing Quebecker simply seizes the heroine, who has been hugging a tree, and makes off with her; pistols are produced and fired; the hero gives chase and the rascal is bested.

From this point on, some combination of tuque, sash, and pipe were considered mandatory for actors playing French-Canadians in the movies. Occasionally, French-Canadians were shown wearing enormous fur hats or peaked habitant caps; but if they didn't wear a tuque, then the sash appeared. Fashions changed over the years: skirts grew shorter, bobbed hair came and went, the New Look appeared on the screen, fedora brims grew wider, then narrower, even cowboy hats changed in style, but the tuque held its own. Jan LaRose wears a tuque in *The Strength of Men* (1913). Gabriel Dupré wears a tuque in *Where the North Begins* (1923). Louis the Fox wears a tuque in *Men of the North* (1930). Pierre wears a tuque in *Pierre of the Plains* (1942). Jules Vincent wears a tuque in *The Wild North* (1951). And the women wear tuques, too. In *The Far*

Country (1954) Corinne Calvet never removes her tuque: she wears it summer and winter, indoors and out, in Skagway, in Dawson, in the mountains, in the saloons, in the mining claim and, presumably, also in bed.

Of all the major stars who have played French-Canadian women, Miss Calvet was perhaps the least tempestuous. Joan Crawford, in the silent version of *Rose-Marie,* was praised for her ability to change her character with a vengeance, "flinging herself fiercely into the wildcat passion of the role of the French-Canadian girl and also into the purring cuteness it called for."[19] Renée Adorée, who was often given French-Canadian roles, was at her most ebullient in *The Eternal Struggle,* leaping up and down in the middle of the street and egging on two fellow French-Canadians to fight over her with knives. And, of course, Lupe Velez, the so-called Mexican Spitfire, fitted easily into the title role of *Tiger Rose,* "The tempestuous French Canadian ward of Hector McCollins of the Hudson's Bay Company."[20] Mexican spitfires and French-Canadian wildcats have been practically interchangeable down through the years. In *Quebec* Nikki Duval was "the untamed spitfire of the Canadian woods."[21]

In Hollywood's Canada, all French-Canadians had brutally simple first names: none of your Jean-Pauls or Jean-Jacques for the movies. By far the most popular Hollywood name, I blush to say, was Pierre. Most of the Pierres were scoundrels: I've counted at least seventeen, including Pierre, the trapper who beats up his wife in *A Pack of Cards;* Pierre Ledoux, another trapper who acts as triggerman for a group of thieves in *North of the Yukon;* a third trapper named Pierre in *Blind Circumstances* who is hired by a brutal skipper to murder the fiancé of the girl he loves. There is also Pierre the Bully in *The Trap* and Bad Pierre in *White Hell.* I have been able to find only two innocuous Pierres. It's obvious that Hollywood found the Bad Pierres much more interesting.

Hollywood's other favourite names, in order of popularity, are Jacques, Jean, Jules, Gaspard, Louis, Raoul, 'Poleon, and Baptiste or Bateese. In the B movies, faceless villains tended to have last names only and these fell into two alliterative families: Dumont, Durand, Duval, Dubec, and Duclos; and Larue, LeBeau, Le Clerc, and LaFarge.

Most of the French-Canadian villains in the early silents were devoid of any socially redeeming qualities. They were, in fact, unspeakable blackguards, consistently unfaithful to their wives whom they beat unmercifully in movie after movie.[22] "Unkempt" is almost too mild a word to describe them. Loup, the wicked and lustful trapper in *North of Hudson Bay,* was a wild man – all hair and beard – with a half-crazy look in his eyes. Joseph Dumont, the murderer in *The Confession,* had a black beard, long greasy hair, and a swarthy complexion. Jean LaFarge, a minor reprobate

83

in *The Calgary Stampede,* was shown as an evil-looking, suspicious man "who guards his daughter and his herds with the same fierce jealousy." In place of a tangled mass of hair, LaFarge sported a drooping moustache and a goatee. He could not be made to look too shaggy, since Hoot Gibson was fated to marry his daughter at the end of the picture.[23]

The latter-day knaves were less interesting. By the late fifties they had lost all personality. The accents vanished along with the Christian names and all that was left were trunk-tag characters, easily interchangeable – LeRoux in *Yukon Vengeance,* LeBeau in *Northwest Territory,* Duval and LeClerc in *Yukon Manhunt.* Hollywood had long since dumped the bestial, wife-beating, sex-mad French-Canadian blackguard for the happy-go-lucky rogue.

At first, the motion picture industry tended to idealize its good French-Canadians,[24] all of whom were carefully barbered – their hair short, slickly groomed, and parted in the middle after the wet-head fashion of the day. They rarely had beards but almost all had small moustaches, turned up at the ends to emphasize their incredible good nature. All had flashing, pearly teeth, which were in constant view. Happy and carefree, they capered through movie after movie, slapping friends and even enemies on the back and giving constant thanks to Le Bon Dieu for their existence.[25] Several of them played the fiddle incessantly, like 'Poleon in *God's Country and the Law,* "with a heart as light as the tunes he plays." In that picture, 'Poleon somehow managed to drive a horse and buggy and a cow home and to play the fiddle at the same time. And while the Wicked Half-Breed, Jacques Doré, was forcing his unwelcome attentions on 'Poleon's daughter inside her own home, 'Poleon was shown prancing about on the road outside, a pack on his back and his fiddle under his chin, oblivious to all marauders.

We can, I think, give Lon Chaney, "the man of a thousand faces," the credit for inventing the stereotype of the happy-go-lucky French-Canadian. He developed it first in 1920 in *Nomads of the North* and perfected it two years later in *The Trap.* In the latter film, Fritz Tidden commented, Chaney "employs 667 of his reported one thousand facial expressions,"[26] possibly because he had been given a role that allowed him to play both hero and heavy.

At the opening of the picture, a print of which has been preserved, Chaney is Gaspard the Good. There he stands in the doorway of his simple cabin, the compulsory tuque crowning his head, hands on hips, head thrown back, laughing uproariously at his good fortune in being alive. The subtitles have him speaking pidgin English to the ever-present priest: "Good fath-aire, I so happy I would geev thanks to Heem who made thees world so beauti-fool." When Gaspard climbs a nearby mountain to his mine, he cannot help kissing his hands and flinging his arms wide as he drinks in the beauty around him.

Alas, the idyll is abruptly ended when Benson, a man from the city (played by a young Alan Hale) steals his mine and his girl. Gaspard the Good becomes Gaspard the Bad, plotting revenge. As the years pass, "lighted only by the never-dimming fires of an all-consuming hate," Chaney gives an animated performance of a Bad French-Canadian trying to act like a Happy-Go-Lucky French-Canadian, in order to dupe his enemy and savour sweet revenge. It was all there for those who followed in his footsteps to study – the malicious grin, the sneaky eyes, the hunched shoulders, the flaring nostrils – and it was put to good use in the years that followed. Nobody, however, outdid Chaney for expansiveness of gesture until Paul Muni hammed his way through the role of Pierre Radisson in *Hudson's Bay* in 1940.

Anyone who examines all of these major French-Canadian performances, from Lon Chaney in 1920 to Stewart Granger in 1951, cannot help but be struck by a similarity of style and gesture. It is as if none of these stars had ever met a French-Canadian, which may very well be true. Lon Chaney and John Carroll were both Americans, Gilbert Roland was a Mexican; Paul Muni was a Jew of middle-European parentage; Stewart Granger was an Englishman; (and J. Carroll Naish, who played the unwashed French-Canadian guide in *Saskatchewan* – with a comic Indian wife, eternally pregnant – was Irish). Some of the best actors in Canada come from the province of Quebec but they have never gone to Hollywood.

Charles Boyer, who has appeared as a French-Canadian in two pictures, *The Happy Time* and *The Thirteenth Letter*, never bothered with an authentic characterization. In both movies he remained a Frenchman with a Parisian accent. This was not the only inconsistency and it brings up a curious Hollywood blindness about French-Canadians in general and the province of Quebec in particular. For years the movies populated Canada with men and women who spoke with French-Canadian accents, confessed to Roman Catholic priests, raised their eyes to Le Bon Dieu and uttered expletives like "By Gar!" The Northwoods were crammed with such people, from Dawson City to Labrador. In *Pierre of the Plains* the screenwriters made the mayor of a Rocky Mountain village a French-Canadian – a comic figure in a wing collar, striped trousers, and a bowler, who was addressed as Your Honour, in the American fashion. But when it came to placing French-Canadians in their own province Hollywood was clearly confused.

The Thirteenth Letter, for instance, produced by Otto Preminger on location in Quebec, must be baffling to any native because, in the small

Quebec town of the story so many of the characters – the chief of police, the postman, all the doctors in the hospital, and most of the hospital personnel – are Anglo-Saxons.

Similarly in Alfred Hitchcock's *I Confess,* shot on location in Quebec City, the chief of police, the judge, many of the court officials, and leading detectives are Anglo-Saxons. In *The Scarlet Claw,* one of the movies in the Basil Rathbone/Nigel Bruce Sherlock Holmes series, all the hotel clerks in Quebec City seem to have English accents; the policeman in charge of the case has a Scottish burr; and the postman arrives at the hotel singing, of all things, The British Grenadiers. And then there is Jules, the French-Canadian youth from the Quebec village in *The Heart of Humanity,* who, dying of wartime wounds, utters a typically Québecois request: "Tell Mumsy I love her!" he whispers as he expires.

In *The Happy Time,* which supposedly deals with the tight French-Canadian community in the Ottawa of the twenties, there is a mixture of accents within the same family. Two of the younger generation don't appear to have anything more than rudimentary French. One, in fact, speaks English with a Harvard accent!

The most curious exhibit of all, however, is again provided by *The Country Doctor,* the over-praised picture about the Dionne Quintuplets. The French-Canadian locale, it will be remembered, was moved from Ontario to Quebec, somewhere north of Montreal. Where, then, are the French-Canadians in *The Country Doctor?* There just aren't any. Slim Summerville plays the town cop with an American drawl. John Qualen plays the quintuplets' father with his usual hick accent. Jean Hersholt, the doctor, speaks with a Scandinavian lilt. The action moves briefly to Montreal where again we hear no French – only the clipped British accents of Montague Love. In fact in the entire picture there is not one soul with a French-Canadian name; even the high Catholic prelates who come to bless the quints' new hospital are Anglo-Saxon. All those trappers and traders and guides, with their tuques and their sashes and their exotic way of speaking, have miraculously vanished and remain hidden away in the chill isolation of the Great Woods.

3: "The volatile blood of the French and the crafty daring of the Indians . . ."

If Hollywood came to view the French-Canadian as a likeable and exotic rogue, it did not show the same tolerance for the Métis. For half a century Canadian half-breeds (to use the universal Hollywood term) were depicted as villains of the deepest dye – sneaky, untrustworthy degenerates who coveted defenceless white women, sold bad whisky to the Indians, and let others take the rap for their crimes. I have turned up more than sixty movies in which this kind of half-breed is cast as the heavy; I have found only four in which the half-breed character might be called "good;" one of those, actually, was a quarter-breed and another was a half-wit.

The dirty, no-good half-breed, of course, has always been a stock Hollywood character. Whether Mexican, American, or French-Canadian – and *all* movie half-breeds are French in pictures about Canada – he is the same person, indistinguishable except for his accent. As Ralph and Natasha Friar point out in their interesting book, The Only Good Indian, the stereotype was lifted by the moviemakers straight from the pages of the nineteenth-century dime novels about the old west.[27]

The half-breed in Hollywood's Canada served the same purpose as the mulatto villain in Griffith's *The Birth of a Nation* (and with much less public uproar) or as the half-castes in a score of exotic films about the Orient. As the Friars have pointed out, the half-breed is living proof of miscegenation, a sin in the eyes of most movie audiences, and was to be treated accordingly: "the term 'half-breed' speaks for itself. For the Hollywood scriptwriter, the half-breed is a great catch-all. Villainy, weakness, and just plain cussedness or their extreme opposites are always attributed to this character."[28]

The Canadian half-breed villain in the movies is clearly an American stereotype but with one difference: his French blood. I have not been able to find a single Anglo-Saxon half-breed in Hollywood's Canada. Again, the familiar names turn up – Pierre, Jules, Baptiste, Jacques, Jean, and Gaspard; and again Pierre is the most popular of these names. There were as many Bad Pierres among the half-breeds as there were among the whites in the movies.

The overtones were very often sexual, especially in the early silents: the half-breed was shown to want a white woman and that very desire made him a blackguard.

Pierre, one of the first of the half-breed heavies in a 1909 film, *The Cattle Thieves*, "has long coveted Mary in his greedy way" and "finding himself near her his passion gets beyond control. He seizes her roughly in his arms. . . ."[29]

In *A Romance of the Canadian Wilds* another Pierre is thrown into a jealous rage when he finds the forest maiden he secretly loves responding to the caresses of a white stranger. He stabs him.

In *The Savage* Monroe Salisbury in the title role "develops a mad passion for a white girl. . . . He kidnaps her but is stricken with swamp fever before he can do her any harm. . . . The clear-headed cool courage of the girl turns the wild creature into her most faithful friend."[30] Friend, yes; husband, no. Marriage by a white woman to a half-breed was unthinkable.

In *Silent Jim* the handsome, smiling Baptiste, a half-breed trader, showers the heroine with presents of rich fur. "But when the test comes she is a real woman,"[31] and a real woman doesn't marry a man of mixed blood.

In *Pierre of the North* two half-breed brothers are enamoured of Marie, the factor's daughter. Naturally, neither can win her. Baptiste, "mad with jealous rage," abducts the girl. Pierre trails him and captures him in a bear trap but is himself caught in another trap laid by Baptiste. Wolves, who live almost exclusively on human flesh in Hollywood movies, make short work of both of them. As one reviewer put it: "Pierre's rough, Indian-like way of making love is the cause of his death."[32]

The movie half-breed was always an alien, a man of degenerate blood, and Hollywood let no one forget it. Those words were actually used in the subtitles of *God's Country and the Law,* which referred to Jacques Doré's "strange heritage of degenerate blood." And when the villainous Doré approached his quarry, the title read: "Across the sunny forest home fell the ugly shadow of an alien intruder."

Similarly, the drunken half-breed in *A Romance in the Fur Country* sees gold in the hands of a trapper and this "arouses all (his) thievish instincts."[33]

The original Pierre of the Plains was a half-breed reprobate "in whose veins the volatile blood of the French and the crafty daring of the Indians are mixed in puzzling proportions."[34]

And then there is Jacques of *Jacques the Wolf,* who sells whisky to the Indians and "even goes so far as to aspire for the hand of one of the officer's daughters." This Jacques, the fans were told, "possesses a complex nature unfamiliar to modern civilization, but, according to authority, it is not uncommon in a land where the Indian has mixed with French and English."[35]

In the silents of the twenties the sexual element was discarded and the movie half-breeds settled down to being normal fiends, like Jules Lagarée in *The Flaming Forest,* whom Louella Parsons described as "an old-fashioned villain without a good quality to his name."[36] The character was loosely based on that of Louis Riel in the Red River uprising of 1869-70; Miss Parsons, in her review, praised the actor, Oscar Beregi, for giving "a uniquely interesting conception of the black-hearted half-breed leader."

The great movie crime was selling liquor to the Indians; it provided the theme for dozens of pictures about the mounted police. In this debauchery, half-breeds were invariably the scoundrels who peddled the

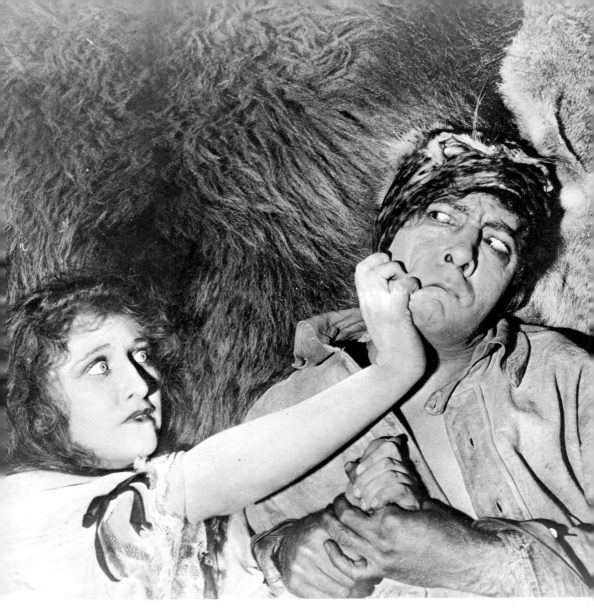

Ruth Clifford as Marie Louise fights off Julio Sandoval (Monroe Salisbury),
the half-breed who attempts to rape her in The Savage, *a 1917 feature.*

The Wicked Half-Breed

There was no other kind as far as Hollywood
was concerned—and he (or she) was always half
French-Canadian.

Above: Movie Mounties were generally shown apprehending movie half-breeds. Here Sgt. Brian Scott, played by Charles Byer, gets the goods on a French half-breed fur pirate in a 1928 picture called Red Riders of Canada.

Opposite: A young J. Carroll Naish plays the sneaky half-breed in Rose Marie *(1936) who steals Jeanette MacDonald's money and leaves her stranded in the Northwoods of Quebec. Fortunately, Nelson Eddy is around to bring the miscreant to justice.*

Villainous whisky-smuggler Jacques Doré, played by William Tooker
in God's Country and the Law *(1921), menaces Gladys Leslie above. He was*
described in the subtitles as an "alien intruder . . . of degenerate blood."

Opposite: George Bancroft as Jacques Corbeau, the half-breed whisky-runner in
North West Mounted Police, *turns the Gatling gun on the Mounties, thereby reversing*
history. That's Akim Tamiroff as Dan Duroc, another wicked half-breed, at the far right.

93

*Half-breed women were generally shown
to be insanely jealous, which is
why so many carried knives. In* Where
The North Begins *(left), Myrtle Owen
as Marie, the half-breed mistress of a
wicked factor, menaces Felice McTavish
(Claire Adams) of whom she is jealous.
Paulette Goddard, above, played the
half-breed girl Louvette in* North West
Mounted Police. *She not only carried a
knife in that picture; in one scene she
apparently tried her best to eat it.*

The last of the movie half-breeds to be featured in a film about Canada
was Thomas Gomez is the role of Natayo Smith in Pony Soldier, *with Tyrone Power.*
Gomez portrayed a sneaky, grasping, cowardly, dirty half-breed.

illicit rotgut. They were the most expendable of all movie characters: there must be at least two dozen films in which hero or heroine, wrongly accused of a base crime, is saved at the last moment by the confession of a captured and often dying half-breed.

These early portrayals helped to freeze the half-breed stereotype for all time. The pattern was set by the time the talkies arrived. The 1933 serial, *Clancy of the Mounted,* is packed with renegade half-breeds who menace the heroine. In *Rose Marie* it's J. Carroll Naish, in the role of a sneaky half-breed guide, who steals Jeanette MacDonald's money and then deserts her. "That's the trouble with these half-breeds, you can't trust them," the local storekeeper tells her.

The main villain in *North West Mounted Police* is a murderous half-breed, Jacques Corbeau, who sells whisky to the Indians. In *Renfrew of the Royal Mounted* one of the villains is Pierre, a half-breed who lures the heroine away with a fake letter and sneakily leaves her, hoping she'll drown in a whirlpool. In *Northern Pursuit* (1943) Monte Blue plays the part of a half-breed traitor, helping Nazi spies in Canada.

The last of the movie half-breeds was probably Natayo Smith, a role taken by Thomas Gomez in *Pony Soldier.* Gomez didn't exactly play a wicked half-breed, merely a sneaky one with long, greasy hair, who wore his cowardice on one sleeve and his avarice on the other – definitely a man not to be trusted.

The half-breed women in Hollywood's Canada were spitfires, like their French-Canadian sisters – but sneaky spitfires who would do any-thing to get and hold their lovers, usually white men. They wore the standard Hollywood Female Half-Breed Costume: long black hair in braids, often to the waist, long necklaces of beads or animal teeth, buckskin or leather skirts, and high boots.

"I die if you not marry me!" cries Marie Beaubien, the hot-blooded mistress of the Machiavellian factor in *The Law of the North* (1917), and she does die after she tries to betray him out of jealousy over a white girl.

Betrayal was standard conduct among such women in the movies. Another Marie, equally jealous, betrays her lover Bateese whom she finds trying to seduce a white woman in *Paid in Advance.* Woolie-Woolie, the passionate half-breed girl in *Men of the North,* jealous of the white hero's love for a white girl, tries to frame him as a thief. In *The Calgary Stampede* Neenah puts the blame for a murder on the cowboy hero to save her boyfriend from the noose, and then betrays her boyfriend when she finds him with another woman.

In the movies half-breed women spelled trouble for white men, as did Marie Duprée, "a capricious coquette" in love with a mounted policeman whom she "torments without mercy"[37] in *The Trapper's Revenge.* Such

97

creatures simply could not control their wild emotions. The half-breed girl in *A Child of the North* saves the life of a white stranger but becomes mad with rage and jealousy when she finds he is preparing for a hasty marriage with a white schoolmistress; so she shoots him.

Hollywood made it clear that it was white men these women were after; it was in their blood. When Babette Dufresne spots Blue Blazes Rawden in the Timber Cove Saloon, knocking back drink after drink and smashing up the furniture, she cannot resist him. As the subtitle puts it: "A savage strain from an Indian mother . . . makes the girl see a master in the forest wolf."

By the time Cecil B. DeMille made *North West Mounted Police* in 1940, it was not possible for an actress to portray a girl of mixed blood in any other manner. Nobody knew this better than Paulette Goddard, who desperately wanted the role of Louvette, the hot-blooded daughter of Jacques Corbeau. In the movie Louvette commits an unspeakable crime: she lures a mounted policeman away from his duty, causing the death of a comrade and precipitating the Duck Lake Massacre that touched off the North West Rebellion.

As DeMille told the story in his autobiography, he had been searching for the right actress to play Louvette with no success at all until, one day, his assistant, Florence Cole, came into his office and said, "Louvette is here to see you." The director was baffled but told her to usher Louvette in.

> Florence stepped back from the door, and a dark girl with eyes that could smolder or melt, came in, made up as a half breed and costumed as such a girl would dress on the wild Canadian frontier in the 1880s.
>
> She gave me an insolent look and said, "You teenk you wan beeg director, hah? Me, Louvette, show you!"
>
> That was enough; Paulette Goddard had the part. [38]

Miss Goddard flung herself into her role with what the distinguished British documentary maker and critic, Basil Wright, called "horrid vivacity."[39] Most reviewers, however, thought she played the role with realistic perfection. The picture itself reinforces all the myths of the infamous, whisky-smuggling half-breed and his treacherous sex-mad daughter. "I told you to forget that klootch," Sergeant Jim Bret warns Corporal Ronnie Logan at the start of the story. "She's poison. Never trust a blue-eyed squaw." But Ronnie cannot forget her: "Listen, you little wildcat," he murmurs to her, "you're the only real thing that has ever happened to me." Louvette is shown to be dishonest early in the movie. When she tries to sell some furs to a stranger, a Scots trader warns him not to buy: "She steals 'em," he explains. At that remark, Louvette rushes at him with a blade. "I t'eenk I keel you!" she cries.

98

DeMille points up the contrast between the unprincipled native and the highly moral white in a scene in which April Logan, the oh-so-English nurse from Nova Scotia – blonde, prim, and perfect (the role was played by Madeleine Carroll) – confronts Louvette in her cabin. "You're a savage, Louvette!" she says, "a vicious, cruel savage. Plotting revenge is all you know – not love." To make sure the audience gets the point, the director shows Louvette tearing apart a prairie chicken with her hands and stuffing it in her mouth.

Ronnie, of course, has been captured by the savage's witchery, though he senses that Louvette is poison. She is, however, "the sweetest poison that ever got into a man's blood." At that point, Louvette moves toward her ultimate treachery. "I got beeg love for you," she tells Ronnie. "My father gone keel me because I love redcoat. We be married tonight or we be married never." That does it. Ronnie leaves his post; his comrade is killed by half-breeds (with an arrow, naturally) and Ronnie is imprisoned by Louvette to spare him from the massacre that follows. It is perhaps unnecessary to add that neither of them survives to the picture's close.

This unrelenting libel on the Métis – a word incidentally that Holly-wood rarely used (although DeMille used it) – can neither be excused by pointing to the tenor of the times in which it occurred, nor explained away by the essential naïveté of the silent films, nor condoned by the need of screenwriters and directors to inject drama and conflict into their stories. *Nobody* – not the blacks, not the Indians – has suffered as badly at the hands of the film makers as have the Métis. To this day the word half-breed conjures up an unpleasant picture. It can no longer be used since it has become – like Nigger, Spik, Hunkie, and Wop – a nasty word, made nasty in this instance by Hollywood. It has been used in this book only because it is necessary to the context.

The historical and anthropological truth about the Métis is almost the exact opposite of the impression conveyed by the movies. To present them as a lawless breed, constantly pursued by the mounted police, is to fly directly in the face of established fact. They did *not* sell whisky to the Indians; that crime must be laid at the feet of the white men – first the great fur-trading companies and later the American renegades who built the notorious whisky forts in what is now southern Alberta.

It was the Métis and not the white men who first brought the law to the untrammelled northwest, building a code based on the sensible and strict orthodoxy of the buffalo hunt. At the Métis community of St. Laurent – where the great Gabriel Dumont ("the prince of the prairies") was leader – the people, unable to wait for the Canadian government to bring the law to the prairie country, set up laws of their own, organizing a local government and a real estate code; fixing penalties for theft, slander, seduction, and arson; establishing a free ferry service; and choosing, in Dumont, a president who made it quite clear that he had no intention of setting up an independent state. And all this took place before the arrival of the North West Mounted Police.

It was not Métis lawlessness that brought the police; it was the depredations of white invaders from south of the border. They murdered Indians, poisoned wolves, exchanged rotgut whisky for furs and were a law unto themselves. Before the police came, the Métis communities acted as the only brake against widespread mayhem instigated by white predators. As John Jennings, a student of mounted police-Indian relations, has explained: "Within Assiniboia, which had an extremely low crime rate, the preservation of order rested mainly on the Métis population, which had a significant stake in the police force." When the force arrived in the west in 1874 they were "thus given the great advantage of dealing with Indians who . . . were enthusiastic about having Canadian law extended to them. It was the American whisky-traders whom the Indians distrusted, not the Canadian 'half-breeds'."[40]

Flamboyant the Métis certainly were. They rode as if they had been born on horseback and they shot straight – at buffalo, not at each other. They loved to dance and they loved to sing and some of them loved to drink and gamble. But they did not murder and they did not steal and they did not seduce. All the evidence shows that they lived by a strict code of laws that encouraged community co-operation. At the forks of the Saskatchewan they were engineering, of their own free will, social change that has generally taken ages to accomplish: the transformation of a nomadic hunting culture into a static agricultural society. They were all good Christians. A Métis would have had to be a hungry man to shoot a buffalo on a Sunday for the laws of the hunt forbade it. And, more than their fellow whites, they believed in and tried to live up to the golden rule. They did nothing to deserve the stigma with which the movies branded them. But, alas, they had no pressure groups to resist it.

It's especially ironic that the American attitude to the half-breed, nurtured first by the inventions of pulp writers like Ned Buntline (the inventor of Buffalo Bill) and later on by the movies, should have become a Canadian attitude. For it wasn't a Canadian attitude in the northwest in the days when the mounted police arrived. The sympathies of the police lay with the Métis, as the official correspondence shows, right up to the eve of the 1885 rebellion. It is quite true that the Orange population of Ontario came to hate the Métis – but not because of their "degenerate blood" and not because they were seen as sneaky, thieving seducers. They were hated because they were rebels and because they were Catholics. Hollywood took no notice of this, of course, and the word half-breed no longer conjures up a mental picture of a Popish rebel. In Americanizing the Métis, the moviemakers even robbed us of our distinctive Canadian passions.

4: "Savage tribes . . . ready to explode . . ."

The Hollywood Canadian Indian differed in no way from the Hollywood American Indian. He even dressed like an American Indian, no matter where his hunting grounds lay. From the rolling Chilcotin country of British Columbia to the forests of Quebec, he was always shown wearing what the Friars in their book call The Instant Indian Kit, consisting of wig, war bonnet or headband, buckskin leggings, with or without matching vest, and moccasins. Blackfoot or Iroquois, Chipewyan or Cree, every Indian shown on the screen looked like every other Indian.

Clifford Wilson, editor of the Hudson's Bay Company's magazine The Beaver, was technical adviser on the film *Hudson's Bay*. He reported that "the Hollywood costumers, like most other people, seem to think that the Indian wore a sort of uniform of buckskin leggings and hair parted in the middle hanging in two plaits." Wilson tried to explain that the hair-do, especially, would be extremely varied, depending on individual tastes. His advice was ignored. "It was so much easier to buy fifty or one hundred wigs all of the same pattern."[41]

The movie braves, when not attired in the cumbersome war bonnets that in real life would make concealment impossible, are invariably shown with bands on their heads, as are all Indian maidens. Actually, as the Friars have pointed out, the beaded headband is a Hollywood invention, not an Indian one. But it has become so engrained in the culture, thanks to the movies, that many young native North Americans on both sides of the border have taken to wearing it, in the mistaken belief that they are preserving a small fragment of their own heritage. The Friars' theory is the headband was first popularized in American wild west shows and later, in Hollywood's early days, to prevent wigs from falling off the actors' heads.

Canadian Indians learned to use firearms almost as soon as the white man landed on these shores; and yet in movie after movie they have been shown with two primitive weapons: the tomahawk and the bow and arrow. In *Yukon Vengeance* twentieth-century "Athabascans" were depicted on a reservation in the Northwest Territories, living in painted skin teepees, wearing buckskin clothing and feathered war bonnets (which are

101

actually Sioux in origin), beating on death drums, and wielding tomahawks. "Soon sun will hide behind mountain in west, then murder of Gray Shadow will be avenged," says Chief Lone Eagle as a Mountie captive is dragged in. A stake is prepared, faggots are piled high, and the policeman is tied to it. "White man die in fire," the chief intones. "Die slow. Much pain." But the chief is persuaded to stage a trial by combat instead – with tomahawks, of course. "Great Spirit tell Lone Eagle who speaks truth," the chief declares. Fortunately, the Great Spirit gives the nod to the Mountie. That movie, in which the Princess Yellow Flower actually uses the phrase "white man's tongue is forked," was made in 1954.

The big Indian numbers staged in the two sound versions of *Rose Marie* are something to ponder on. In the 1936 picture, which is clearly set in Quebec, Nelson Eddy as the mounted policeman tells Jeanette MacDonald (Rose Marie) that a big Indian festival is about to be staged down by the lake: "We only thank one God, they thank everybody. The corn, the sun, the rain, their ancestors. . . ." The Indians, he adds, come from miles around to take part in it. And they certainly do. The dance that follows seems to borrow something from every Indian culture: there are Plains headdresses, Mexican shawls, Aztec breech clouts, medicine men with gigantic beaks, squaws with papooses on their backs, naked Indians, buckskin-clad Indians, west-coast totem poles, drums twelve feet high, and the Great Spirit knows what else – an aboriginal mulligan stew that makes a joke of Canadian Indian culture.

In the 1954 version the same number was staged by Busby Berkeley, who threw everything into it except a burning stake. He had one of the biggest totem poles ever seen in the movies, a Sioux medicine man with black horns, a bevy of naked Aztec-style Indian girls waving immense pennants, and a chorus of braves in breech clouts all shouting something that sounded like "Gitchi Gooma." The background was about as far removed from the Canadian Rockies (where the scene was supposedly set) as Montreal is from Banff. The flat rocks, arranged in a kind of vast circle, were apparently meant to suggest the mesa country of the American southwest. The only items missing in the entire production were a genuine Canadian Indian and a genuine Canadian Indian costume.

But who really knew what a genuine Canadian Indian looked like? Certainly not Hollywood costumers and probably very few Canadian moviegoers. For years in the late twenties and early thirties, a blue-eyed Scotsman named Archie Belaney fooled an entire continent into believing that he was an Indian named Grey Owl. He wrote books in which his picture appeared, made several movies in which he was shown with his friend the beaver, and went on exhausting lecture tours throughout Canada, the United States, and England, and *everybody* who saw him thought he was an Indian. Nobody twigged to the fact that he was a white man. Hardboiled newspapermen thought he was an Indian. Officials in the national parks thought he was an Indian. Even his publishers thought he was an Indian.

How could this be? He looked no more like an Indian than the Governor General did. He lived among the Ojibways, but he didn't look a bit like an Ojibway. He claimed to be part Apache, but he didn't look anything like an Apache. With his thin nose, his ascetic face, and his blue eyes he looked like a Britisher with a public school background which, in essence, he was. Why, then, did everybody believe the story that he was an Indian?

The answer must be that Belaney looked like a *Hollywood* Indian. Indeed, he was invariably pictured wearing the Instant Indian Kit, complete with black hair, braided and parted in the middle, and buckskin jacket. For years nobody really looked at Indians in Canada, although there were plenty to look at. They looked at Indians in movies about Canada. And that was the secret of Archie Belaney's masquerade.

In Hollywood's Canada, as in Hollywood's USA, the Indian was a primitive savage. He attacked wagon trains, burned down settlers' cabins, and did his best to torture people at the stake. There was a significant difference, however, between the Indian stereotype and that of the half-breed. The Indians were almost always given a motivation for their actions, which, if it didn't excuse their savagery, at least explained it: they wanted to stop the march of civilization across their hunting grounds; they had been fed liquor by a renegade half-breed, which turned them into wild men; or there was a radical minority among them who prevailed over wiser heads.

The half-breed, on the other hand, acted out of pure cussedness; he was evil because he liked to be evil; unlike the Indian he knew the difference between right and wrong, which is why so many silent pictures were able to show half-breed villains repenting and confessing on their death beds.

There was an even greater difference in the silent pictures' treatment of Canadian Indian women. Unlike their hot-blooded half-sisters, the Indians were portrayed as small, gentle creatures, like little Fawn Afraid in *The Trail of the Silver Fox* or Little Snow Bird in *The Lure of Heart's Desire*, who carries the hero safely out of a blizzard and then dies of grief when he marries a white girl. Indian maidens were generally pictured as victims of unrequited love, who nursed white men back to health, as Singing Pine did in *Unseeing Eyes* or as Wauna did in *White Hell*. These lovely, sad-eyed creatures with their beaded headbands, single eagle feather, buckskins, and braids – so different from the knife-wielding Louvettes and the passionate, treacherous Woolie-Woolies – succoured their hero only that he might marry into his own race.

In the very early days of the silents there were a few bad Indians who tried to steal furs or white girls; and there were a few good ones, too. (*They* knifed half-breeds.)[42] But with the development of a Hollywood mythology of the old west, the Indians in the movies ceased to act as individuals and were seen as members of a band, pounding on tom-toms in front of their teepees, swooping down on horseback to attack white settlers, and generally whooping it up. Like Wolf Pelt in *Susannah of the Mounties,* Black Bear in *Perils of the Royal Mounted,* or Konah in *Pony Soldier,* the Indian heavies operated within the tribe, stirring up the braves to fight against the better instincts of the chiefs. By the use of this device Hollywood was able to show plenty of Indians shedding white blood without appearing to be anti-Indian.

Nonetheless, Canadian Indians have been atrociously libelled by the American motion picture industry. The nation that suffered most at the hands of the screenwriters was the great Blackfoot Confederacy of the western foothills. Hollywood fell in love with the word Blackfoot in the very early years and sprinkled the country with Blackfoot Indians. They turn up in a 1911 movie in French Canada, of all places, and they turn up forty years later in the Chilcotin country of western British Columbia! There is a Blackfoot Indian "on the edge of the great woods" in *God's Country and the Law* and several more in Hudson Bay territory in *The Primal Lure.* Then there is the town of Blackfoot, Canada, in *Bulldogs of the Trail,* set somewhere in the Canadian northwest, "where strenuous incidents in life are quite common;"[43] and the town of Blackfoot Crossing in the mining country of *Fangs of the Arctic.*

Throughout the history of Canadian-subject films, the Blackfoot were shown as vicious savages. In *True to His Trust* (1910) they attack a settler's cabin, loot it, and set it aflame. In *For the Flag* (1911) they capture and condemn the heroine's lover to death. In *The Flaming Forest* (1926) they battle the mounted police. In *The Primal Lure* they do their best to burn William S. Hart at the stake. In *Susannah of the Mounties* they attempt the same thing with Randolph Scott and in *The Cariboo Trail* (1950) they make a second attempt on Scott who, having been saved by the last-minute intervention of Shirley Temple in one film, is saved by the timely arrival of a vicious mule in the other.

All of this is historical twaddle. The Plains Indians in general and the Blackfoot in particular did not torture white men or burn *anybody* at the stake. It was not part of their culture. Nor did they attack wagon trains, sack settlers' cabins, or do battle with the mounted police. The Blackfoot, under their great chief, Crowfoot, were the most peaceful of all the Plains

Indians. They signed one of the earliest western treaties and shunned the repeated abjurations of the Crees and Métis to join in the rebellion of 1885.

But Hollywood has made little distinction between Canadian Blackfoot and Cree on the one hand and American Apaches and Comanches on the other. "This is the story of the old North West Territories of Canada – the earliest days of the North West Mounted Police," Tyrone Power as Constable Duncan MacDonald announces in the opening commentary of *Pony Soldier*. (The disembodied voice makes it sound like a documentary.) ". . . We were trying to bring the law and keep the peace throughout thousands of square miles of Indian territory. . . . In those days it was a powder keg. Savage tribes in the mountains were ready to explode into bloody war. To prevent that was our job. . . ." And later, another piece of unadulterated fantasy: "All warlike Canadian tribes were restless. . . ."

Any Canadian schoolchild knows that it was not the Indians whom the Mounties were sent west to subdue, but the whites. "How do you keep your whites in order?" was the wistful question asked by the US Secretary of the Interior to his Canadian counterpart in 1877.[44] The answer to that question is central to an understanding of the essential differences between the two frontiers. For it was the whites and not the Indians who committed the worst crimes in the Canadian northwest and caused the major problems to the mounted police. And it was the Indians who kept the peace. To quote John Jennings again: "It is not too much to say that the mounted police could not have functioned without the rapport that was built up between officers of the force and Indian chiefs."[45]

Yet *Pony Soldier* shows Canadian Crees swooping down on a US cavalry detachment, attacking a wagon train, killing or capturing its members, and attempting to execute a white man by spread-eagling him among four horses. Chief Standing Bear is depicted as a man unable to hold a young radical, Konah, in check (Hollywood's copout again) until MacDonald of the Mounted appears and brings matters to a successful if bloody conclusion. The crowning insult is a suggestion at the end of the picture that the events portrayed actually happened.

The Indian attack on the settlers' wagon train has long been a standard Hollywood western cliché, so it is not surprising to see these scenes repeated in movies set in Canada. Shirley Temple was the only survivor of a wagon-train massacre in *Susannah of the Mounties* and so was Shelley Winters in *Saskatchewan*. Later in that movie she learns that Alan Ladd himself was found under a flaming wagon when a child and brought up by the Crees. None of this makes much sense. Wagon trains were all but non-existent in Canada, since there were no settlers or homesteaders in the far west before the police arrived; and there is certainly no shred of historical evidence to suggest that any wagon train was ever attacked by any Canadian Indian band.

Nor did Canadian Indians ever attack the Canadian Pacific Railway, although that idea is central to the plot of the two American films about the building of the CPR. "The Indians resented the coming of the railway," the opening subtitle of *Susannah of the Mounties* declares, "and only the vigilance of the North West Mounted Police forestalled open warfare." Again, this is pure bunk. Chief Crowfoot, who rightly resented the railway builders crossing his land without a by-your-leave, cheerfully accepted a trade-off from the government and spent his declining years riding back and forth on the trains using a free pass given him by the CPR. The only other protest, that of Chief Piapot, lasted exactly fifteen minutes. Yet in *Susannah of the Mounties* there is a full-dress Indian battle – a bloody attack on the police post and on the railway, buildings aflame, tom-toms beating, smoke signals of course, Randolph Scott with both feet in the faggots, native warriors leaping around the stake, and the usual last-minute rescue.

Scott escaped unscathed to return in *Canadian Pacific,* which is the kind of movie that has white men greeting Indians with the salutation "How!" This picture, too, reaches its climax with half-naked, feathered savages whooping and hollering, brandishing tomahawks, and shooting flaming arrows into a barricaded work train in the heart of the Rockies. The mayhem is relieved by a comic scene in which Scott's sidekick, played by J. Carroll Naish, perpetrates a cunning trick on the redskins, who have captured him. He hands each brave a stick of dynamite and the dumb Indians light up, believing that he is giving out cigars. That is the end of the Indians but not of Naish, who miraculously escapes.

Scott turned up next in *The Cariboo Trail* and was once again beset by aborigines. The story has him taking part in the gold rush of 1862 in the Chilcotin country of British Columbia where, once again, the Blackfoot are busily at work in their Instant Indian Kits and war paint, having been conveniently moved several hundred miles west across three ranges of mountains from their traditional prairie hunting grounds.

These Indians, wielding the usual Hollywood tomahawks and bows and arrows, are presented as scalpers. "White man come Indian land. Indian kill white man. White man no come," the chief tells Scott, explaining why he is going to burn him up. Fortunately Scott's comic sidekick, Grizzly, played by Gabby Hayes, has a mule that kicks every time Grizzly asks him to; there follows another hilarious scene in which the mule kicks several of the dumb Indians to death.

The picture's climax features the usual battle, with Scott and his friends barricaded behind covered wagons, picking off their attackers

106

with rifle fire until help arrives. It turns out that the Indians were put up to this outrage by the villain of the story played by Victor Jory, who was also typecast as a provocateur in both *Canadian Pacific* and *Susannah of the Mounties*. Once *he* is disposed of, the Blackfoot give no more trouble.

If Hollywood's favourite Canadian Indians were the Blackfoot, its favourite American Indians were surely the Sioux (although a case can be made for the Apaches). The Sioux under Sitting Bull wiped out Custer, so it was natural that Hollywood should follow their further adventures after they crossed the Canadian border. Three major pictures dealt with this incident in history, *Fort Vengeance, Saskatchewan,* and *The Canadians*. The first two libelled the Sioux and the last one (as will be seen later) libelled the Mounties.

Both *Fort Vengeance* and *Saskatchewan* completely reversed history by turning Sitting Bull and his followers into villainous invaders, bent on rousting out the Canadian tribes to attack the mounted police and eradicate white influence in the Canadian Northwest.

In *Fort Vengeance*, Sitting Bull tries to persuade Chief Crowfoot to join him in a massacre. When Crowfoot demurs, Bull decides to stir things up himself: "You, Broken Lance, take some braves, find the white settlers, kill them, burn their homes, strike swiftly, and return here. When a few of the white settlers and their squaws are killed, the redcoats will come here seeking vengeance and when that happens, Crowfoot's tribes will be angered enough to fight."

The stock Hollywood-style atrocities follow (more blazing wagon trains). In the picture's climax Bull comes within a whisker of getting Crowfoot to help him wipe out the NWMP, since one of the Blackfoot braves is about to be executed for a crime he didn't commit. Fortunately Sergeant Ross of the Mounted arrives at the last moment with the real miscreant, Pierre Louboque – the standard unkempt trapper – and Sitting Bull's plan is frustrated.

In *Saskatchewan* the story is similar. Sitting Bull and his vandals are swarming into Canada and this time it's the Crees whom they want as partners in a massacre of whites. Bull's advance guard has already annihilated Shelley Winters' wagon train and now the conquerors of the Little Big Horn are dogging Alan Ladd's trail. "There are enough Indians out there to take over the whole western Canada," says Ladd's comic French-Canadian sidekick, played by J. Carroll Naish. Fortunately, the Sioux's innate treachery – they also intend to wipe out the Crees – is discovered by Ladd, who averts a bloodbath and saves the Canadian west from predatory Indians.

Hollywood presented *Saskatchewan* to moviegoers as the real thing. As part of the main title, this message appeared:

The motion picture you are about to see was photographed in the locale where the original events upon which it is based occurred – events that gravely threatened the peaceful development of Western Canada.

To put the final seal of approval on the documentary nature of the movie, there was a note at the end thanking "Canadian friends for their generosity and co-operation."

The geographical mumbo-jumbo did not fool Canadians. The locale was all wrong and everybody knew it. But what about "the original events" which threatened the development of the west? Nothing remotely resembling them ever took place. Indeed, the peaceful movement of the Sioux across the border after the battle with Custer is one of the remarkable chapters in the history of the Canadian frontier. Never at any time was there the slightest suggestion of bloodshed by Sitting Bull or his Sioux. On the contrary, the Indians fled across the "medicine line" to seek the protection of the Queen and to escape massacre by the US military. The force first met up with the Sioux at a place called Old Wives' Creek during the famous march west. The Indians were treated with dignity and pomp, including a fanfare of trumpets. The police were drawn up in their dress uniforms and the Sioux were given presents. In return the Sioux danced and sang for their hosts.

The first Canadian official to shake the hand of Sitting Bull after he and his followers crossed the border was the legendary superintendent, James Walsh. The famous medicine man told Walsh that he had buried his weapons before coming to the land of the white queen and that he desired to know her laws. He had not come to Canada seeking blood, he said – "The grass in Canada is not stained with blood" – all he wanted to do was rest and be relieved of war. For several years, before they returned to the United States, he and his people were model refugees. Their memory deserves something better than the cheap posturings of Hollywood bit-players in their Instant Indian Kits.*

---

* I have not dealt in this chapter with the treatment of the Canadian Eskimo by Hollywood. There have been only about a half-dozen pictures and all have been filmed in the Arctic, using native Eskimos as actors in semi-documentary fashion. Selig made two films in Labrador in 1911, *The Way of the Eskimo* and *Lost in the Arctic*. Then, following Flaherty's *Nanook of the North* in 1924, Earl Rossman, a big game hunter and explorer, made *Kivalina of the Icelands* in 1925. W. S. Van Dyke, who had worked with Flaherty in the south seas, took almost a full year in the Arctic to make *Eskimo* for MGM in 1933, based on a story by the famous explorer, Peter Freuchen. Because the producers were working under real conditions with the actual people, all these films portrayed the Eskimos both realistically and sympathetically. (It was palpably impossible to try to simulate high Arctic conditions in California.) In *Eskimo* the theme was that of the corrupting influence of white civilization on a peaceful and charming primitive people. The story lines of *The Savage Innocents* (1959), a non-Hollywood production, and *The White Dawn* (1974) followed in the same tradition.

PART THREE

Perils
of the
Royal Mounted

1: "Broken hearted, he carries out orders . . ."

Of the 575 motion pictures that Hollywood has made about Canada 256 have featured the Royal Canadian Mounted Police or their predecessors, the Royal North West Mounted Police, or *their* predecessors, the North West Mounted Police. Hollywood hasn't always got its nomenclature straight. Some movies refer to the Royal Mounted Police, or the Canadian Mounted Police, others to the Royal Canadian North West Mounted Police, or even the North West Canadian Mounted Police; but the movie industry's unrequited love affair with the force has been passionate and long-standing.

The number of Mounted movies noted above covers only those in which the mounted police are central to the story. In most pictures about Canada there's at least one Mountie to be seen somewhere, and always in his scarlet uniform. In the opening scene of *The Happy Time,* for instance, a whole gallop of Mounties passes by, almost knocking Charles Boyer to the ground. In *Scandal at Scourie* one turns up on a railway platform in western Ontario, an unlikely place to find a member of the force at the turn of the century. In *I Confess* Mounties form a kind of background frieze.

To an international audience, Canada and the mounted police are inseparable. Hollywood has banished them from the screen only in those pictures where shoot-ups were required and the presence of the law would wreck the plot. Even then, as in *North of Hudson Bay,* sometimes a stock Mountie – shoes glistening, dress uniform brushed – pops in and out of the picture long enough to register the fact that this is indeed the Northwest, and then conveniently vanishes, allowing the wicked factor to get on with his dirty work.

The movie Mountie was almost invariably brave, noble, honourable, courteous, kind, and trustworthy – all the standard Boy Scout qualities, to go with the hat. There have scarcely ever been any bad Mounties or even droll Mounties in the motion pictures, at least not intentionally. In a comedy like *Dangerous Nan McGrew* the Mountie gets the straight lines. He is the quintessential hero and he always wins. He gets his man and he

111

usually gets his girl (or nobly gives her to another). "All Canadian heroes belong to the Royal Mounted,"[1] one reviewer commented in 1919, with only the tiniest touch of irony. For half a century that was Hollywood's credo.

When the first Mountie movie, a one-reeler titled *The Cattle Thieves*, was released by the Kalem Company in 1909 the advertising was ecstatic: "This marvelous production introduces for the first time to the American public the heroes of the NORTHWEST MOUNTED POLICE, generally conceded to be the most wonderful organization of trained men in the world."[2]

This hyperbole continued for more than a decade. G. F. Blaisdel, reviewing *Silent Jim* in 1912, wrote that "this wonderful constabulary . . . has had a history which is the pride of the English speaking race."[3] And in 1922 the press sheet for *Man's Law and God's* pulled out all the stops when it hailed the RNWMP as "the most dapper police organization in the world, the most famous, renowned for their gallantry, their valor, their courage, their traditions, and their esprit de corps. . . . Honor is placed above life itself and duty above dictates of the heart."

At that juncture Hollywood had produced no fewer than 188 Mountie movies, forty-eight of them the feature-length variety that came into vogue after 1914. Then, in a single record year in 1922, the production houses ground out twenty-three more. This glut caused critics and exhibitors, if not audiences, to become more than a little jaded. "Keep down the RNWMP angle and play up the snows and fights,"[4] exhibitors of *Man Trackers* were warned in 1921. "Ignore the Mounted Police angle. . . ."[5] the trade suggested when *The Silent Vow* was issued in 1922. "Impersonally considered, the story of the Northwest mounted police is, by now, almost devoid of novelty,"[6] Moving Picture World reported in June of that same year.

"The poor Canadian mounted police!" wrote Charles Larkin, another reviewer. "What lives they must lead if we are to believe all the things depicted on our shadow stage. It seems that when stories run low, someone is always called in and taking the usual formula dashes off a tale of the Mounted. Of course there is a great deal of romance connected with these sleuths of the snows, but it is getting a bit monotonous watching this everlasting effort of a trooper 'getting his man.'"[7]

The critics might carp, but the public continued to flock to the Mountie movies. "It was generally supposed that the last Northwest Mounted Police story had been filmed and shown months ago, and that no more were to be inflicted upon the public,"[8] a pained New York Times movie critic wrote in 1923. The supposition was dead wrong. Over the

112

next eight years – to the end of the silent era – the motion picture industry made forty-one *more* features about the Mounties, almost as many as it had turned out in the first eight years of the feature film cycle, before that record year of 1922.

When sound came in Variety again curtly dismissed the Mountie movie. Its reviewer, reporting on the 1930 production of *River's End,* pointed out: "It's the Royal Northwest Mounted. That immediately implies B house classification. . . ."[9] Little did the show business Bible realize that the biggest and most successful Mountie movies, with the biggest and most successful star names, were yet to come.

So used did the moviegoing public become to seeing Mounties in northern pictures that some producers even tried to sneak them across the border. Mae West's *Klondike Annie* was set in Nome, Alaska, about 1,500 miles from Canadian jurisdiction, but Inspector Jack Forrest looks suspiciously like a Mountie in this film. He wears the familiar Stetson, the buffalo coat, the unique breeches with the wide stripe and high leather boots. He also falls in love with Mae West. He and his colleague wear no insignia and are identified only as police, but since no such costume existed for the men who kept the peace in Nome, it's obvious the producers were fudging a little: enough to fool the Toronto Daily Star's reviewer, who described Forrest as a "young Yukon Mountie,"[10] and no less a critic than Graham Greene, whose review in The Spectator referred to Forrest and his colleague as "the Canadian police."[11]

The "trooper" who always got his man, of whom Charles Larkin wearily complained, has long since become part of the Hollywood mythology about Canada, so much so that the makers of *Find Your Man,* a 1922 movie starring Rin-Tin-Tin, were driven to explain that "contrary to what might be inferred from the title . . . [it] has nothing whatever to do with the Northwest Mounted Police."[12] And one RCMP official was forced to explain to a Hollywood producer that the force's motto was *not* "Get Your Man" but "Maintain the Right."

O'Malley of the Mounted, a William S. Hart thriller, even opened with a scrap of Get Your Man doggerel:

> There's no hiding place for me
> South or North of '53
> For a Mounted Man's been told
> To bring me back

The police were seen as supermen, free of normal human appetites when on the trail of their man. When Warner Brothers was making *Heart*

113

of the North in 1938 the technical adviser on the film, a former mounted policeman named Bruce Carruthers, suggested a sequence in the movie which would allow six redcoats to stop for what the force calls "noon camp;" after all they had been chasing a group of desperadoes through the snows of the far north for days without even taking time out for a cheese sandwich. The director rebelled at the suggestion. "My God," he said, "these men are Mounties and they are out to get their man – they haven't got time to stop to eat!"[13]

The apotheosis of the Get Your Man movie was probably a 1917 picture titled *Until They Get Me.* The theme was described as "the doggedness of the Canadian Mounted Police, how they never give up hope of tracking a wanted man though years may pass and love make the capture undesirable. . . ." Actually, the picture, to modern eyes at least, comes dangerously close to being a comedy (although it wasn't so intended) since it deals with an unfortunate member of the force who, try as he might, just can't seem to *get* his man.

Constable Richard Selwyn, who is a pretty scruffy looking Mountie, as most movie Mounties were in the early pictures, is just too soft-hearted to get his man. It is, after all, his first day with the force and so he allows his quarry, a murderer named Kirby, to play upon his sympathy. When the murderer asks permission to take one last look at his dead wife, who has expired in an adjacent room, Selwyn relents, and then goes after the wrong man, believing that Kirby has escaped through a window. Firing wildly (from horseback, of course), Selwyn almost shoots down a passing Indian whom he believes to be the escapee, only to realize that he has been tricked and his man has got away.

The rest of the film deals with the tragedy of a Mountie who fails to get his man. "You blundered," his superintendent tells him. "We of the Service sometimes do that. But – we always get our man, no matter how long it takes." He grasps the young constable by the shoulder, stares fixedly into his eyes, and sends him off on the hunt.

Months, possibly years pass, and the wretched constable cannot seem to Get His Man. His colleagues give him odd looks. His future is clouded. "There's only one mark against your record, Selwyn," the superintendent tells him. "I know you are doing everything you can to erase that."

Poor Selwyn falls in love with Margy, "the sweetheart of the post," who had come to work for the superintendent and his wife. He'd like to pop the question but he can't because He Hasn't Got His Man. "There is one thing I have yet to do before I ask anything of man or woman," is the way he puts it. Little does he know that Margy has accidentally met his quarry south of the border and has promised to keep his secret: that he sneaks back to Canada every September 7 to see his small, motherless son.

114

A typical ad for a typical Get-Your-Man Mountie movie. Hollywood nurtured the myth that Mounties who failed to get their men were instantly dishonoured.

115

More time passes. Other Mounties get their man but Selwyn is still in disgrace and Margy waits for his proposal in vain. "I'm going away tonight," he tells her. "There is something I would ask you if I could. . . ." His face falls: he can't ask her anything unless he returns with his man. Then, in a moment of miscaution, she blurts out her secret. By a happy coincidence it is September 6: Selwyn can get his man the following day! He is rapturous but she is remorseful: "You would take advantage of my broken promise? You would take the man that way?" Without a second's hesitation the Mountie chooses duty over love: "Though it means losing my life. Though it means losing you, I must do this thing. We of the Service are sworn to pry, search, follow and take, at whatever cost of happiness. There stands our honor, beyond which we may not think nor feel until that first be served," and off he gallops as a subtitle, "True to the Traditions of His Service," flashes onto the screen.

At the last moment, Selwyn relents but Kirby the fugitive has had enough. "Take me," he says wearily, "I'm done. You've wore me out."

Selwyn brings in his man and offers to resign: "I made a blunder in the beginning and here is a bungled end of it," he tells the superintendent, handing over his gun. "I wish that I might have taken you fairly in action," he tells his prisoner, "but that does not matter now." The superintendent, however, will have none of this. Selwyn has brought in his man and that's what matters. He hands him his gun and claps him on the shoulder as Margy leads him away by the lanyard.

Far-fetched though this sounds, movie audiences gobbled it up. The theme of the Mountie disgraced because he doesn't get his man recurred in the years that followed. It provided the plot for *The Man She Brought Back,* a picture about an adventurer who joins the force, is given a chance to get his man and thereby win his stripes (always cause for promotion in Hollywood movies), and is then discharged in disgrace when he fails. Thirty years later, a similar theme was to be found in the opening sequences of *Pony Soldier,* in which Tyrone Power as Constable MacDonald is given a dressing down for not getting his man. In expiation he goes on a dangerous, perhaps suicidal, mission into the country of the hostile Crees.

"Inject in the picture the 'get-your-man' slogan," wrote Matthew A. Taylor in Moving Picture World in 1921, "and . . . it is fairly certain the feature will have a strong audience appeal."[14] Producers were still following that advice in 1938 when *Heart of the North* appeared. The picture, which is dedicated to "this courageous group of men [who] have won the admiration of the entire civilized world," starts out by showing an authentic-looking bronze plaque on which is engraved the crest of the RCMP and these words:

You are the agent of justice.
Where the law is unknown; make it known.
When the law is broken; get your man.

Col. John French

The plaque and the quote were both phoney. French, the first commissioner of the NWMP (whose Christian name was George, not John)* never said anything of the sort. The force, over the years, has come to hate the phrase Get Your Man almost as much as it despises the abbreviation Mountie. Neither is ever used by any member of the RCMP.

C. S. Sewell, reviewing *Prisoners of the Storm* in 1926, commented on the fact that the hero, Sergeant "Bucky" Malone, a totally innocent man, was saved only at the last minute "The fact that this time, the Northwest Mounted is shown to be working entirely on the wrong trail is certainly out of the ordinary and adds an element of novelty. . . ."[15] As a movie reviewer Sewell could not have been too perceptive; for the truth of the matter is that in Hollywood's Canada the Mounties very seldom tracked down their man. In scores of movies the police work was of the most elementary kind. In picture after picture, the Mounties got the *wrong* man (or the wrong woman), who was snatched from the gallows at the last moment, not by clever detective work on the part of members of the force, but by that creaky motion picture device, the last-minute confession.

There was a reason for this plot twist. It lay in the other great theme of the Mountie movies – the theme of Love versus Duty, or Friendship versus Honour. In movie after movie, the Mountie was required to track down his sweetheart, his brother, his best friend, or somebody else close to him, usually his sweetheart's father or brother or best friend. This, of course, put him into immediate conflict with the heroine. In most cases duty won out. As a synopsis of *Northern Hearts* (1913) phrased it, "the brand of duty has burned so deeply that nothing can swerve him from orders."[16] A standard gesture evolved among those silent actors faced with the conflict of Love versus Duty, which appeared as early as 1913 in *Big Hearted Jim*. Ordered to bring in a Loved One, the Mountie's eyes widened, then narrowed as he clutched his hand to his breast and breathed deeply. Then, stiffening, he snapped to attention, saluted, did a right-about whirl and headed off into the wilds.

It was, of course, unthinkable that the girlfriend's father *or* her brother *or* the Mountie's brother *or* his best friend should turn out to be the heavy, which explains the last-minute confession by the repentant half-breed. "Broken hearted, he carries out orders only to find she has

---

*His brother was John, but he wasn't a colonel and he didn't say it, either.

117

been wrongly accused,"[17] reads part of the plot description for *The Wolf Hunters* (1926). And a similar synopsis for *The Blood Hound:* "McKenna arrests his brother and brings him back and the Captain produces a half-breed who confesses he murdered Rambeau."[18] In that case, as in many others, the bloodhound was sniffing up the wrong trail.

The real mounted police history provides some extraordinary cases of fine detective work, such as the famous O'Brien murders in the Yukon in 1900. A mounted police constable and a detective, working for six weeks in intense cold, conducted what has been called "one of the most thorough inch-by-inch searches in the history of crime detection,"[19] digging and sifting three feet of snow from half an acre of forest to find the evidence that sent a murderer to the gallows. But nobody has thought to make a picture about the apprehension of George O'Brien.

Instead, Mountie movies concentrate on the chase, such as the one in *The Eternal Struggle,* in which the heroine flees to Herschel Island. "Why, man, she loves you. Do you mean to take her back to prison?" asks the astonished sea captain on whose ship the beautiful Andrée Grange has taken refuge. Constable O'Hara nods grimly and off he plods with his prisoner into the mountains. "Give me strength to do me duty," O'Hara prays when they reach the first, lonely supply station. By this time Sergeant Tempest, also on the trail of the fugitive, has caught up with both of them. He, too, loves Andrée and he, too, struggles with his conscience.

Holed up in the supply station with the other two, Tempest finally breaks. He wants O'Hara to flee to safety with the girl: "I can't stand this any longer! It's torture. . . . Listen to me, Bucky, I'm going to let her go. Go! I give her to you."

But O'Hara is the stronger of the two: "Every fibre of my being, every beat of my heart cries out for you," he tells the girl; but he knows his duty. "She is not mine and she is not yours," he reminds Sergeant Tempest. "She belongs to the Crown and she's going back!"

That night the sergeant helps Andrée escape by canoe and once again the chase is on, enlivened by all those stock Hollywood adventures: the perilous journey through Devil's Cauldron, "a six mile gash through solid granite;" the obligatory plunge over the giant cataract; the dizzy rescue leap from the cliff to the foaming waters below. By now everyone – even Andrée – is reconciled to the concept of Duty. But on arrival at Grey Wolf Landing the Mounties discover that this particular trip has not been necessary: the girl they love isn't a murderess after all; she only *thought* she killed the lecherous Barode Dukane. Actually he was merely stunned; the fatal knife was wielded by beautiful, mysterious (and jealous) Camille Lenoir.

There were at least thirty of these Love versus Duty movies made by Hollywood. Here is how they broke down:

Mountie is ordered to bring in his

Sweetheart's brother 9
Sweetheart's father 6
Sweetheart 5
The man his sweetheart *really* loves 4
Own brother (apart from twin) 3
Best friend 3
Twin brother 2
Sweetheart's sister's boyfriend 1

This kind of movie never went out of fashion. All three versions of *Rose Marie*, for instance, made use of the theme, even though the stories are strikingly different. (Film buffs will recall that it was Jeanette Mac-Donald's brother, played by a young James Stewart, whom Nelson Eddy was required to bring to justice.) And when in 1940 Cecil B. DeMille decided to make his blockbuster, *North West Mounted Police*, he, too, for all his protestations about breaking new ground with a different kind of Mountie movie, fell back on the same device.

2: "Fights, thrills, fast riding, gunplay . . ."

The real mounted police had every reason to hate the Mountie movies. Hollywood was getting everything wrong. In about a dozen films, even the ranks were wrong; the moviemakers kept using American military terms such as private and trooper instead of constable. This Americaniza-tion of a proud force, sensitive about its quasi-military origins, was carried into the uniform. In the early silents the famous dark breeches with their broad yellow stripes came out grey with dark stripes. In some films – *Big Hearted Jim* is an example – Mounties turned up in several kinds of breeches. Lewis Stone, who probably played more Mounties than any other actor in the silents, never quite managed to look like one. When I saw him in *Nomads of the North* in his miner's hat, his rumpled jacket, his wrinkled khaki breeches, and his back pack, I thought at first that he was a prospector; as a matter of fact he looked more like a Klondike miner than most Hollywood miners in Klondike movies, who were generally dressed up as cowboys. Then I realized he was supposed to be a Mountie.

In movie after movie, the Mounties acted like Americans. They wore their chevrons upside down, saluted with their hats off and fired their pistols from the back of a horse. Hollywood cannot be blamed for putting them into dress uniforms, even under the most rugged conditions, be-cause that is the way the force is depicted in Canadian tourist promotion.

But I did think it was going a little far in *Until They Get Me,* when the constables were all shown sitting down to Christmas dinner, booted and spurred, with their pistols jutting from their holsters.

Hollywood's real problem has always been the Stetson hat. The force is very particular about these hats, which are now manufactured by the Biltmore Company, with equipment purchased from Stetson. In fact, the RCMP specifications for "hats, felt" run to eight close-typed pages with diagrams. The hats are made from rabbit fur blown onto a large cone, which is then shrunk through several processes until it becomes solid felt. It is hydraulically shaped on aluminum moulds and blocked twice, first to a solid oval and then to the indentations, as in the final product. The brim and crown are treated with two different kinds of shellac. The force's inspection department rejects any hat that is substandard and the inspection is a fierce one. I happen to own an RCMP hat which seems to me to be perfect in every detail. It is, however, a second. The Biltmore inspector found a little wiggle in the brim and threw it out.

In the movies the Mountie hats have more than wiggles; they have waves. In *River's End* the hats look more like the snap brims affected by movie gangsters of the thirties. Renfrew of the Mounted appears to be wearing a slouch hat. When William S. Hart stepped into the role of O'Malley of the Mounted, "veteran of a thousand trails and a man who has never failed," he apparently continued to wear the identical battered Stetson that had made him famous in westerns.

It is a matter of visual record that the hats worn in Hollywood westerns have gone through fashion cycles. In the Hart period, the cowboys wore the pointed Stetson, like a Boy Scout hat. In the Tom Mix era, the ten-gallon hat came into vogue. Later on, the crown grew much smaller and flatter. Hollywood seems to have followed this fashion cycle when dressing its Mounties. In some of the twenties silents the Mountie hats had very high crowns, similar to the prevailing ten-gallon style; but later the crowns dropped and the famous pointed peak all but vanished. In the Mountie serials of the 1950's, for example, the crowns are flat and so rounded that the policemen look a bit like grown-up Buster Browns.

When I screened *The Law of the North* I was baffled by the Mountie uniforms. They were all wrong and yet they were oddly familiar. The police were shown wearing light breeches, long khaki raincoats, and limp, flimsy Stetsons. It finally came to me that these men were really dressed as American doughboys in the Great War. The picture had been made in 1918 and the costume department either raided a war surplus warehouse or subconsciously dressed its Mounties as Yankee cavalrymen.

The Stetson did not come into widespread use until the turn of the century and that has been a problem for the historical film makers. The

120

original pillbox, which tended to make mounted policemen look like bellhops, was rarely shown: it has turned up only twice in the movies. The white helmet, which replaced it, appeared only once. In other movies about the early days of the force, Hollywood either ignored history or invented fur hats of its own design, as Cecil B. DeMille did for *North West Mounted Police*. These hats, which bore little relation to the real fur hats that the RCMP uses in cold weather, were so successful that the Paramount costume department rented them out to other production companies so that moviegoers became used to seeing Mounties galloping about in the sweltering heat of the summer with their heads encased in fur.

In the majority of the movies the Mountie was little more than an American sheriff in a scarlet tunic. The point is made by Alan J. Barbour in a nostalgic book about western movies, *Days of Thrill and Adventure*: "Whenever the studios wanted to add variety to their production schedules and still maintain relatively low production costs, they would make a non-Western by converting the hero from a fighting cowboy to a gallant Mountie. Aside from the change of costume and change of location . . . the films remained western in flavour."[20]

By switching the sheriff over to a Mountie, Hollywood still retained the essential ingredients of the classic western: blazing guns and thundering hooves. If the federal Canadian police had not been mounted, would a single movie ever have been made about them? I doubt it. It doesn't matter that the RCMP long ago discarded their steeds. In Hollywood's Canada, the Mounties were always shown on horseback.

There is an hilarious scene in *Renfrew of the Royal Mounted*, set in the late 1930's not far from the Canadian-US border, in which a local detachment of mounted police have been invited to an outdoor barbeque. The entire troop of them gallops up to the picnic grounds on horseback singing at the top of their voices.

Even when automobiles were present, movie Mounties did not deign to use them. In *Dangers of the Canadian Mounted*, a serial with a post-World-War-Two setting, a Mountie on a horse is shown chasing a car down a highway. The car is driverless, with the heroine tied up in the front seat, and it's heading for a truck loaded with explosives. At the last moment the Mountie draws abreast of the speeding auto, sweeps the girl into the saddle, and spirits her to safety just before the truck blows up.

In *The Cyclone* Tom Mix, in the role of Sergeant Tim Ryerson of the mounted police, working undercover, discovers the location of a Chinese gambling den. He returns to headquarters, gets into his dress uniform, leaps onto his horse, and gallops off to make the bust. He rides noiselessly up three flights of stairs and then crashes through to the cellar, still on horseback, to capture the lawbreakers.

Horses were ridden under the most improbable conditions in Mountie movies – over the tops of mountains, through jungle-like forests, off the edges of cliffs and, of course, through the eternal snows of the Great Woods. The blizzard scene in *Men of the North* provides a pretty good example. The heroine and her father have set out for their mine in a horse-drawn cutter. Louis the Fox, betrayed by a half-breed girl, is sensibly making his escape by fast dogteam. A terrible storm springs up and an officer who fears they may be in danger from the blizzard orders his corporal to go after the couple in the cutter. The corporal salutes, does a neat about-turn, steps outside the post into the swirling curtain of snow, and immediately mounts his horse, just as if he were heading down the main street of Dodge City. Off he canters through the howling blizzard, his steed knee-deep in the drifts, following the nearly obliterated tracks of the sleigh, obedient to the Hollywood dictum that a Royal Canadian Policeman must always be Mounted.

But the scenes that have maddened the real mounted police more than any others have been those showing the capricious use of firearms by members of a force which from the very beginning has specifically tried to shun violence. When Ralph Connor, the internationally famous Canadian novelist, was ushered into the White House to meet Theodore Roosevelt, the American president greeted him with his usual robust verve, exclaiming about "the big, raw West country, with its vast possibilities and its perils," about which Connor had written in his novels.

"It's a great country," Roosevelt exclaimed, "but it is wild, the 'wild west' alright, with its lawlessness and –"

Connor ventured to interrupt. "Lawlessness? Why, Mr. President, the law runs in the western country that I know just as it does in Toronto. I never saw a man offer resistance to one of our Mounties. And what's more I never saw a Mountie pull a gun to enforce the law."

The President was clearly taken aback: "Never pull a gun in making an arrest? You amaze me! And you have seen men arrested?"

"Yes," Connor told him, "and gunmen, too, from across the line. They do come across, you know, Mr. President."

"Your Mounties hold down that country amazingly," Roosevelt remarked.

"Hold down? Not exactly. Why those laddies are like dry nurses to the community. They are everybody's friend. They look after the sick, they rescue men from blizzards, they pack in supplies to people in need."[21]

But in Hollywood's Canada, Mounties drew their guns on the slightest provocation. "Fights, thrills, fast riding, gunplay . . .,"[22] ran the exploitation for one of Ken Maynard's last films, *Wildcat Trooper*, in which the great western star switched to a Mountie costume. The phrase could just as easily have fitted any of his American westerns.

Almost all of the stills from Mountie movies show the policeman hero with a drawn gun taking a bead on his prisoner. The Mounties have consistently been shown by Hollywood as trigger-happy cops, firing from horseback at the nearest moving target, quite often an innocent by-stander. A movie Mountie could not search a cabin without drawing his pistol, as in *The Man in the Moonlight,* and he certainly could not be seen making an arrest without pulling a gun on a prisoner, as Wendell Corey did in *The Wild North.*

Movie Mounties always shot first and asked questions later. In one popular serial, *Canadian Mounties Versus the Atomic Invaders,* a constable returning to his post on horseback and suspecting an intruder, reaches for his gun and opens fire as soon as he gets to the door. In *The Eternal Struggle* Bucky O'Hara sees a movement at a window and begins banging away, almost murdering an innocent woman. In *The Confession* a constable enters a private home and, suspecting that the man he wants may be hiding in a closet, blasts away at the closed door. Movie Mounties always pulled their pistols from their holsters before knocking on doors and there was never any "Halt or I'll fire" nonsense. On seeing a body lying in the snow they blasted away at the nearest target, like the corporal in the 1918 version of *The Law of the North.*

The Criminal Code of Canada makes it clear, of course, that excessive force must not be used by any police officer in the pursuit of his duties. The mounted police go further than that. The Constable's Manual warns that "unnecessary violence should be studiously avoided" and then goes on to say that "only in the last extremity should a peace officer resort to such a dangerous weapon as a revolver in order to effect an arrest or to prevent escape by flight." This has been a tradition in the force since the earliest days; and it was central to the original idea of a Canadian mounted constabulary. It wasn't the six-shooter in the hands of a single individual that cowed potential lawbreakers in Canada; it was the symbol of the law and all that stood behind it that kept the peace in the northwest. But then Hollywood Mounties were never Canadians; they were simply hard-riding, hard-shooting cowboys from the American wild west, thinly disguised in scarlet and gold.

3: Louis B. Mayer always gets his man

Since the days of the silent feature the mounted police have done their best to discourage motion pictures about the exploits of the force and, when that has been impossible, to withold any co-operation with the moviemakers. In this latter endeavour they have been only partially

123

successful, for Hollywood was often able to exert subtle pressures which forced the various commissioners to give in to its importunings.

In one area only was the force able to have some effect on the screen image of the mounted policeman. If the Mountie has rarely been depicted as a villain or a dissolute in the movies, that was partly due to RCMP pressure on Hollywood through the early censor boards. In 1919 a former member of the force wrote from Yorkshire, England, protesting a Lasky film, *Tyrant Fear,* which showed a mounted policeman drinking in a brothel. The force acted on the complaint through Colonel E. J. Chambers, chief wartime censor for Canada. Chambers persuaded the censor boards of Ontario and Quebec to condemn the movie. Famous Players, the distributors, withdrew it from circulation and the British Board of Film Censors, also prodded by Chambers, ordered "considerable alterations, one being that all references to Canada must be deleted."[23]

"My Board fully appreciates the fact that respect is due to such a body as the Royal North West Mounted Police," the secretary wrote to the Canadian High Commissioner, "and our Policy is to discourage any reflections on the reputation of that body. . . ."[24]

Although censor boards eventually lost their power to clip films for anything other than sexual immorality, Hollywood after that was always careful about how it handled mounted policemen. As time went on and more attention was paid at least to superficial authenticity, it needed official mounted police help. Even more important, producers desperately strove for some sort of official seal of approval that would aid the box office.

In the very early days, the police, dazzled perhaps by the idea of pictures that moved, gave whole-hearted co-operation to the Edison and Kalem one-reelers. But by the end of the first decade, disillusionment set in and the force turned its back on Hollywood. It didn't like the way Mountie stories were handled and it considered movie producers a time-wasting nuisance, as Cosmopolitan Productions discovered in 1922 when they wired Commissioner A. Bowen Perry, asking for permission to film at the Banff barracks for Curwood's *The Valley of Silent Men.* The request was the precursor of dozens of others down through the years, full of the flattering phrases and pledges of good intentions that a succession of commissioners would receive from a succession of producers: "We desire above all to show for once the force perfectly costumed, disciplined, etc. We are trying to do this wonderful story on real locations and feel your co-operation would help to make a Mounted Police picture correctly. . . . Money and talent have not been spared,"[25] etc. etc.

The commissioner wasn't moved. He shot off a one-sentence refusal and scribbled a memo of explanation to his subordinates:

I have refused permission for this for two reasons:

1. The Force has had quite enough advertising in moving pictures, some of it damaging.
2. Curwood's Valley of Silent Men contains a libellous representation of the Officers of the Force.[26]

The producer went over the commissioner's head to the Minister of Justice (as future producers would do) but the mounted police could not be budged. From that point on they decided to stay away from the movie people.

There were other requests. All were turned down. The new commissioner, Cortlandt Starnes, wouldn't even supply photographs to Vitagraph as background for its production of Curwood's *Steele of the Royal Mounted.*

... I regret to say that in the past, the presentation of the Police in Motion Pictures has, with very few exceptions, been most unsatisfactory, and as a result of this, we have been obliged to refuse to supply Pictures, Rules and Regulations, and photographs.... I further regret that I am obliged to write you in this strain, but this decision has been arrived at through long experience.[27]

Starnes suggested the production company send a man of its own to Regina; in other words: do your own research.

The following year, 1926, Metro-Goldwyn-Mayer, which was contemplating a film about the formation of the NWMP, requested information through its research department. Starnes again turned them down.

The big studio didn't leave it at that. It unearthed an ex-Canadian army officer, G. L. McDonell, whose brother had served in the force and who had come into contact with some of Starnes's men in the war. McDonell was persuaded to wire Starnes personally. Unluckily Western Union listed him as a mere lieutenant instead of a lieutenant-colonel and Starnes, who didn't recognize the name, sent back his bluntest reply yet:

MOUNTED POLICE WOULD APPRECIATE BEING LEFT ALONE BY MOVIES. HAVE NO INTENTION OF ASSISTING.[28]

McDonell, maintaining a stiff upper lip, replied by mail, listing his credentials and adding a softener: "There are many of us from Canada resident here who loath the pictures that have already been made dealing with Police in Western Canada and we are anxious to see that the thing is done right when the movie Powers that be do such pictures."[29]

Starnes, who had also been approached on the same matter by A. W. Neill, a Vancouver Island Member of Parliament, grudgingly sent along some information on early uniforms. McDonell wrote him an enthusiastic letter, explaining that the picture would deal with "the Blackfoot trouble of 1874 and will be made in the State of Wyoming. I understand that the Indian part will be carefully and thoroughly done by ex-US officers with long frontier and Indian experience."[30]

At this point more pressure was put on Starnes from a new source: the Canadian Government Motion Picture Bureau. While the mounted police had been doing their best to fend off movie companies, the bureau under its director, Ray Peck, had been going cap-in-hand to Hollywood, trying to interest American producers in making motion pictures on location in Canada. In back of the idea, Peck told Starnes, was his belief that Hollywood later on would "very probably make a certain quota of their pictures representing Canadian history and modern Canadian life."[31]

Because M-G-M was now promising to make the picture in Canada, Peck wanted Starnes to bend the rules and lend the company "every encouragement and assistance."

> Aside from the propaganda value of the picture, if it is done on a massive scale and produced correctly, is the fact that a large sum of money will be left in Canada by the Metro-Goldwyn-Mayer Company while the picture is being produced.[32]

Again Starnes was forced to bend to pressure and reluctantly offer considerable help, including an RCMP instructor to train the Hollywood performers when they arrived at Regina, and the loan of considerable equipment, rifles, and even horses. M-G-M also got all the research it had originally requested and which Starnes had so bluntly refused. As soon as this was forthcoming, M-G-M announced that the picture wouldn't be produced in Canada after all but in its own studios.

The result was *The Flaming Forest,* a total distortion of the history of the Canadian northwest and of the mounted police and a libel on the Métis and Canadian Indians. The picture was billed as an authentic account of both the first Riel uprising of 1869 and the formation of the North West Mounted Police in 1874 – two events that had absolutely nothing to do with each other.

Briefly, the story was this: Jules Lagarre, a half-breed brigand, undertakes to dominate the Canadian Northwest with the aid of cut-throats and Indians whom he incites to revolt against Dominion authorities. He shoots down André Audemard and his wife, making orphans of Jeanne Marie and her brother, and driving out the settlers except for Jeanne Marie, on whom he has Evil Designs. Meanwhile the North West Mounted Police have been formed and are on their way to the Northwest to erase lawlessness. Braving a ring of fire touched off by the villains, who have set the forest aflame, they scatter the renegades, rescue the heroine and allow the settlers to return to their homes.

This nonsense, purporting to be about an historical event in which scarcely a drop of blood was shed (the uprising of 1869 was marred only by the execution of Thomas Scott), was foisted on the public as the real thing. Louella Parsons, whose boss, William Randolph Hearst, owned Cosmopolitan, the producing company for M-G-M, was predictably enthusiastic:

> James Oliver Curwood . . . knows his Northwest so well that any fiction of his is invested with an undoubted authenticity. Waldemar Young, in his adaptation . . . has capitalized on all the highlights, by keeping intact the history of these sturdy pioneers who made Canada habitable for decent men and women. This emphasis on the underlying reasons for the organization of the Northwest Mounted Police I thought especially interesting, since no motion picture ever has revealed the origin of these fearless soldiers.[33]

The North West Mounted Police, of course, were organized for exactly the opposite reason: because a posse of white Americans had ruthlessly murdered on Canadian soil some thirty Assiniboine Indians in what came to be known as the Cypress Hills Massacre of 1873. No one knows what Cortlandt Starnes, many of whose colleagues had been members of that original force, thought of the movie he was forced into aiding. He probably never bothered to see it.

Nonetheless, with the rule against co-operation abandoned and with men like Peck urging more aid and comfort to Hollywood, there was no returning to the old inflexibility. Over the next decade, Starnes and his successor, Sir James MacBrien, submitted to film company requests for information, manuals, technical advice, and even drill instructors, whose presence pleased the press agents because they lent a quasi-official seal of approval to the Mountie movies.

"Personally, I think Police pictures have been overdone,"[34] Starnes wrote testily to one producer; but police pictures continued to pour out of the Hollywood mill. The one liberty, however, that the force would not allow was the presence of real mounted police on the commercial screen – not at least until Louis B. Mayer entered the lists.

In 1935 Metro-Goldwyn-Mayer, then the most powerful studio in Hollywood, decided to make a sound version of *Rose Marie* with Jeanette

MacDonald and Nelson Eddy. This was the third time the studio had launched the production. M-G-M had purchased the rights to the Rudolph Friml musical in 1926 and proceeded to make a lavish silent version with Ralph Forbes, the star of *The Trail of '98*, and Renée Adorée who, with a succession of French-Canadian parts behind her, seemed right for the title role. Something went wrong, however. After spending $50,000, M-G-M scrapped the picture, engaged a new director and a new cast, and started all over again with Joan Crawford as the wild girl from the mountains. The result, even without songs, was so successful that it made good commercial sense to re-make the picture in sound.

In the original musical, however, and also in the original movie (which differed substantially from the stage production) the Mountie was a secondary character who didn't get his girl. In the silent film, Sergeant Malone is required to go after Jim Kenyon, the man that Rose Marie really loves and who is wanted for a murder he didn't commit. Malone is wounded before the picture ends, and Rose Marie gets her man when it is revealed that the real killer is a villain named Black Bastien.

In order to build up the part of the policeman and give Nelson Eddy a starring role M-G-M took this stock Mountie tale and transformed it into *another* stock Mountie tale. In the new version of *Rose Marie* the locale, the plot, and the names were changed; only the clichés and the Indian Love Call remained. In this version, Marie de Fleur is no backwoods wildcat but a cultured and pampered Montreal opera star who goes to the North-woods to try to save her brother, who has escaped from a Quebec penitentiary after killing a Mountie. In the woods, she takes a job singing in a saloon and meets Sergeant Bruce of the Mounted who falls in love with her. When he figures out who she is he faces the terrible choice of either bringing in the brother of the woman he wants to marry or courting dishonour. In the classic Love versus Duty conflict he opts for duty but is finally forgiven in a confusing curtain scene that appears to take place in a Rocky Mountain tourist lodge.

For the new production of *Rose Marie* the studio head, Louis B. Mayer, was determined to have real Canadian policemen, with Nelson Eddy galloping at their head, singing Here Come the Mounties. The RCMP, of course, flatly refused to have its members appear in the picture and so informed Mayer. Accordingly, Mayer wrote to a Canadian government official he knew, the Commissioner of Income Tax, C. Fraser Elliott. Elliott owed a favour to Mayer who had given him VIP treatment at the studio during a Hollywood visit. He immediately phoned Major-General Sir James MacBrien, Starnes's successor as RCMP Commissioner. Mac-Brien countered by suggesting that M-G-M use the existing newsreel foot-age.[35] Elliott wired Mayer immediately and followed up with a letter in

This typical scene from God's Country and the Law *(1921) shows a Mountie in the Northwoods arresting a French-Canadian for cattle-thieving.*

Movie Mounties

They're mainly American sheriffs
dressed (often inaccurately) in scarlet
tunics and funny hats.

*MOUNTIES' HATS never looked quite right in the movies,
as this collection spanning a quarter-century
demonstrates. The permanent wave at the upper left
belongs to* Channing of the Northwest, *a 1922 picture
with Eugene O'Brien in the title role. The wave was still
there fourteen years later in* Code of the Mounted,
*top centre. That's Tom Mix, the great cowboy star,
with the fancy hatband in* The Cyclone *(1920) and Buck
Jones in the modified ten-gallon at centre left in* McKenna
of the Mounted *(1932). Two distinct versions of the Stetson
showed up side by side in a 1953 serial,* Canadian Mounties
Versus the Atomic Invaders *(centre). The pointed job at
centre right made its appearance in* False Clues *(1943),
while the Buster Brown number at bottom right was part
of the get-up of* Renfrew of the Royal Mounted, *the
radio hero who made his motion picture debut in 1937.*

130

These are Mounties? So the caption writers claim. The scarecrow figure above made his appearance in 1919 in The Confession. *The great D. W. Griffith is responsible for the strange characters below, who look more like American doughboys. The picture is* Jordan is a Hard Road, *made in 1915.*

FUR HATS came in as many designs as did the more familiar Stetson in Mountie movies. The sergeant in the ill fitting number on the right is trying to arrest Gilbert Roland in Men of the North (1930). His constable, shown in a still from the same film (immediately below) sports a totally different design. Neither are regulation gear—nor is the one worn by James Hall in the 1930 comedy Dangerous Nan McGrew, in the photograph at the bottom of the page.

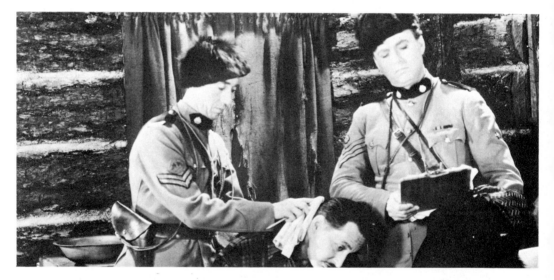

Cecil B. DeMille invented a fur hat for Preston Foster (shown above with Gary Cooper) to wear in North West Mounted Police. *Paramount got its money back renting them out for other Mountie movies, such as* The Canadians *(below) with Robert Ryan (centre). Police were shown in fur hats on the hottest July days.*

133

Mounties only draw their guns in the movies; in real life it's taboo. Above,
Forrest Stanley, as Sgt. Michael Devlin in Tiger Rose (1923), must bring in
the girl he loves (Lenore Ulric) and her boyfriend. Below, in the 1928
version of Rose-Marie, House Peters as Sgt. Malone pulls a gun on the boyfriend
of the girl he loves (Joan Crawford). In both pictures the Mountie
lost the girl to a man accused—unfairly, of course—of murder.

Hollywood's favourite Mountie of the silent films, Lewis Stone, holds two
unarmed Oriental miscreants at bay with his service revolver in the 1920
version of James Oliver Curwood's River's End. Below, Wendell Corey in the
role of Constable Pedley menaces his quarry, Jacques Vincent, played by
Stewart Granger in The Wild North (1951). In real life, the guns would stay
in the holsters. The real Pedley never had the need to draw his weapon.

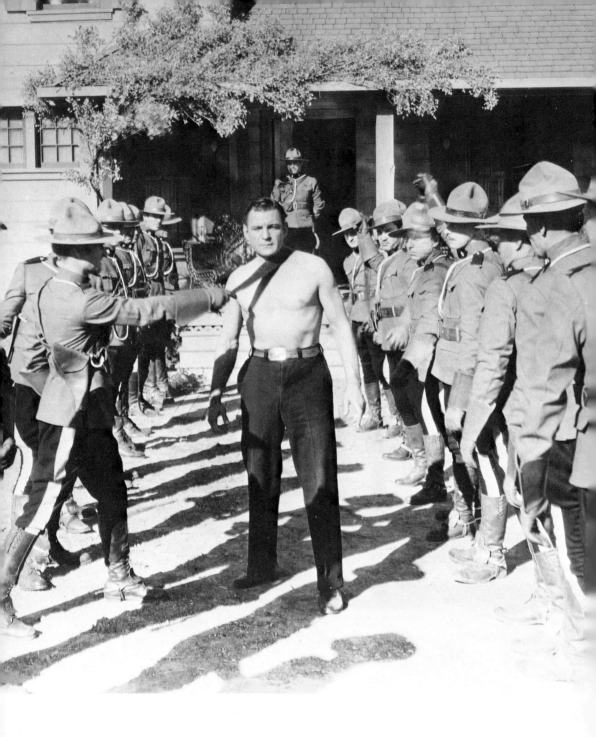

According to the caption supplied with this still from McKenna of the Mounted, *"Buck Jones' brother Mounties look on while he takes the traditional lashes of a man dishonorably discharged from the Mountie service." Hollywood made it all up of course. A similar scene occurs in* River's End.

which he said he was certain that Mayer's purpose "will in due course be accomplished to your complete satisfaction."[36]

With his foot lodged in the door Mayer wrote to MacBrien. He wanted an absolute minimum of fifty mounted men going through their exercises in front of the Vancouver barracks, with Nelson Eddy singing the Mountie song. The scene, he said, would "reflect all possible credit on the RCMP."[37] MacBrien bluntly refused but, to mollify Mayer, offered the services of a technical director.[38]

Mayer sent an underling, Billy Grady, directly to Ottawa to see MacBrien personally. Grady promised that none of the force would be used in the actual telling of the story but would be seen merely going through a series of mounted manoeuvres. He promised that the footage thus taken would be presented as a gift to the force and that the studio would use only those shots in the picture of which the commissioner approved.[39] MacBrien hedged, or pretended to hedge, using the excuse that the matter would have to be decided by the Minister of Justice, the Honourable G. R. Geary. As soon as Grady got back to New York he received a telegram from MacBrien, which said in effect: nothing doing. Grady pleaded for a change of mind in a lengthy wire but there was no reply.[40]

The studio accepted the offer of a technical advisor in the person of Inspector William Grennan, who had done a similar job for *Rose Marie*'s director, W. S. Van Dyke, when Van Dyke directed *Eskimo*. Grennan, whose expenses were paid by the movie company, enjoyed himself and wrote a spirited account of his Hollywood adventures for the RCMP Quarterly.

But Louis B. Mayer had not given up on his intention to have real live Mounties in the picture. Somehow, he got to Prime Minister R. B. Bennett (probably though Colonel John Cooper of the Motion Picture Distributors and Exhibitors Association). Bennett fired off two pro-M-G-M telegrams to the Minister of Justice and the commissioner, urging that the scenes be allowed "in the interest of accuracy." "It is certainly desirable," Bennett wired MacBrien, "that Canada should put her best foot forward if pictures such as this are to be shown around the world."[41]

MacBrien, however, held his ground. The force, he said, was dispersed for other duties. A Canadian moving picture company had just made a similar request and had been refused. It would be unwise to give preferential treatment to a non-Canadian firm and, if a change of policy was contemplated, the Canadian company should be the first to benefit. Besides, MacBrien indicated, blurring the real situation slightly, M-G-M seemed perfectly satisfied with the technical advice it was getting from Grennan and the only problem appeared to be William Grady, "a professional picture taker of New York who has not ceased to try to upset the arrangement made with the corporation."[42]

In the face of this, the Prime Minister withdrew his request. But M-G-M wasn't finished. One of its New York executives, William Orr, went to see F. C. Badgley, Peck's successor as director of the Canadian Government Motion Picture Bureau, and asked for his help in changing MacBrien's mind. Badgley also owed M-G-M a favour; the studio had co-operated on the official Canadian war film *Lest We Forget,* placing all its footage at the bureau's disposal free of charge. Badgley made a strong pitch to Mac-Brien and MacBrien weakened.[43] He agreed finally that, if the movie company guaranteed not to make any mention in its advertising or publicity that members of the force had been used, the scenes could be shot in Vancouver – but only if a cover story was put out that the scenes in question were being made by the Canadian government and not by a Hollywood studio.[44] Thus Louis B. Mayer got his way and an American film company was secretly granted a privilege that a Canadian film company had been denied.

Commissioner MacBrien and his staff went to see *Rose Marie* when it was completed and they liked what they saw. The mounted police in the picture were properly drilled, properly uniformed and, in their view, properly portrayed. They received some letters of protest, however, including one from a man in Pennsylvania who wrote directly to the commissioner to ask "if it is reasonable for a 'Sergeant' to go after his 'man' singing at the top of his voice to the sister of the criminal with whom he has fallen in love?"[45] To which MacBrien's deputy replied in his stilted policeman's style:

> In answer to your letter of the 20th April, it is not likely that a member of this Force would go about a case of the kind you mention singing in the manner alleged, but I dare say it is necessary both on the legitimate stage, as well as on the silver screen, to permit certain departures, which may appear to be needed either from the point of view of pleasing an audience, or for some other motive.[46]

As the years went by, members of the force grew less enamoured of *Rose Marie.* That vision of Nelson Eddy singing at the head of all those Mounties continued to haunt them. Mountie movies came and went but it was *Rose Marie* that everybody remembered – and with more and more laughter. It's not too much to say that, in the end, the mounted police came to loathe *Rose Marie* and the image it gave them.

In 1954 M-G-M decided to make another *Rose Marie,* this one in Technicolor with Howard Keel, Ann Blyth, and Fernando Lamas. Again, the story was changed but all the clichés of the Mountie movies down

138

through the years were retained: the Mountie who loves the wild child of the forest and knows he must lose her because she, in turn, is in love with the man he must bring in for murder; the happy-go-lucky French-Canadian trapper, falsely accused of a crime; the savage Indians who almost burn a white man at the stake; and the last-minute confession by an Indian maiden which saves the hero from the gallows.

The picture wasn't the success its predecessor was. Everybody still remembered Nelson Eddy warbling the Indian Love Call, the wooden quality of that performance long forgotten in the mists of nostalgia. In 1969 Prime Minister Trudeau in a public speech remarked that Canada was about to shed her "Rose Marie image," a feat more easily described than accomplished. This promptly drew a letter from Rudolph Friml's secretary who wrote Mr. Trudeau with some asperity: "Shame on you!" said she. "Swinging is great, and I'm sure it's here to stay, but the beautiful legend of ROSE MARIE is as much a part of Canadian history and tradition as is the French language in Quebec."[47]

I don't know how the Prime Minister replied but he could easily have retorted: "No doubt. But to *which* beautiful legend of Rose Marie do you refer? There have been so many of them."

4: Trials of a technical director

Chastened, perhaps, by his experience with *Rose Marie,* Commissioner MacBrien co-operated with Hollywood movie companies for the remainder of his term in office. He gave them access to research, supplied them with technical direction, and allowed them to make photographs of RCMP posts. But after his sudden death in 1938 the new Commissioner, S. T. Wood, clamped down again. Wood decided to enforce a one-year moratorium, at the very least, on all assistance.

When 20th Century-Fox, making *Susannah of the Mounties,* asked for "your co-operation and supervision as was supplied a few years ago,"[48] Wood told them curtly that no assistance could be given because "during recent years we have had far too much publicity."[49] Instead, he proceeded to fob off all requests onto Bruce Carruthers, the former mounted policeman who had set himself up as a freelance technical director in the movie capital.

A technical director is a man with special knowledge who tells scriptwriters and directors of movies when they're making terrible errors. Sometimes the movie people listen to him and sometimes they ignore him. A lot of the time they hassle him, but then a lot of the time he hassles them. But they like to have his name on the movie because it lulls the audience into the belief that everything has been carefully checked and what they've been looking at is "authentic" – a favourite Hollywood word.

Carruthers's technical expertise was sought in two areas: the mounted police and the Canadian north. A reading of his personal papers suggests that he saw himself in the role of the Lone Defender, fighting an uphill battle against Philistine forces of commerce who were, in his view, determined to sully the reputation of his native land in general and the force in particular.

"I love the Royal Canadian Mounted Police and Canada and its people and I am idealist enough to believe that Right can win out against Greed and Ignorance . . .,"[50] he once wrote to a Canadian committee set up to co-ordinate censorship in Canada.

Occasionally, in letters to Commissioner Wood, Carruthers poured out his feelings about Hollywood, a community with which he enjoyed a love-hate relationship.

"If there is anything I detest," he wrote one time, "it is the arrogant attitude of an individual or group of individuals who believe that because of the millions of dollars they have back of them that they can get anything they want, PARTICULARLY when it concerns my Force!"[51]

Part of this, I think, was Carruthers's way of letting the RCMP brass know he was on their side. He needed mounted police co-operation and he got it from the commissioner far more easily than the studio heads did: after all he *was* Carruthers of the Mounted. "I still serve in my own way," he once told a Hollywood columnist. "The Mounted Police and what our organization stands for is my religion. . . ."[52] His letters to his former superiors were always couched in strict RCMP fashion: every paragraph numbered and the commissioner addressed repeatedly as Sir (once a Mountie always a Mountie). The style, however, was more passionate and more gossipy than the clipped officialese of the replies:

> It is quite a strain endeavouring to convince people who know absolutely nothing about the Police as to how they should be portrayed and that Canadian people DO have respect for law and order and the Courts, that they do NOT hate the Police and that members of the Force do not talk out of the corners of their mouths, can speak correctly and are courteous in public. . . .

> . . . To become established has taken much time and effort and I am constantly accumulating material and information regarding the Force. I have always loved the Service and Canada and, though I am no longer a Member of the Force, I am a constant student and feel as though I am

still on the strength except for the wearing of the uniform. . . . I have grown to look upon this work of mine as a 'one man detachment' and the greatest thrill I have received from it was . . . when Sir James MacBrien referred a studio to me for information. It was somewhat like getting an approval of my work.[53]

No doubt a good many producers thought of Carruthers as a necessary evil – a hairsplitter who always seemed to want to ruin a perfectly good yarn by raising silly objections. He was told more than once: "What the hell do we care whether Canada or the Police like it or not, we don't get much money out of your Country, anyway!"[54] Sometimes when he tried to hire himself out, he got a curt brush-off: "We can get the information we want about Canada and the Police because we are quite a power in Canada."[55] And scenes which he wanted to change for accuracy would be retained with the casual remark: "It doesn't matter, the kids will like it."[56]

But Carruthers persevered in spite of the rebuffs and his name can still be seen on the TV re-runs of several big movies, not only as technical director but also occasionally as an actor. When he was hired for a bit part in *King of the Royal Mounted* in 1940 the director told him quite honestly that he knew the story was all wrong from an RCMP point of view and that he himself knew nothing about the force but his budget didn't allow for any expert advice.[57] Carruthers took on the job without extra pay.

Carruthers was a Prince Edward Islander by birth. He enlisted in the mounted police in Battleford, Saskatchewan, in the summer of 1919 as soon as he reached the required age of eighteen. He served in Regina and then in Whitehorse and Dawson in the Yukon, and when he retired from the force in 1923 he had been promoted to corporal, with his conduct during service listed as "very good." He knew how to handle a dogteam and a canoe. He knew exactly how northern police posts operated. He understood the difference between placer and hard-rock gold mining (something Hollywood was never able to get straight). He knew how northerners dressed and acted; and of course, he had a meticulous knowledge of mounted police procedure. In short, he had all the proper qualifications for the job which came his way purely by happenstance.

When Carruthers left the force, he travelled extensively in Latin America. He was on his way back to Canada again when he stopped off in Los Angeles, met a girl, married her, and settled down in the movie capital. At this point he was in his early thirties, a tall young man, ramrod straight, with a lean, handsome face and the pencil-thin moustache made popular by every matinee idol from Warren William to Warner Baxter.

In Hollywood Carruthers began to see a lot of Mountie movies and what he saw he didn't like. At last, having reached "the limit of my endurance," he dashed off a heated letter to Irving Thalberg, the so-called boy wonder who was head of production at Metro-Goldwyn-Mayer. Hollywood, wrote Carruthers, had made "some very idiotic and disgusting pictures portraying the Force." To his surprise Thalberg's response was an invitation to come to the studio. There, Carruthers told him that movies "should be made educational as well as entertaining and sometimes they ceased to be the latter and became only disgusting in their lack of authenticity."[58] Thalberg promptly offered him the job of technical director on M-G-M's next Mountie movie, which turned out to be *Rose Marie*. Carruthers found himself with a new career, and within a short time RCMP headquarters in Ottawa was using his presence in Hollywood as a convenient excuse to keep at arm's length from the moviemakers.

In the summer of 1937 Commissioner MacBrien had referred Al Herman to Carruthers, no doubt as a convenient way to get Herman out of his hair. Herman's production was *Renfrew of the Royal Mounted*, a Republic cheapie based on the highly popular kiddies' radio serial of the same name. Herman didn't want any part of Carruthers. He couldn't afford a technical director and besides he said he'd "made Mountie pictures before."[59]

"The confidence of some of our producers is pathetic," Carruthers wrote to MacBrien, "they make pictures pertaining to a subject foreign to them and think they know all. . . ."[60]

At this point Carruthers was given a bit part in *Barrier*, a film about the Klondike gold rush of 1898. He'd tried two months previously to be taken on as an adviser but was told, again, that there was no budget. The picture was being shot halfway up Mount Baker, in the State of Washington, an environment that the producer apparently considered typical of the Yukon. When Carruthers, the old Yukon hand, arrived on the scene he was properly horrified.

The company had spent thousands of dollars hauling in fake logs over sixty miles of mountain roads to cover cabins that didn't require any renovation, and had then built an additional dozen, "not one of which was correct in appearance." The director had ordered eighteen totem poles built in California at a cost of $200 each. These were also hauled in at heavy expense and then discarded because there are no totem poles in the Klondike. Carruthers, who figured he could have shaved the budget by $50,000 by eliminating expensive and incongruous props, remarked in a letter to MacBrien that "the financial angle is the least of it. . . . The dialogue . . . is truly laughable, no, I should say lamentable as it places Dawson in Alaska and refers to the way we hang people in Fortymile – where we were stationed at the time of the story, 1898 – thereby placing it also under US jurisdiction. There are other errors, too numerous to mention, but which will make a half-million dollar production a farce."[61]

In the spring of 1938 Warner Brothers hired Carruthers for some technical advice on a forthcoming production, *Heart of the North*. They told him the story was perfect – all they wanted him for was to check on the police uniforms and to make sure the actors acted like real Mounties. But when Carruthers read the script he hit the roof. And, following a script conference, he was virtually apoplectic: "The writers and PARTICULARLY the director come from East Side New York and they can't get their minds out of the gutter and they know absolutely nothing of the mental workings of those who spend their lives next to Nature."[62]

Some items were easily corrected: Carruthers got the Mackenzie River flowing the right way, substituted river boats for ocean steamers and managed to scale down the size of the huge sacks of gold the miners were shown lugging onto the vessels. But when he tried to change the character of the mounted police inspector, he met a stone wall of resistance. The writers had made the officer a sex-crazed Englishman who knew nothing of the north, who had been given his job through political pull, and who was doing his best to have his own sergeant killed off by criminals so that he could enjoy the favours of the two white women at the post.

Carruthers managed, after a long verbal wrangle, to get the inspector's character sandpapered down. But he immediately encountered another example of lèse majesté: the writers had a Mountie bribing an Indian into silence with a bottle of whisky. Carruthers patiently explained that mounted policemen didn't act that way.

That scene went, too, but the writers, growing more and more frustrated as they watched page after page of their script disappear into the wastebasket, rebelled when Carruthers tried to tinker with the climax of the movie. The plot called for the Wicked, Sex-Mad Inspector to arrest the father of the sergeant's sweetheart, give him the third degree, order a court rushed in from Edmonton and, to curry favour with his superiors, have the prisoner tried and hanged within twenty-four hours.

This was too much for Bruce Carruthers, former RCMP corporal and loyal Canadian. He tried to explain, patiently at first and then with rising phlegm, why this monstrous perversion of justice, perfectly acceptable of course in movies about Dodge City or Tombstone, Arizona, was more than slightly at odds with the Canadian – and the RCMP – way of doing things.

Finally after a verbal tussle he won his point, only to discover that the writers had sneaked another un-Canadian scene in its place – that good old frontier standby, the necktie party, complete with torches. Carruthers, struggling manfully, got *that* toned down to an attempted lynching.

143

His final battle was fought over a dramatic scene in which the inspector is drummed out of the force, his insignia of office torn from his uniform in the kind of public ceremony familiar to all students of movies about the British Army in India. Carruthers was forced to break the news to the writers that no such rite had ever occurred in Canada. Again, they gave in.

When the film was finished, Carruthers continued to view it with misgivings. "I removed 95% of the filth," he reported to Commissioner Wood in Ottawa, ". . . but the remaining 5% is quite noticeable. . . . All that I can say is that I did my best, the opposition was terrific and I won most of my points."[63]

The movie company, however, had its revenge. Somebody, possibly a press agent or perhaps one of the thoroughly frustrated members of the writing team, noised it around that somebody in high places in Canada had threatened to ban the entire picture if the mounted police in the film were shown in a bad light. Several columnists picked up the story and ran it. Erskine Johnson claimed that the Canadian government had insisted upon deleting all references to bad Mounties. Jimmy Fidler reported that the RCMP high command was responsible. Walter Winchell in New York carried a similar item: "A Mountie may never be shown in a flicker as a villain. Warners had to rewrite the entire story of HEART OF THE NORTH because originally the villain was a Mountie, and Canadian authorities warned that unless the character was changed, the picture would be banned in the entire British Empire."[64]

All this brought about a mild blast from The Halifax Daily Star, which sympathized with Hollywood producers for being hamstrung by taboos, and charged that "the redcoats would appear to be arrogating to themselves even wider powers than they now possess – movie censors, no less."[65]

But it was only Bruce Carruthers trying, as best he knew how and in the face of fearful odds, to Maintain the Right.

He moved almost immediately to the 20th Century-Fox lot as technical director on *Susannah of the Mounties,* the picture which Commissioner Wood had refused to help with. Wood had naïvely suggested that the studio contact Muriel Denison, the author of the original book, Susannah: A Little Girl with the Mounties, who could probably supply the research department with everything it needed; but, as Carruthers noted, the studio wanted to stay as far away from her as possible, "as they will probably have the story so changed for their production that the author will not recognize it."[66]

Wood had recommended Carruthers and Carruthers responded by keeping Wood fully informed of what was going on: "This will be my heaviest assignment yet," he reported. "The Writing and Wardrobe Department will fight me tooth and nail to put over THEIR ideas. . . . The Indian situation will be one of my troubles as it is difficult for the people of this Country to picture treatment of Indians other than the way the US Cavalry handled the situation in this Country with much blood-shed."[67]

Carruthers won his battle, if there was one, with the wardrobe department; the Mounties in the picture all wore the authentic pillbox hat, standard issue for 1883. He only partially succeeded with the script, however. Nobody had the slightest intention of deleting the stock attack on the wagon train, even though Carruthers explained that "there is no record of a wagon-train being wiped out on the Canadian plains prior to or after the coming of the Mounted Police. In CANADA the Police came before the settler."[68]

He was able to tone down some of the Indian savagery by putting the blame for the Indian attacks on a minority of malcontents led by a renegade. He did get rid of cerain Americanisms and he succeeded in preventing the writers from having the police seize an Indian boy as a hostage whose life would depend on the good behaviour of his father, a Blackfoot chief. "We have never been so low as to use a child to pay a debt for the father, in fact it is against the law," he told the studio.[69]

Altogether, Carruthers did his work well. He turned in twenty-three close-typed pages of comments on a scene-by-scene basis. But he could not change the basic plot, which turned the Canadian west into the American west.

The most outrageous scene of all was shot only after Carruthers had finished his work and left the lot – the sequence in which the Blackfoot chief condemns the Mountie hero to be burned at the stake. That upset Carruthers almost as much as an apparent error in the credits. He had tried to make it clear that, as technical adviser, he should be referred to as "formerly of the RCM Police," but, either by accident or design, somebody dropped the word "formerly" and so *Susannah* was made to look like an officially approved movie.[70]

Carruthers encountered similar frustrations as technical adviser on *Northwest Rangers,* another M-G-M Mountie movie, which opens with the usual attack on a settler's cabin by drunken, half-naked Canadian Indians somewhere in the north. Carruthers pointed out scores of inconsistencies, paradoxes, and straight errors in the movie, including a major one, in which the mounted police allow a fourteen-year-old to play a roulette wheel in a saloon. But his suggestions for plausible changes in this and several other areas were rejected with the laconic comment: "Ah, nobody'll know the difference."[71]

Not all of Carruthers's experiences in Hollywood were as frustrating

145

as that. Some directors were happy to accept his recommendations, and there's no doubt that most of the movies he worked on were improved in some way, at least from the mounted police point of view, because of his script suggestions. (A water cooler in a remote northern outpost, he told the director of *Northern Pursuit,* was "more out of place than doilies on a police desk.")[72]

It's not hard to sympathize with the screenwriters who were confronted with Carruthers's intransigence. His holier-than-thou attitude shows through in his correspondence with Ottawa; his was more than a job – it was almost a crusade. And sometimes he couldn't see the woods for the trees, splitting hairs over a minor detail of police dress while ignoring the overall effect of an historically impossible plot. He must have been a pain in the neck, especially to journeymen screenwriters, trying to pump some drama into a B movie about a foreign land. On the other hand, no one can fault his dedication or his very real efforts to improve the Hollywood product, at least from the point of view of the force and the country he loved so much.

He also loved his work, but towards the end the frustrations grew more inhibiting. During the shooting of *Johnny Belinda* he let his hair down to a new commissioner: "I will be very happy when I can bow my way comfortably out of this inharmonious, disloyal and unintelligent industry,"[73] he wrote. That time was not long in coming. Six years later he was dead at the age of fifty-four.

5: The gospel according to DeMille

Commissioner Samuel Taylor Wood, who succeeded General MacBrien as the top mounted policeman in Canada, had been born into the force. His father, Zachary Taylor Wood, one of the great heroes of the Klondike stampede, had risen to assistant commissioner, a post he held until his death. The younger Wood, who was a great-great grandson of Zachary Taylor, twelfth president of the United States, had a quarter-century of service in the force and was all policeman. When he took over in 1938 he had no intention of buckling under to the kind of Hollywood pressure that had embarrassed the mounted police for some two decades.

At that point, however, Wood had not yet encountered Hollywood power in the person of Cecil B. DeMille, who was planning his sixty-sixth motion picture and his first in Technicolor. It was logical that DeMille should choose Canada to provide a background for what was still a relatively novel process. If we believe his press agents, DeMille even day-dreamed in colour, seeing in his mind a moving procession of red-coated riders, brilliant against the stark white of the Canadian snows. No doubt he also saw those snows stained with Technicolor blood, but the press releases do not go into gory detail.

DeMille had made one previous movie about Canada in 1914 – the Hudson's Bay Company story titled *The Call of the North*. His publicized specialty then, as later, was absolute historical accuracy. Press kits for DeMille's historical pictures were always loaded with stories about the master's scrupulous fidelity to the smallest detail.

The mounted police might have been more suspicious of DeMille's protestations about accuracy at the outset if they had read one of the several trade descriptions of *The Call of the North*, or seen the film, a print of which reposes at George Eastman House in Rochester, New York. This was the first of the movies to deal with La Longue Traverse, or Journey of Death. We have already seen that the moviegoing public accepted this legend, aided by DeMille's own assurances that "no stone was left unturned to make the picture absolutely true to the life it portrayed."[74] Much was made of the fact that, to add a touch of authenticity, DeMille had imported "15 big Tiger Indians with authentic canoes from Ahitiba, Canada, far north of Winnipeg."[75] A search of the most detailed gazetteer fails to turn up any community called Ahitiba, while the definitive list of Indian bands in Canada makes no mention of any Indians who called themselves or were called Tiger.

DeMille's knowledge of historical and contemporary Canada can be gauged from a conversation he had with Clifford Wilson of the Hudson's Bay Company. His original plan, he told Wilson, was to make a picture about the great fur company, choosing the period of strife with the rival North West Company before 1821. "He explained to me, however, that he would have to take sides and show the North West Company as the villain of the piece. And certainly he didn't want to offend the North West Company!"[76] At that juncture, the North West Company had been defunct for more than a century.

DeMille wanted something more than mere mounted police co-operation in making his picture. He wanted to make it look like an officially sanctioned film, stamped with the force's seal of approval. His desires were made clear in a wire that Paramount sent to its Toronto office manager, M. A. Milligan, in May of 1939:

WHILE WE WISH TO MAKE NO PRESENT PUBLIC ANNOUNCEMENT CECIL DEMILLE PLANS AS HIS NEXT BIG EPIC PICTURE A STORY OF RCMP FOR WHICH HE IS NOW STARTING PREPARATIONS STOP NATURALLY THIS

PICTURE WILL BE A TREMENDOUS INTERNATIONAL SUBJECT ESPE-
CIALLY FOR CANADA AND BRITISH EMPIRE IN GENERAL ALSO MARVEL-
OUS PUBLICITY FOR RCMP STOP DEMILLE IS ANXIOUS TO SECURE FULL
COOPERATION CANADIAN GOVERNMENT AND RCMP AUTHORITIES
STOP HE SPECIFICALLY NEEDS WHOLEHEARTED ASSISTANCE OF MEN IN
CHARGE OF THIS ORGANIZATION FROM WHOM HE WANTS NOT ONLY
DATA BUT COOPERATION IN PHOTOGRAPHING MOUNTED POLICE
THEIR HEADQUARTERS EQUIPMENT ETC AND SCENERY ALL THROUGH
WESTERN CANADA AND CANADIAN ROCKIES STOP CAN YOU ARRANGE
ABOVE IMMEDIATELY. . . .[77]

The studio's assumption that the mounted police were hungry for publicity and would jump at a chance to see themselves on the screen was a widely held notion in Hollywood, where everybody thrived on publicity, good or bad. One director put the attitude succinctly to Bruce Carruthers: "Bruce, where would the mounted police be if it wasn't for motion pictures?" As Carruthers later remarked, "I naturally cleared up this point for him rather quickly."[78] The RCMP's attitude, of course, was the antithesis of Hollywood's. The force didn't want publicity and when Milligan passed the Paramount request on to Commissioner Wood in Ottawa, Wood's reply was guarded.

Wood's one-year moratorium on aid to Hollywood was up and he didn't object to helping in a minor way, but only if the force had total script control. The studio must also promise that no attempt would be made to suggest that the movie was made with RCMP co-operation. Finally no mounted policeman could turn up at any première to add colour to the proceedings or suggest official recognition.

DeMille now decided to come to Canada himself, and to Ottawa, a visit Wood attempted to discourage. Paramount announced that the picture would be called *Royal Canadian Mounted Police* and that it would be filmed on location at Banff. DeMille's associate producer, William Pine, was already in Canada during that July of 1939 – the year of the Royal Visit – along with Frank Calvin, Paramount's research chief. Calvin's stay in Regina produced a flutter of exclamatory news features all stressing DeMille's much-publicized passion for accuracy.

"In preparing an historical picture, such as the proposed picture dealing factually with the story of the Mounted Police, everything possible is done to assure accuracy of the material," The Regina Leader Post reported in a lengthy interview with Calvin. "The language, the costumes, the customs are the subject of painstaking study."

"As a rule, in a DeMille production, people in the audience are usually wrong if they question something, because he goes so thoroughly into everything," Calvin told the interviewer.[79]

At this point, DeMille had no story and no cast. He had a vague notion in his mind that he might somehow tie the mounted police in with the Bengal Lancers. This idea was sketched briefly to Commissioner Wood whom Pine visited in Ottawa. Wood did not like that idea at all, nor did he like DeMille's proposed title. It would, he wrote to Pine, "be inaccurate and inappropriate as a picture such as you described to me could not possibly portray an outline of the work of the Force, and frankly I cannot see the parallel you draw between the Royal Canadian Mounted Police, which has multifarious duties, and the Bengal Lancers, which is a fighting unit of the British Indian Army."[80] Pine and DeMille had hit the commissioner in his most sensitive spot by voicing the firmly held Hollywood misconception that his men were soldiers rather than policemen. Wood then went on:

> I trust you will forgive my frankness if I explain further that the type of picture you have in mind appears to be one more attempt of the melodramatic type, and I cannot refrain from feeling some disappointment as I had imagined you had an opportunity of making a better picture, showing the spirit and history of the Force, than has heretofore been produced, but this does not seem to be what is intended.[81]

Pine responded with hasty assurances that the "few words of description I gave you . . . was no more than a mere thought of possible action."

"I can assure you, however, of one fact," he continued. "Any motion picture Cecil B. DeMille produces will be true in detail and based on fact. *He never garbles facts or distorts history.*" (The italics are mine.) Pine then added that DeMille hoped "to evolve a story out of some historic occurrence that will portray the spirit that has made the Force the outstanding organization of its kind in the world."[82]

In Regina Frank Calvin had been keeping a file on the two Riel rebellions and by the end of July it began to appear that one of these would form the historical basis for the script. That intelligence dismayed the mounted police hierarchy. "The last thing I should like to see is to have your picture placed in the North West Rebellion period," the departmental secretary, G. T. Hann, wrote to Pine. "The old-time stories of the pill-box period have been told so often that I feel certain that I did not advise that. . . ."

Hann suggested something more modern that would show a case of mounted police detective work: "To be quite frank with you, I feel your opportunity is not in something of the old days, but in something much more modern."[83]

These suggestions were politely ignored. DeMille himself was already on the site of Duck Lake, Saskatchewan, the scene of the so-called Duck Lake Massacre that touched off the rebellion of 1885. The picture, he told the press, would star Clark Gable.[84]

By September, when the war in Europe broke out, DeMille had four writers working on the script. "As far as his next picture is concerned, Cecil B. DeMille is just going to pretend there isn't any war," a press release announced. The title of the film had by now been changed to *North West Mounted Police* and the press was reporting that "full co-operation in the making of the picture had been promised DeMille by officials of Canada's famous mounted police."[85] DeMille also announced that he planned to shoot a good portion of the picture on location in Canada.

The report about full co-operation obviously bothered Wood, who had not even seen a script. Until he did, he wrote Pine, the force would not consider any kind of co-operation. But the script wasn't in any shape to be seen. Carruthers, whom DeMille refused to use in spite of Wood's recommendation, reported to the commissioner on November 27 that "he now has five writers working, none of whom know what they are doing and they are in constant trouble."[86] Carruthers also reported Hollywood gossip that Wood *himself* would be technical director on the picture – a rumour Wood hastened to deny. "We have lost considerable interest now that we know it is only to be 'another picture' of the Force," he told Carruthers.[87]

DeMille, however, hadn't lost interest in the mounted police. He wanted to tie the RCMP as closely as possible to the picture in the public's mind. When the script was finally in shape a few days before Christmas he did not mail it to Wood; he sent Pine by air to Ottawa to deliver it personally. This gesture produced the expected results. The Ottawa Citizen, in a story picked up nationally by the Canadian Press, reported:

> . . . Wm. H. Pine, Mr. DeMille's associate producer, arrived by plane from Hollywood this morning, script in bag, ready to submit it to Commissioner S. T. Wood of the RCMP for his approval. Scriptwriters and workers have been engaged on the story since last June, receiving the collaboration of "the silent force" in their task. . . .[88]

This was too much for Wood. He flatly refused to have anything further to do with the production unless Paramount agreed to stop publicizing the fact that the script was being vetted by the RCMP or capitalizing on that fact in any way. Paramount agreed and the commissioner, mollified, made a series of suggestions, most of them dealing with the removal of American military terms. The larger implications went unremarked or unnoticed.

In February Wood went so far as to lend the production a training instructor from Regina, Sergeant Major G. F. Griffin, to put the actors through their paces. By this time DeMille had been forced by Paramount's budget control to abandon any location shooting in Canada; the movie would be shot on the studio's backlot. Clark Gable wasn't available for the leading role and neither was Joel McCrea, whom DeMille had hoped would play a Texas Ranger in the movie. Gary Cooper was cast for that part; Preston Foster would play the mounted policeman.

The publicity mills began to grind as soon as the cameras did. Carruthers, still ignored by DeMille, was approached on the quiet by two Paramount publicity men to get his reaction to a series of ideas they were working on to sell the picture. What, for example, did he think of their plan to hold the world premiere in Canada, with the RCMP and possibly the prime minister in attendance? Carruthers, who was embittered by DeMille's rebuffs, replied that he couldn't see anybody from the Canadian government enthusing over a picture "which portrayed the police as deserters and nincompoops." The ex-corporal had managed to sneak a copy of the script out of the Paramount lot – not an easy thing to do because, as he said, "Scripts are guarded in studios like state secrets." He did not like what he read. He was certain that the script was a more recent one than the copy that had been shown to the commissioner and that it contained sequences that Wood hadn't seen.

The publicity men had some other ideas. They wanted to set up Junior Mounted Police Clubs across the United States with Carruthers's help. (Carruthers said DeMille didn't have enough money to buy his services.) They wanted to set up a monument to the mounted police in Canada. (But, said Carruthers, the Force isn't dead.) They suggested that DeMille present a set of colours to the force, but the idea bogged down because they had no idea exactly *which* colours to proffer. And perhaps, they suggested, the RCMP band might tour the United States to help exploit the picture.

Carruthers reported all of this to Wood in a confidential letter: "As it is customary to figure on 12% of the production cost for exploitation, DeMille will move Heaven and Earth with $240,000.00 to get publicity in any and every way possible,"[89] he warned.

Hann, the departmental secretary, in a memorandum to Wood also advised that "it is obvious that the original script has been changed and that Mr. Cecil B. DeMille is likely to make very strenuous efforts to make unusual requests for publicity."[90]

In Hollywood that spring Sergeant Major Griffin was drilling his Mountie actors. That fact did not escape the notice of the Paramount publicity department who lost no time in sending out a release that again suggested an official tie-up between DeMille and the RCMP:

> DeMille, a demon for authenticity, wants his troops to do credit to the real mounted police, who are co-operating in the production. . . .[91]

To understand exactly what it was that Cecil B. DeMille was doing to Canadian history, it's necessary to recall briefly the events surrounding the North West Rebellion of 1885.

Louis Riel, whose earlier uprising in 1869 had earned him the title of The Father of Manitoba, was teaching school in Montana when a group of Métis rode across the border in the summer of 1884 and asked him to return to Canada to help them present their grievances to the Canadian government. The grievances of these French-speaking mixed bloods, who lived around St. Laurent on the South Saskatchewan River, were real ones, no less impassioned than those of the English-speaking Protestant half-breeds, the Indians and the whites, all of whom were in ferment. Ottawa, however, ignored all petitions and protests, and the Métis' intention (which was also Riel's) to proceed peacefully and legally was eroded.

At last, Riel set up a provisional government of his own at Batoche. Bloodshed was inevitable and it came at Duck Lake, largely as the result of a mounted police blunder. Inspector Leif Crozier, blocked from getting supplies and ammunition from the Duck Lake store, impetuously ordered a detachment of mounted police and white volunteers to proceed to the scene by sleigh, rather than waiting for a column of reinforcements to arrive. A parley took place near the Duck Lake store between the NWMP and the Métis. It is unclear who fired the first shot – it was, apparently, the result of a misunderstanding – but in the fracas that followed the Métis were better deployed and the police, although they had superior weapons including a cannon, were defeated. Three mounted policemen and nine volunteers were killed in addition to eleven wounded. The Métis suffered five casualties.

This incident touched off a widespread prairie revolt. The Canadian government dispatched some 7,000 militiamen on the still-unfinished Canadian Pacific Railway to do battle with Riel's forces, who were joined by Cree Indians under two great chiefs, Poundmaker and Big Bear. Outnumbered and outgunned, the natives fought skilfully but the issue was never in doubt. The troops had not only modern rifles and cannon on their side but also three Gatling guns – the first successful machine gun ever devised – being tested in battle for the first time by an American cavalryman and Indian-fighter, Lieutenant Arthur Howard. The hostilities lasted from March until June, by which time all the leaders had surrendered including Big Bear, who was the last to give in.

Cecil B. DeMille (seated, left of camera, with hat) recreates Fort Carlton on the Paramount backlot. The set was scrupulously accurate; the history was myth.

Myth and Reality

So powerful was the Hollywood image
of Canada that in many cases it was accepted
as the real thing—even by Canadians.

153

Hollywood Myth

The moviemakers saw the Klondike in the same way
they saw Tombstone or Dodge City—as a glamorous
corner of the old west. The well-scrubbed men above
in their cowboy hats are living it up in Hollywood's
version of a Dawson City saloon and gambling house.
The movie, made in 1942, is called Northwest Rangers.

154

Klondike Reality

This is what the inside of a Klondike gambling house and saloon really looked like. It's the famous Monte Carlo, photographed in Dawson City in 1899. The rough characters shown here make the slickers opposite look like cream puffs; but then these men and women have actually climbed the Chilkoot Pass.

How Could A Blue-Eyed Scotsman Fool An Entire Country Into Believing He Was An Indian?

That's Archie Belaney, above, wearing a Sioux head-dress. Back in the thirties everybody thought he was an Indian named Grey Owl. He didn't look a bit like an Indian, as the photograph of the real Indian at left indicates. But he fooled the country. How did he pull it off?

Answer: Because He Looked Exactly Like A Hollywood Indian.

The man in the photograph above isn't Grey Owl and he isn't an Indian, either. He's Victor Jory playing a Hollywood Indian. Nobody looked at real Indians in the thirties; they looked at Hollywood Indians. Even Lord Tweedsmuir, the Governor General, looked like a Hollywood Indian when he put on the head-dress.

Hollywood Athapaskans

Indian maidens were generally portrayed in the movies wearing fringed buckskin and feathers in their hair, like Yellow Flower (left) played by Carol Thurston in Yukon Vengeance, *made in 1954. Cyd Charisse, a Hollywood dancer, also played a glamourous Athapaskan maiden in* The Wild North, *made about the same time.*

Real Athapaskans

These two photographs of Athapaskan Indian women were taken by the author about the same time the two Hollywood pictures were being made, allegedly about the same region. Both pictures were taken at Fort Rae on the shores of Great Slave Lake in the summer of 1954. There is no glamour in these conditions.

Bruce Carruthers, the ex-mounted police corporal who acted as technical advisor on so many movies about Canada, often fought vainly to try to make movies about Mounties, Indians, and the Canadian north more authentic.

160

DeMille did more than twist these historical facts to suit his purpose. He turned them inside out. From the very opening of the film, with its introduction voiced by DeMille himself against a background of snow-capped Rockies, everything was wrong:

> The Canadian Northwest! Here the first traders from the Old World intermarried with the Indians of the plains and the forests and founded a new race, the Métis of Canada. Here for two centuries these half-breed hunters and traders multiplied and prospered, a law unto themselves. Then surveyors and homebuilders pushed westward, bringing laws of land and property, which threatened to end forever the free ways of the wild. . . . In 1885, resentful and confused, the half-breeds under the leadership of Louis Riel revolted against the advance of unwelcome law. At that hour a handful of hard-riding men in scarlet coats, the North West Mounted Police, stood between Canada's destiny and the rebellion that was being kindled across the border in a little Montana schoolhouse.

DeMille's opening suggested that the Métis were opposed to the idea of Canadian law as represented by the police. Nothing could be farther from the truth. The mixed bloods welcomed the extension of Canadian law to the plains and, if anything, wanted more (to prevent undisciplined buffalo hunters from destroying the herds, for example). Their quarrel wasn't with the NWMP but with an unbending and distant government that refused to give them title to lands which they had farmed for years. The impression that a handful of redcoated police managed to contain the rebellion, and not an overpowering military force, was continued throughout the picture. But there was worse to come.

Louis Riel, who was nothing if not dynamic, was presented by DeMille as a weak, indecisive puppet, controlled by the villainous Jacques Corbeau. In the movie it is Corbeau who masterminds the entire rebellion, over Riel's weak protests, in order that he may be free to sell whisky to the Indians. "I'll let you lead my people," he tells Riel, "all I want is the whisky business." Riel goes along with him. But in real life it was Riel who restrained the more impetuous Métis from shedding unnecessary blood.

The Gatling gun was introduced in the picture's opening sequence, but in DeMille's version of Canadian history it was Corbeau and his Métis who had the weapon and who used it. "I got a gun that shoots a thousand slugs a minute," Corbeau tells Riel. And Duroc, his sidekick, played by Akim Tamiroff, remarks gleefully: "Trust Corbeau to know the newest way of killing."

Throughout the picture the Métis were portrayed either as blood-thirsty killers or comic buffoons. One of the buffoons was Shorty, played by Lon Chaney, Jr., who appeared to be frozen into his earlier performance as Lenny, the half-wit in *Of Mice and Men*. When Shorty's wife presents him with a baby boy early in the movie, he dances about in the street in childish delight and then looks puzzled when shown the infant: "She not very beeg. How you make sure she boy?" Everybody has a good chuckle over that one.

Corbeau is shown as the mastermind and leader of the revolution that follows. In Riel's presence, he shoots down two Mounties who get nosey over the hiding place of the Gatling gun. Then he seeks out Big Bear and, demonstrating the gun, attempts to get the Cree chieftain to join him in the forthcoming bloodshed. The chief is impressed. "Redcoats no longer our friend," he says. "This is our friend who fights with a thousand teeth of fire." Sergeant Jim Bret of the Mounted is present, but makes no attempt to arrest Corbeau, a failure that would have lost him his stripes in real life.

The Duck Lake affair, which followed these scenes, was presented as a treacherous and unprovoked ambush in which hundreds of Métis, armed with the Gatling gun, mowed down and killed some fifty redcoats, including the inspector in charge.

It is unnecessary to follow the rest of the picture in detail. Its polished production and big names only partially obscured the fact that Hollywood's most publicized director had employed the same clichés that had been standard in Mountie movies since the early days: the wicked half-breed who sells booze to the misguided natives; the passionate half-breed girl who loves not wisely but too well; and the grim-faced policeman who is forced to bring his sweetheart's brother to justice, even at the risk of losing the woman he loves. ("When this is over I'm going to get him . . . if I have to follow him over the ice caps!") Suffice it to say that the mounted police single-handedly put down the revolution in a matter of days, partly because Dusty Rivers, the Texas Ranger, destroys the Gatling gun, and partly because Sergeant Bret in a face-to-face confrontation with Corbeau, persuaded Big Bear *not* to join Riel – another historical right-about-face.

The Métis see the error of their ways and are shown, in a comic scene, straggling back to their homes. "You come home. I'll give you all the fight you want," says big Shorty's tiny wife as they march down the trail, defeated. And so the picture moves to its romantic conclusion with the Mountie and not the Ranger getting the girl.

Even while the picture was still before the cameras DeMille's press agents were describing scenes from the script to reporters, inviting columnists onto the set to watch the shooting, and assuring everyone that the movie was a totally authentic account of the Canadian rebellion.

One seasoned columnist, who swallowed it all, was Virginia Wright, the drama editor of The Los Angeles News. Miss Wright, one of a dozen key journalists who were invited to the set early in May, wrote an enthusiastic description of the six-acre forest that DeMille had created on the Paramount backlot – a pine forest, of course. She was present when the big scene with Big Bear was filmed – a scene in which the Indians are about to join Corbeau, only to realize that he has lied to them. Wrote Miss Wright: "Because he lied the Indians refuse to be a party to any half-breed revolt. If this episode sounds like phony dramatics, DeMille has the facts to prove that it happened during the Real [sic] rebellion in Saskatchewan."[92]

The publicity men fed another anecdote to the press party, which Miss Wright also reported as fact:

Indicative of the sort of thing to expect from this latest DeMille opus is the producer's insistence that the Indian chief change his name. History has him down as Little Bear. DeMille as you might expect, christened him Big Bear.

That story kept turning up in newspapers all over the continent, even including the scrupulous New York Times, whose Hollywood man also accepted DeMille's version of the Duck Lake Massacre without a raised eyebrow.

With the picture nearing completion Paramount stepped up its publicity campaign. It badly wanted to hold the première in Ottawa and to turn it into "an international celebration sponsored by the Canadian government." The plan was to get Canadian National Railways to place an entire train at the studio's disposal, to be called "The North West Mounted Special." The train was to transport some sixty stars and studio officials across the United States and Canada, with celebrations at every whistle stop.

The CNR apparently was partially convinced by R. C. Moriarty of Paramount, who told the railway publicity director, W. S. Thompson, that the film was "the first serious attempt to present on the screen the authentic history of the North West Mounted Police and we have produced it in close co-operation and with the approval of Commissioner Wood and officials directly connected with the Royal Canadian Mounted."[93]

Thompson checked with Wood who replied that "the picture does not portray any such history but is simply another melo-dramatic romance woven around the name of the North West Mounted Police."[94] Wood saw no reason for helping at all, nor did G. H. Lash, the government director of information, who replied that "there is much more important work for us to do."[95] There was, after all, a war on.

163

With Ottawa out of the picture Paramount opted for Plan B. For some months the Regina Board of Trade had been lobbying to have the première held in the Queen City, long the headquarters of the mounted police. The vice-president of the board, J. Alex MacKenzie, had been dispatched to Hollywood for that purpose and had returned with glowing accounts of DeMille's "devotion to accuracy"[96] in making the picture. Now, with Wood cold to any official help, the studio seized on the Regina offer and with good reason: if the board of trade was pulling the strings, it would be impossible for the mounted police not to be front and centre.

Wood had already warned the commanding officer at Regina that "the claims for the picture are extravagant" and that he mustn't provide escorts "or anything of that nature" without permission from headquarters. But then he was forced to add: "Of course if the Board of Trade at Regina are very anxious to have the première showing in Regina we cannot very well refuse to attend if we are invited. . . ."[97] And that, of course, was exactly what the studio wanted.

The board now mounted a massive campaign around the première. Festivities were to last for several days. Storefronts were to be covered with log slabs to suggest the pioneer era, with prizes for the best display. Life-sized replicas of mounted policemen were provided to all merchants. The local daily, The Leader Post, published a special thirty-two-page souvenir edition of mounted police history. Paramount announced that four of the picture's stars, and possibly DeMille himself, would be present for the opening.

The results probably surpassed what the studio publicity department had expected. Regina went wild in a three-day celebration, climaxed by one of the biggest parades in its history as well as the première of the movie. DeMille did not appear but William Pine and the four stars all turned up. Madeleine Carroll, whose British connections in this time of overseas crisis were not overlooked (her sister had just been killed in the London blitz), presented a cheque to the RCMP on behalf of Famous Players Canadian Corporation, the picture's distributor. The cheque was actually for the Red Cross but, by making the presentation to the RCMP, the movie company managed to get two assistant commissioners of the force on the theatre's stage and in the press photographs.

By this time the mounted police, for all their reluctance, had become thoroughly involved in the affair, sucked in in spite of themselves. They could hardly refuse the board of trade's invitation to lead the parade on horseback. They were needed at the première to help hold back the crowds who jammed the streets outside the theatre. And they couldn't very well turn down the board's invitation to aid in a worthy cause. The press photographs of the event give the distinct impression that the mounted police are not only committed to the film but are also actually

164

running the celebration. As The Leader Post put it: "Scarlet-coated Mounties, stern-faced and straight-backed, were the guiding light of the entire procession. The renowned Redcoats led the parade on their dancing horses, and the riders carried lances and flags that stood out in the line as a sunset in an artist's pictures."[98]

Thus Cecil B. DeMille managed to achieve all his objectives and get what he demanded when he first set out to make a movie about the mounted police, especially the undeniable visual evidence that convinced the average moviegoers that this was an official motion picture, blessed by the top officers of the force.

The question of historical accuracy was not seriously debated. Frank Morriss, The Leader Post's critic, neatly side-stepped the issue: "The matter . . . will have to rest with Hollywood and the mounted police experts who were on hand when the cameras ground in the movie capital,"[99] he wrote, again suggesting official RCMP approval. Roly Young, in an enthusiastic review in The Globe and Mail, Toronto, did not even mention the problem. "There have been plenty of movie yarns about the Mounties in the past," he wrote, "but they fade into insignificance when compared to DeMille's production."[100] It was, he added "a film that will make Canadians want to stand up and cheer." Jack Karr, in The Toronto Star, pushed aside any petty problems regarding accuracy: "Out of the pages of Canadian history comes this tale of Saskatchewan of the days of the Riel rebellion. And while those pages may have become a trifle blurred through the sights of a motion picture camera, sufficient authority has been observed to persuade even the most devout scholars of Canadiana to put any stray lapses in the field of fact on the entertainment side of the ledger and let it go at that." The picture, he wrote, was "like no other film ever built around this vast and colourful country of ours. . . . The ball has now been set rolling. Canada has finally been recognized by Hollywood as worthy of something better than routine treatment. . . ."[101]

In the United States the picture was widely praised as DeMille's best effort in years, and accepted, without demur, as historically accurate; "predicated on actual historical events,"[102] as Variety put it. The Hollywood Reporter called it "the true saga . . . of Canada's amazing organization . . . when there were a scant 500 of the Mounted all told and barely more than a handful of these by sheer, intelligent bravery, crushed the uprising of thousands of Indians and half-breeds under white leadership which threatened to slice half the Dominion from the British Empire."[103] And The Motion Picture Herald wrote that "the picture is a dramatisation of the Riel Rebellion of 1885 which threatened to destroy Canada and was put down by fifty North West Mounted Police in a manner celebrated by Canadians in song and story."[104]

DeMille's version of Canadian history even reached some of the classrooms of the United States. Photoplay Studies, a weekly group-discussion guide, published in New York and recommended by the Motion Picture Committee of the Department of Secondary Teachers of the National Education Association, devoted an entire issue to the picture, with photographs of the stars, a detailed synopsis of the story, a list of historical questions based on the movie, and some other features in which the long arm of the Paramount publicity department was apparent.

Only Charles Jefferys, the Canadian historian and artist, seemed to have realized the lengths to which DeMille had gone to change history. "Only a genius could have evolved from historic facts such a masterpiece of misinformation,"[105] he wrote in The Canadian Historical Review.

That kind of comment, of course, didn't bother the great director. When somebody asked him why he had switched sides and given the Gatling gun to the Métis, he brushed the question aside. He had to do it, he explained, in order to increase the odds against the North West Mounted Police and make them look like greater heroes.

★

PART FOUR

★

Canadian Co-operation, Hollywood Style

★

1: The seduction of Donald Gordon

By the fall of 1947 the flow of cash out of Canada and into the United States had reached alarming proportions, Canada's supply of American dollars and gold had melted away – from $1,045 million at the end of 1945 to a dismaying $300 million two years later. To prevent the immediate devaluation of the Canadian dollar the government acted on November 17 with sweeping import restrictions on a wide variety of American imports, including automobiles, some food, and certain non-essential consumer items. Pleasure travel to the United States was severely restricted and a special program was created to increase the export trade.

The one luxury import that wasn't affected in this austerity program was the motion picture. It was obvious, however, that Hollywood movies would be next on the list. At the very least, it was thought, the government would establish some kind of quota system to force Hollywood to invest part of its box-office profits in Canada. In fact, some said, this might mean the beginning of a genuine Canadian film industry.

The Canadian Moving Picture Digest made matters plain in its issue of November 29: "Canada appears to be heading for a quota system of film imports from the United States under the austerity measures of the Dominion government. . . ."

C. D. Howe, the American-born Minister of Trade and Commerce, controlled imports of motion picture film. Under the dollar conservation program he was also given the job of trying to get more movies made in Canada – a prospect that alarmed the American motion picture industry. That year it had taken seventeen million dollars out of Canada. The last thing it wanted was any form of government restriction.

The papers were scarcely on the streets announcing the new Canadian policy when Eric Johnston, president of the Motion Picture Association of America, set up a committee to lobby in Ottawa against any government action. The committee included his own vice-president, Francis Harmon, and J. J. Fitzgibbons, president of the American-controlled Famous Players Canadian Corporation, the most powerful exhibitor-distributor in Canada.

169

The committee's task was to head off the kind of specific proposal for redressing the dollar balance that Ross McLean, Commissioner of the National Film Board, was urging. McLean made two proposals to his political superior, J. J. McCann, the Minister of Revenue. First, that American film companies be required by law to reinvest a proportion of their annual revenue, say four or five million dollars a year, in making films in Canada for international audiences; second, that the Hollywood-controlled distributing companies be "induced to offer effective United States distribution each year to forty or fifty or more short subjects"[1] produced by private Canadian companies and by the National Film Board.

McLean had put his finger on two of the chief barriers to a home-grown film industry: the lack of experience and the lack of a climate in which to make films (the presence of experienced film makers in Canada could help seed a movie industry) and the impossibility of cracking the solid wall of distributor resistance to Canadian product. As McLean put it, "except for the Soviet Union the United States market is probably the most difficult to break into." And that market, of course, was completely under Hollywood's thumb.

"Sooner or later," McLean wrote, "they are simply going to have to discover the logic of international trading, that it is not and never can be for long a one-way traffic. The process of learning has already proved to be a painful one for them. Something which would speed up the process would be useful both to them and to us."

But not in Hollywood's eyes. Fitzgibbons acted swiftly to head off this form of government control. He arranged an immediate meeting with C. D. Howe, followed by a luncheon at the Rideau Club in Ottawa on January 14 with Fitzgibbons, Harmon, and a Canadian group that included Donald Gordon, Deputy Governor of the Bank of Canada; Lester B. Pearson, Secretary of State for External Affairs; and Ernest Bushnell of the Canadian Broadcasting Corporation.

These Rideau Club get-togethers are an Ottawa institution. The club itself, set in the most strategic of all locations directly opposite Parliament Hill, fairly reeks of influence. The élite dine there: Cabinet ministers, top civil service mandarins, leading members of the Press Gallery, and visiting power-brokers. This is where decisions are made, policies formulated, news stories leaked. The atmosphere really is clubby: everybody knows everybody else; first names sprinkle the conversation; public adversaries become private cronies. It isn't in the lobbies that the lobbyists seek to weave their spells; it's here, in the leather-chair, white-linen atmosphere of a gentleman's private retreat, with the sound of the carillon echoing sweetly in their ears.

This particular luncheon must have been even cosier than most because the Canadians, in the end, bought the entire tinselled package that was offered to them. Actually the Americans gave no guarantees of any kind. The idea of a scheme that would force them to leave a specific percentage of their earnings in the country to contribute to the development of Canadian films does not seem to have been seriously discussed. Instead, they offered an ingenious alternative: rather than leave money *in* the country why not attract more American dollars *to* the country in the form of tourist travel?

What they promised to do was to increase Canadian publicity in the United States by means of the motion picture; and that was *all* they promised. They would make a special documentary explaining the dollar deficit. They would try to get more newsreel coverage. They would try to get more short subjects about Canada released in American theatres. They would look at NFB films to see if they were suitable for US release. They would make an effort to insert various Canadian references into Hollywood features. They would get big stars to make radio recordings about Canada. And finally – a really hollow promise – they would "undertake a program designed to insure proper selection of product"[2] for release in Canada; translation: no cheapie second features. "I can well understand the desire of our Canadian friends to avoid dollar-expenditure by Canada for gangster films or other pictures of a low-toned nature,"[3] was the way Eric Johnston put it in a letter to Fitzgibbons designed for Howe's eyes.

As an article of good faith, Fitzgibbons told Howe after the Rideau Club lunch, the Canada-boosting had already begun. Hollywood was rushing a beautiful blond bombshell, in the person of Miss Joan Caulfield, all the way to Mont Gabriel Lodge in the Laurentians for some snow shots to be inserted in US newsreels. Also Universal, which was completing a short subject titled *Snow Capers,* had been persuaded at huge expense to revise the commentary to include a mention of Banff and the Rockies as winter vacation spots.

On the wings of these triumphs the great Canadian Co-operation Project was launched. It offered very little and much of what it did offer was valueless. There isn't any evidence that the tourist trade was affected by stray references in feature films or newsreels or by the sporadic production of short subjects about snow. And there isn't any evidence that the dollar balance was helped. Pictures of "a low-toned nature" continued to pour into Canada, as they always had. Motion picture producers continued to make occasional movies in the Banff-Lake Louise location, as they always had – although the CCP grabbed the credit for persuading them. And if the number of NFB shorts released in American theatres increased the increase was a relatively minor one.

The project was falsely sold to the public as a boost for film production

171

in Canada and, by corollary, as a way of launching a Canadian film industry. Early in April, Harmon, Fitzgibbons, and other members of the Motion Picture Association of America met in Ottawa for what the press described as a roundtable discussion "concerning the production of movies in Canada."[4] Howe had already told the House of Commons that the government hoped to encourage more film making within the country. CANADA-US TO COOPERATE/EXPECT INCREASED PRODUCTION, ran the headline of The Canadian Moving Picture Digest on April 17, reporting another Ottawa meeting. In late June the same trade paper acted as if the matter was a fait accompli, announcing that the American motion picture industry was already diverting some of its production to Canada.

The hard truth is that the industry never had any intention of increasing production facilities in Canada or of making any more than the usual minimum number of films on location. Its purpose, in fact, was the exact opposite – to stifle any nationalistic outcries. More than a month before those smokescreen meetings in Ottawa J. J. Fitzgibbons had stated the problem bluntly in a letter to Spyros P. Skouras, the president of 20th Century-Fox:

> There are people in Canada – as in every other country where American films are released – who insist upon American companies building studios all over the world and scattering their production activities in an uneconomic fashion. If we are to avoid extreme pressure for expensive and expansive studio operations in Canada, then we must demonstrate to the Canadian government our capacity really to do a job for the Dominion. . . .[5]

From start to finish, the Canadian Co-operation Project was a public relation man's boondoggle. But from the point of view of the American film industry, it was remarkably effective. It prevented a quota system and thwarted any wistful hopes there might have been for a home-grown motion picture industry. The money taken out of the country by Hollywood movie companies continued to increase year by year. In 1947, as we've seen, seventeen million dollars left the country. Of that sum seven million came from theatre and other property rentals and ten million from film rentals. By 1963 rentals to Canada had increased to $16.8 million. Ten years later the figure jumped to $39.5 million, making Canada Hollywood's second largest international customer. (Then in 1974 Canada became Hollywood's largest foreign customer.)

But in 1948 Canadian government officials were enthusiastic about the CCP. Donald Gordon led the pack in shouting hosannahs about American co-operation. The hard-nosed banker was softened up at a luncheon at the Harvard Club in New York, where senior executives of

MPAA fed him, along with the lamb chops, statistics about Canadian references in newsreels and a glowing account of the production of short features such as *Quaint Quebec*. They also remarked on the possibility, never fulfilled, of one company making ten pictures in Canada. The company was Monogram, known as the lowest-budget studio in Hollywood; its quickie releases were scarcely designed to fulfill the high-toned expectations whetted at that first Rideau Club get-together.

Gordon, however, was positively starry-eyed, especially after being shown *Neighbour to the North*, a short subject about Canada's dollar deficit starring the American comic actor, Walter Abel, which had been rushed into production and obviously made, in The Ottawa Citizen's caustic phrase, "to please C. D. Howe."[6]

Gordon, who was invited to speak at the luncheon, described the CCP as "an excellent indication of the imaginative spirit rather than legal restrictions, as well as an outstanding example of good neighbourliness."[7] On his return the banker immediately wrote to Howe's deputy, M. W. Mackenzie:

> These and other tangible results of the effort so far indicate that earlier expectations have already been fulfilled or give firm promise of being fulfilled. This was encouraging to me, but no less encouraging were the impressions I formed of the spirit with which the executives of the Industry were pursuing the matter. In my opinion, we are obtaining, through the Canadian Co-operation Project, service beyond valuation by any conceivable commercial criteria and one which any government or any country would consider itself fortunate to obtain.[8]

Howe echoed these sentiments in praising the establishment of the co-operation project in the House of Commons.[9]

There was one dissenting voice, however, and it belonged to the sole government official who knew something about the film business. Ross McLean, the film commissioner, was more interested in results than promises, wasn't so easily seduced by statistical puffery, and cared more about film quality than Monogram quantity. Shortly before Gordon's Harvard Club luncheon, McLean had written to Harmon of the MPAA:

> I have been studying the results of the project as closely as possible over the last period and my own feeling is that while there is a good deal of good will evident, this good will has not so far been translated into concrete results or plans. It is true that a number of short pictures are projected and a number of these will no doubt be made. Some plans, too, appear to be developing for the production of feature films in Canada or on Canadian themes.

Unfortunately, in my view, too many of the producers who think in terms of Canadian stories think first of crime pictures or other forms of 'cops and robbers' motif. I am sure there are innumerable other kinds of stories which when filmed would do a better job, not only for this country but for the people of the United States and the rest of the world. I do not mean to say that a limited number of pictures on the work and traditions of the Royal Canadian Mounted Police would not be useful and interesting but surely there are to be found by digging, a great many other stories springing from the development of Canada's national life during the last three centuries. This aspect I feel the producers have not studied adequately.

There is another aspect of the co-operation project about which I am very concerned myself. That is the distribution in the United States of pictures produced by Canadian companies in this country. The results so far achieved through the co-operation project, during the last three months, have been anything but encouraging. I myself find it difficult to believe that subjects which are of great interest to people in this country would not be found to be also of considerable interest to people of the United States if they were given the opportunity to see them. Certainly if we are to assume that the people of the United States are interested only in themselves and cannot be brought to consider the attitudes and interests of neighbouring peoples when presented on the screen, it does not promise particularly well for the future development of a co-operation project. I do not, of course, subscribe to this view, but I know of no other way of allowing the people of the United States to show their reciprocal interest except by giving them an opportunity to see pictures from elsewhere. This the film industry of the United States is alone equipped to do.

I do not want to minimize all that has been done or what is expected may be done, but in the light of the opportunity which presents itself as between our two countries I cannot think that developments so far offer anything like what we might hope for.[10]

Ross McLean was obviously going to be a problem to the Americans. They raised that problem during their luncheon with Donald Gordon. It had been taken for granted, initially, that the National Film Board would be the co-ordinating centre for the entire CCP. But in the light of McLean's resistance, the Americans wanted him out.

Gordon was easily won over: "Recent occurrences," he wrote to Howe, "have suggested that the National Film Board has reservations as to the effectiveness of the programme, and views expressed on its behalf to the Industry do not seem calculated to contribute to results."[11]

Howe got the message and in a polite but firm letter to McLean's minister, J. J. McCann, on July 13, he announced that his own man,

Archibald Newman, would replace the NFB as the liaison between the Canadian government and the CCP. McLean, the film maker, was out. Newman, the public relations expert, was in.

It was now clear which way the CCP was being steered. Originally, according to Donald Gordon, the government had agreed with the Americans that the project have five objectives:

1. Obtaining more American production in Canada.
2. Purchase of more Canadian films for the American market.
3. Opportunity for Canadian capital to participate in American production.
4. Promotion of American tourist traffic to Canada.
5. Presentation of general information about Canada to the American public.

Following his seduction at the Harvard Club, Gordon in his report to Howe made no bones about what the priorities should be. The most importance, he said, should be placed on objectives four and five. These were not McLean's priorities, but McLean didn't have Gordon's clout. The Canadian Co-operation Project was to be what the Americans had always wanted it and intended it to be, a public relations operation and nothing more.

2: The tribulations of Constable Pedley

One of Archibald Newman's first official acts as liaison between the Canadian government and the Americans was to shoot off a cordial telegram to welcome Randolph Scott at the Banff Springs Hotel. The western star, who was appearing in *Canadian Pacific*, replied in kind, remarking that "all of us feel that through the film of CPR the rest of the world will gain something we were fortunate enough to experience."[12]

What the rest of the world gained was another Americanized view of Canadian history, which bore even less resemblance to the facts than DeMille's earlier opus on the North West Rebellion. *Canadian Pacific* was a second-rate American western and was so described in the critical American press. It came complete with gun-fights in saloons and shoot-'em-ups with Indians and half-breeds. But to the Americans it was "the cornerstone of the Canadian Co-operation Project."[13]

The picture was in the planning stage before the CCP came into being and would have been made regardless of the project, but the CCP took full credit for it, as it did for the same producer's follow-up movie, *The Cariboo Trail,* another American western with Randolph Scott, which again blurred the differences between the two national identities.

In fact the CCP, in justifying its existence, took credit for *everything* the movie people did in Canada – which did not differ appreciably from what they had been doing since the early days of the silents. Those records that still remain, detailing the triumphs of the project, make such amusing reading that it's not surprising so many of them have vanished. After all, civil servants are enjoined to burn up all embarrassing documents to prevent them from being examined by hostile eyes.

We do, however, have a copy of Archibald Newman's report for the first quarter of 1950, a masterpiece of public relations obfuscation. To the untutored eye, the report may have looked impressive, although it's difficult to believe that a skilled Ottawa mandarin wouldn't have seen through it.

Newman reported first that the five American newsreel companies had released a total of fifty-one "sequences," or less than one sequence a week per newsreel, about Canada; but he didn't say exactly what these sequences were or exactly what the subject matter consisted of: fires? explosions? floods? plane crashes? bathing beauty contests? freak accidents? pet shows? Uncle Louis St. Laurent shaking hands with visiting royalty? The emphasis, as always, was on quantity not on content – the Hollywood obeisance to the *mention,* good or bad.

Newman then reported that four short subjects about Canada had been released during the first quarter. Two, however, contained only brief sections about Canada. *Women of Tomorrow,* for instance, had a so-called Canadian sequence about the Girl Guides. The other two, one about skiing and one about hunting wild geese, were black-and-white short subjects. Newman's report didn't say what kind of US distribution they received.

In discussing feature production Newman was even more evasive: "More feature picture productions about Canada are scheduled to be made in Hollywood during 1950 than ever before." The weasel word was "scheduled." The fact is that fewer pictures about Canada were made by Hollywood in 1950.

"References about Canada are *constantly* appearing in feature pictures," the report went on. The italics are mine, because Newman was able to list only two examples:

> THE TATTOOED STRANGER – RKO – recently released – contained references about Canada.

> SQUARE DANCE KATE – Monogram – about to be released contains two songs by Canadians and purchased by Monogram.

Newman's report avoided noting whether or not the songs used in the Monogram picture had anything to do with Canada. (They didn't.) Nor did he detail the exact dialogue from *The Tattooed Stranger* which was supposed to bring tourists rushing across the border to spend their dollars, although he knew what it was because RKO had sent it to him in March:[14]

TOOMEY:

He shipped out on the "Granger Valley," all right . . . and the "Granger Valley" *did* go down . . . but Al Raditz wasn't on her.

DEL VECHIO:

He wasn't?

TOOMEY:

He and two other hands jumped ship at Halifax. He turned up in Toronto under another name.

(to Corrigan)

Where's that wire from Central Repository in Ottawa?

CORRIGAN

Here it is. . . .

(He reads)

"Arrested for Robbery under Arms . . . got ten years in an Ontario Prison . . . paroled on seven . . . violated parole and believed to be in the States."

Newman was careful not to mention another dialogue reference inserted into a movie called *Louisa* in which Edmund Gwynne, in the role of a gourmet, gloats over some game from Canada served in a classy restaurant. Taylor Mills, the MPAA man in New York, was enthusiastic over this coup, but Newman and Leo Dolan of the Canadian Government Travel Bureau weren't exactly rhapsodic.

"This is very bad," Dolan informed Newman, explaining that Canadian game laws prohibited the sale of both game fish and game animals for the market. "This is the sort of thing the conservationists would jump on with both feet."[15] It was too late to change the dialogue, which Mills had already declared "gets over very well in the picture . . . and . . . hits harder than would appear from the printed sheet." Newman made it clear that "Laura [sic] would not be included on the list of achievements."[16]

Newman himself kept an eagle eye out for any opportunity to slip a Canadian reference into a Hollywood picture. One night in April 1950 he and his wife went to see *Love Happy*, the last of the Marx Brothers pictures. He immediately wrote to Don Henshaw of the MacLaren advertising agency in Toronto, which had been engaged by the Americans to represent their cause north of the border:

This feature, as you know, contains a very unusual title sequence. In this sequence Marx tells about the difficult diamond robbery he is working on, saying in part that Scotland Yard and the FBI have been unable to solve it.

In this feature, Don, the producer might possibly have considered the addition of the RCMP to the dialogue.[17]

The RCMP, as a result of government pressure, were now reading and commenting on all scripts sent them through the CCP – a happy by-product of the Canadian dollar deficiency as far as Hollywood was concerned. The force did the job with its usual precision, carefully going through each script scene by scene and even shot by shot with only a few wry asides: "The plot is a bit far-fetched," commented Sergeant H. J. F. Ade, who vetted the draft script for Republic's *Secrets of the Mounted Police*, "and while it might be quite interesting and full of suspense to an audience, I find it a trifle amusing."[18] The picture was never made, at least not in that form.

But even the patient RCMP rebelled when faced with the script for *Gene Autry and the Mounties*.

"To make a picture suitable to this Force, the whole script would require rewriting," Deputy Commissioner C. K. Gray advised Newman. "It is hopeless to make comment that would improve the present script. From your letter . . . it is noted this Force is not asked to play any part in the production of this picture, and this is wholly concurred in, as for this Force to take any part whatsoever in such a screen play, would not be in its best interest."[19]

The picture was made anyway, without RCMP help, and was released in 1951 by Columbia. The CCP had the taste not to include it in its annual list of triumphs.

The establishment of the co-operation project didn't put an end to perennial RCMP problems with Hollywood. Actually, it tended to exacerbate them. This was especially true in the M-G-M film *The Wild North*, supposedly based on an authentic case from the mounted police files about a remarkable winter patrol made by Constable A. Pedley in 1900.

Even in Pedley's own unassuming report the story has all the earmarks of an intriguing and off-beat motion picture. Pedley's assignment was to convey "an unfortunate lunatic"[20] in the dead of winter from Fort Chipewyan in the Northwest Territories to Fort Saskatchewan, some 800 miles to the south. He travelled with his charge in two dogteams, up to his knees in slush and water for the first five days. At Fort McKay the sick man's feet, badly frostbitten, had to be specially wrapped. But Pedley struggled on through Weechume Lake to Lac La Biche and finally reached his destination.

At this point the insane man was suffering terribly from frostbite and exposure. His feet were frozen and his tongue was so badly frost-bitten he couldn't speak. He was given such good care, however, that he was eventually discharged from the hospital with only the loss of the first joint of his big toe, "and his mind and speech were as good as ever."[21] Pedley, however, did not fare as well. Having done his job, he turned right about and headed back north to his post as his orders required, even though he was in a bad way. By the time he reached Lac La Biche he, too, was violently insane, partly because of the hardships of the journey and partly over anxiety for the safety of his charge.

The constable was brought back to Fort Saskatchewan and trans-ferred to an institution at Brandon, Manitoba, where, after six months of treatment, his mind returned. He was given three months' leave and then went back for another tour of duty. He was retired and living in England when M-G-M decided to film his story and to pay him one thousand pounds for the privilege of using his name.

About all that emerged from the film *was* the name. The screenwriter changed the story drastically to turn Pedley's quarry into a perfectly sane trapper – French-Canadian, of course, complete with tuque – who is suspected (wrongly as usual) of the crime of murder. Pedley was played by a freelance actor, Wendell Corey. The trapper, Jules Vincent, was por-trayed by an up-and-coming contract performer, Stewart Granger, whom the studio was anxious to develop into a star. The task of the scriptwriter was to build up the part of the hunted man at the expense of the Mountie.

In his report of March 1949 Archibald Newman, lauding the work of the CCP, had written:

> In addition to its positive results, the Canadian Co-operation Project can be credited with making Hollywood so Canada-conscious that inac-curacies and unfavorable impressions about Canada are no longer likely to find their way into US Theatrical films. For example, any producer contemplating an RCMP movie now makes use of the Project channels to have the script checked before shooting. The Project also has caused the appointment of competent technical advisers in Hollywood.

In 1950, more than a year after those words were written, Hollywood was turning Pedley the Mountie into a dunderhead, totally outclassed by the man he has been sent to capture. In the movie the prisoner convinces Pedley that he knows nothing of the north, then gets him lost, makes a fool of him and, as he disintegrates, begins to take command. The climax comes when the usual pack of Hollywood wolves, slavering as always for human flesh, surrounds the camp and attacks the two men. As a result of this incident, Pedley is shown going insane. His prisoner, the trapper, becomes his captor and brings him in.

This was the story that M-G-M desperately wanted Commissioner Wood of the RCMP to approve officially. Carruthers, who was technical adviser, had had most of his major demurrals brushed aside, including his objection to the characterization of Pedley. The studio was counting on the Canadian Co-operation Project to force an official blessing out of the RCMP – a feat that would allow the studio to present the movie as a true story, with resulting commercial benefits. To this end M-G-M approached Colonel Blake W. Owensmith, the man appointed by the CCP as its Hollywood liaison, to take the script directly to Ottawa and convince Commissioner Wood that he should give it his okay.

This was the one privilege the force would not grant. Wood didn't want the slightest public suggestion that the RCMP had anything to do with any Hollywood movie or was even reading scripts. He had been warned of Owensmith's impending visit and knew he'd have to see him because of the co-operation project, but he had no intention of going further than making a few informal and unpublicized suggestions.

Then, out of the blue, there landed on his desk a press story, originating with Owensmith in Hollywood, reporting that the Pedley film had not only been officially sanctioned but also that the commissioner was quite pleased with it. I can only guess at Wood's private reaction; publicly and in his correspondence he never lost his cool. But he wrote at once to Carruthers to ask, in effect, what the hell was going on. Carruthers, in his best gossipy style, replied with an incisive, if prejudiced, three-paragraph character study of Owensmith:

(a) This man is a rather likeable chap . . . who for some reason beyond my knowledge except that he has an English accent was made head of the Canadian Co-operation Project of the Motion Picture Producers' Association.

(b) He has little first-hand knowledge of Canada and no understanding of the psychology of a Canadian and it is quite apparent that he is of the same impression as many Englishmen who live in this area: That we are a bunch of colonists who should jump to comply with his requests.

(c) I have known Owensmith for a year, have always found him a pleasant individual except for his overbearing attitude and absolute lack of understanding of the Force, Canadians and Canada, the three things which are required in order for him to hold this position and to do his work efficiently.[22]

Owensmith had apparently gone to Ottawa with the script but had declined to meet with the formidable Wood, preferring to leave the document with the friendlier Archibald Newman, who gave it to an RCMP sergeant. But when he returned to Hollywood, Owensmith had indicated

180

he'd seen the RCMP commissioner – "a 'face-saving' expedient, very common in this industry," as Carruthers explained.

This teapot tempest had scarcely blown over when Jeff Hackett's Hollywood column for the Canadian monthly New Liberty announced that the M-G-M script "already has the approval of Commissioner Wood."[23]

That was really rubbing salt into the wound. Wood wrote a stiff denial to the magazine's editor, Keith Knowlton. Knowlton checked with his Hollywood man who wired back that "both M-G-M and Blake Owensmith, Canadian Government representative [sic] in the Johnston office in Hollywood, insist script has RCMP approval."[24] Knowlton suggested Wood write a letter to the editor to clear things up.

The incident brought another immediate press attack aimed directly at the commissioner. Jack Hirshberg, a syndicated columnist whose work appeared in Canada in the Montreal tabloid The Monitor, wrote:

> Ottawa headquarters of the RCMP seem unable to make up its mind on whether or not an okay has been accorded Frank Fenton's script of "Constable Pedley" for M-G-M.
>
> . . . Canadian Department of Trade and Commerce liaison with Hollywood's studios says the screenplay received Commissioner Wood's approval. . . .
>
> Wood says he hasn't seen it, let alone given it his blessing.
>
> What probably happened was this: Some government officials have a high-hat attitude towards motion pictures and relegate such matters to the attention of a subordinate. However, when the final okay comes through it is usually issued over the supervisor's signature. Thus Commissioner Wood may have okayed "Constable Pedley" without knowing it.
>
> In any event it is high time the RCMP realized that motion pictures offer the Force and the nation a valuable opportunity for high standard public relations. The Mounties may always get their man, but what their leaders don't know about the fine art of making friends for Canada would fill an encyclopaedia. It would seem that the scarlet-coated mounted policeman has become an international symbol for law enforcement despite, rather than because, of the public relations policy of Force leaders. At a time when Canada is attempting to attract extra American dollars this policy could stand revision.[25]

What the public and the RCMP did not know was that Jack Hirshberg, the author of the attack, and Jeff Hackett, the New Liberty columnist, were one and the same man – not a bona fide journalist at all but a paid Hollywood publicist and spokesman for the big studios where he earned his living. The attack was a concealed attempt, apparently inspired by the

CCP, to force the mounted police into playing Hollywood's game. The real reason why the force had become, in Hirshberg's phrase "the international symbol for law enforcement," was because of the remarkable feats of men like Constable Pedley, whose exploits M-G-M was in the process of distorting, and not because of the flackery of movie press agents.

As a result Wood put his foot down. He would have nothing to do with the M-G-M script. His suspicions were further aroused by a letter from Owensmith, pre-dating the press attack, attaching an M-G-M statement that "we may be called upon to request permission to refer to the co-operation of the Royal Canadian Mounted Police on the main title of our picture and possibly to use their seal as a background for such main title. . . ."[26] To Wood, this was the most revealing part of the letter, since it suggested the studio's real reason for wanting script approval was to commercialize the fact that it had been passed officially by the force.

The pressure on the mounted police didn't let up, however. Again, using the CCP as a convenient lever, M-G-M put the heat on the Canadian Department of External Affairs through the Interdepartmental Committee for Information Abroad. The committee was totally on the side of M-G-M. A memo from Arnold Heeney, a top Ottawa mandarin, written on behalf of the committee to Lester B. Pearson, the Secretary of State for External Affairs, praised the idea of the picture. Heeney pointed out that it was "based on a dramatic manhunt by a member of the RNWMP in 1900 . . . a technicolor thriller, the principal merit of which will be to portray for American audiences, in a favourable light, an exclusively Canadian story."

He went on to press the Hollywood case, using Hollywood's own arguments:

> Hollywood films about the RCMP can be produced with or without official approval but, since the Force has become for people abroad a symbol of Canada, it is important that this symbol be presented as clearly and creditably as possible. . . .
>
> The Committee, while sympathizing fully with the Commissioner's view, nevertheless feels that it is important, when the opportunity arises, to cooperate with the industry and to influence it as much as possible the Canadian way. It believes therefore that an attempt should be made to have Commissioner Wood reconsider his stand and at least see the script before arriving at a final decision. . . .[27]

The memo suggested that, "in the general interest of the Canadian Co-operation Project," Pearson try to persuade the Minister of Justice, Stuart Garson, to change Wood's mind.

But Wood and the man who was about to succeed him, L. H. Nicholson, were wise by now in the ways of Hollywood. They refused to be budged and Garson backed them up in his reply to Lester Pearson:

182

the fact that movies could easily be made without RCMP approval, "merely confirms the view that official sanction is desired merely for its box-office value."[28] After all, Hollywood had plenty of research experts and technical advice. And why bother to look over a script, Garson added, when Hollywood could always change it later? The mounted police had had plenty of experience in approving scripts that bore no resemblance to the finished product.

The RCMP now had ample and justifiable reasons for refusing to deal further with Hollywood, a situation that Hollywood could not tolerate. At a meeting of the same inter-departmental committee in the spring of 1952 the agency man, Don Henshaw, representing the CCP suggested the force send a man to Hollywood "to meet with scriptwriters and editors."[29] The following day a letter of invitation was on its way from Eric Johnston to Commissioner Nicholson.

Nicholson was unenthusiastic. He told Johnston bluntly that the force's experience with Hollywood had been disappointing, that its advice was frequently disregarded and that the police were no longer surprised by movies that showed them in "an utterly fantastic light."[30] He didn't see what a Hollywood visit could accomplish, but he had also been prodded by C. H. Richardson of the Bank of Canada. He agreed to send a man down in the fall when the Musical Ride would be appearing in Los Angeles. The man he chose was Inspector R. S. MacNeil.

The inspector took his job seriously. He spent two days in New York talking to motion picture executives there and then went to Hollywood, where Owensmith took him in tow. MacNeil was given a royal reception and met many producers and directors, including Aaron Rosenberg, "a very important and certainly intelligent producer." Rosenberg "was quite taken with the word 'Saskatchewan' as a title for a feature film dealing with the Force." Rosenberg told the inspector that he intended to make "the great epic picture of all time" about the mounted police. MacNeil, however, had read the script the night before and discovered to his distress that it dealt with a psychopathic superintendent in an isolated outpost who hates one of his own sergeants so much that he taunts him with court martial and eventual execution.

"I informed him that in its present form the script simply would not do. . . ." MacNeil noted. After two hours of see-saw argument, the studio agreed to have the script rewritten. Rosenberg played the earnest and dedicated producer:

"[He] told me that he is prepared to have the script written again and again and to have rough prints of the film sent here as often as necessary in order to produce a really great film which will be acceptable to this Force," MacNeil reported.

MacNeil was won over by the reception he was given in the movie capital:

"I was surprised to encounter. . . a genuine desire to show the Force in a more realistic light. . . . I was listened to with the utmost courtesy. . . . I feel that due to my visit the people who count in Hollywood have a very different conception of what this Force is. . . ."[31]

"Clearly a most worthwhile trip," Nicholson commented. The Hollywood Public Relations mill, skilled in its handling of a VIP, had won the day. Once again, the RCMP began to co-operate with American film makers.

But Rosenberg's picture, *Saskatchewan,* when it was released, was a disaster from everybody's point of view except the producer's, whose easy promises at that Hollywood luncheon were swiftly forgotten. Although the writers tinkered with the script, the unflattering superintendent figure was retained – more imbecilic than psychopathic, more moronic than vile. His men were shown in an act of unthinkable mutiny and he taunted his sergeant (played by Alan Ladd) with court martial as in the original plot line.

The geographical gaffes were such that the picture became in Canada a national joke, but from Hollywood's point of view it was an enormous success – one of the year's top grossers. To the police the title replaced *Rose Marie* as a kind of epithet. S. T. Wood, who had retired to Fort Walsh in Saskatchewan, used the phrase when he wrote to a later commissioner, Clifford Harvison, about the plans of another Hollywood director, Burt Kennedy, to make a film titled *The Canadians.** "No idea what the script will be like," Wood commented. "My past experience makes me suspect all US movie people and I fear another movie like *Saskatchewan.*"[32]

With *The Canadians* history repeated itself. Kennedy had already been to see Harvison, who used both *Saskatchewan* and *Rose Marie* as horrible examples and issued the usual statutory warning that he must see a script before approving production. Kennedy responded with the usual earnest promises. Harvison found himself under pressure from both the federal and provincial governments because the company was employing a number of Canadians and spending $400,000 in Saskatchewan. As he put it to Wood: "The 20th Century-Fox people have been through the mill many times and know precisely where to go in order to get pressures applied. . . ."[33]

Harvison was prevailed upon to lend sixty men and horses together with his deputy commissioner, George B. McClellan, as senior technical

---

*Strictly speaking this was not a Hollywood film but an international production. The difference, in this case, was purely academic. Producer, director, studio, and star were all Hollywood products.

adviser. The picture was supposedly based on the Cypress Hills Massacre of 1873 but as McClellan later recalled: "Twentieth Century-Fox weren't satisfied with that alone. They had to get Sitting Bull into Canada with his several thousand Sioux warriors. . . . Actually Sitting Bull didn't arrive until 1879 but for the purposes of this turkey of a picture, Twentieth Century-Fox made them contemporary with each other. The result was an absolute mishmash of history."[34]

The RCMP, however, didn't object to that. What concerned Harvison and McClellan was a scene in which three prisoners, accused of murder, managed to escape from their police escorts. They had spent three days on the trail under heavy guard. Suddenly the leader of the trio pulled a sawed-off shotgun from the slicker roll on the back of his saddle, held up his captors, and all three criminals fled.

"This idea struck horror in the mind of the commissioner," McClellan recalled. "The very idea that the police would arrest a motley crew like this and escort them for three days without a complete search of their whole gear was utterly ridiculous. It was contrary to every possible teaching and instruction that had ever been given on the guarding of prisoners. When the commissioner and I were constables there was simply no excuse for losing a prisoner, unless you were unconscious or dead."

McClellan rejected the scene out of hand and said he'd have no part of the picture if it were retained. A long argument followed. "Both the producer and the director gave us a firm commitment that the scene would not appear," McClellan remembers. On that condition, Harvison extended his co-operation.

But 20th Century-Fox did not keep its part of the bargain. Having got its sixty men and equipment and its senior technical adviser, it shot the scene anyway behind McClellan's back and inserted it in the picture which, in its closing credits, thanked the "Northwest Mounted Police" for their co-operation.

Burt Kennedy, the director, tried to wiggle out of responsibility for the deception in a letter to Harvison in which he claimed he had not had a chance to view the finished movie, "as the major part of the technical work on the film was done in London." The studio, he said, "had me pretty much between the devil and the deep blue sea on some story changes, and it simply came down to being told flatly No by Fox on some of the things they wanted – all of which is by way of passing the buck but I would much rather have the RCMP after the studio than me. . . ."[35]

Of course it *was* passing the buck and Harvison made no bones about that in a brief and chilly response: "I was very disappointed that despite the very considerable co-operation and assistance extended to you . . . and despite assurances that changes would be made, certain scenes were allowed to remain in the picture. Since I made my objections very clear to you, as had Deputy Commissioner McClellan . . . I can't take the charitable view that there was a misunderstanding."[36]

So much, then, for Archibald Newman's boast that the Canadian Co-operation Project could be credited with making Hollywood so Canada-conscious that inaccuracies and unfavourable impressions would no longer creep into movies about the country. *The Canadians*, a weak, dull picture, was almost universally panned. But it did have one dubious claim to fame. It was probably the last Mountie movie Hollywood would ever make.

3: Red-wing orioles from Canada

In the press-agent game, which is sometimes called the public relations profession, there is a widely used technique which, although transparently thin, seems to work. The PR man will tell the client that in the period January 1 to March 31, say, he has been able to arrange 2,307 column inches of publicity in daily newspapers with a circulation of more than 100,000; when translated into paid advertising space, that would amount to so many tens of thousands of dollars.

The PR man even flashes a clipping book, showing that he's kept meticulous count of all the stories he's planted in the newspapers about the client. There is a catch, however, which the unenlightened never seem to cotton on to. In many of the stories, the client may be mentioned by name only as part of a list in the second last paragraph; or he may be a face in a large crowd of executives photographed at a banquet; or the reference may even be a derogatory one. It doesn't matter. The PR man clips the whole story and the entire three-column photograph and lumps all those column inches into his statistical summary.

That was the technique that the American CCP and its Canadian advertising agency used, year after year, to lull the government into the belief that the project was an important factor in solving the dollar crisis.

The annual reports of the CCP (there are only three extant)[37] are apparently the work of the agency and the executive in charge of the CCP account, Don Henshaw. They are crammed with graphs, statistics, charts, ad man's padding, sheer nonsense, irrelevancies, and unintended humour. The 1951 report even drags in Winston Churchill for an opening quotation that is given a page all to itself: "Upon the whole surface of the globe there is no more spacious and splendid domain than Canada open to the activity and genius of free men." This is followed by a full-page photograph of Wendell Corey in his Mountie costume sitting on a horse. In short, these are not reports at all but presentations that any ad man makes to a prospective client or that a would-be film producer puts into the hands of prospective backers.

The 1951 report is a classic example of a whole series of tried and tested PR techniques:

1. **Flatter the client with a puff opening.**
   The motion picture industry is proud to report to its friends in Canada that the Canadian Co-operation Project has completed its fourth successful year.

   Canada's economic expansion and recovery from its financial travail of only a few years ago – its present position as one of the few nations of the world with a free currency – has been without precedent.

   There is no precise yardstick for measuring the contribution of the motion picture industry to Canada's tremendous development during the past five years. However, during the life of the Canadian Co-operation Project nearly 700 separate topics about Canada have appeared, not only on American screens, but also on the motion picture screens throughout the world. Though some of these topics may have been brief items about Canada as a delightful vacation land, others have been twenty-minute subjects dramatizing in full color the industrial potentials and business opportunities in this rising young nation. Canada with its breathtaking scenery, its wealth of opportunity for outdoor sports in summer and winter, its importance as a source of wood pulp, news print, aluminum, nickle, iron ore, uranium, oil and gas, and grain – all these have been mentioned, not once, but many times in films distributed throughout the world by American motion picture companies.

2. **Use as many official names as possible.**
   Working closely with Canada's Department of External Affairs, Trade and Commerce, and the Canadian Government Travel Bureau, the National Film Board and with several Consulates throughout the United States, the Canadian Co-operation Project has endeavored to portray the important message of Canada as a partner in defense and in peace and a great and growing nation to the North.

3. **Put the best possible face on bad news.**
   Though the amount of Canadian material shown in US newsreels during 1951 showed ten fewer sequences than last year, the material used was of a highly significant nature[38] and included fewer items dealing with unfortunate floods, fires and airplane accidents. . . .

   Only fifteen shorts were actually released during 1951 compared to sixteen in 1950. However, four additional subjects are completed and ready for release early in 1952 and six more are already in various stages of production.

4. **Dazzle the client with big numbers.**

   A given sequence included in all five newsreels is estimated to reach an audience of some 50,000,000 people during its theatre run. Through the medium of US newsreels during the past year, 1,500,000,000 audience impressions about Canada were brought to US theatre audiences.

.5. **Create pseudo-events to impress the client.**

   Indicative of the kind of support given the project by the studio heads in Hollywood, a visit to the M-G-M studio is a case in point. In order that the work of the project be brought to the attention of all of the producers on the lot a luncheon was arranged by Mr. Doré Schary and L. K. Sidney. This luncheon was attended by twenty-eight M-G-M producers – every producer on the lot. The group was addressed by Mr. J. J. Fitzgibbons of Canada, Taylor Mills, New York Co-ordinator for the project, and by Col. Owensmith. The studio heads enthusiastically endorsed the project and recommended that all producers give it their full support.

6. **Convey an impression of furious activity even when it produces no results.**

   Arrangements made to obtain stills, information and research on logging activities and operations on Vancouver Island for Pine-Thomas productions in connection with the possible production in that locale of a logging story.

   In conjunction with Toronto Associate, arrangements made for M-G-M representative to visit Canada to secure permission from Banting and Best families and the University of Toronto etc., for production of MIRACLE AT MIDNIGHT, the story of the discovery of insulin.

   Screened short subjects and obtained research material for Walter Wanger Productions in connection with their forthcoming feature picture YELLOWKNIFE, part of which is tentatively scheduled for production on location in and around Yellowknife.

   Obtained research material on the Hudson's Bay Company and submitted to Doré Schary, production head of M-G-M, for consideration as a possible feature production by Carey Wilson, producer at that studio.

   Submitted research material on displaced persons in Canada to Leon Gordon, producer at M-G-M, for consideration as the basis of a future picture.

Words such as "consideration," "tentatively scheduled," and "possible production" loom large here. Actually not one of these pictures, listed as part of the section entitled Other Activities, was ever produced.

Again, under the heading Co-operation with the National Film Board, the report gives the impression of extraordinary exertions on behalf of the NFB, one of the world's great documentary producers.

(a) Arrangements for theatrical showing of ROYAL JOURNEY and MAN IN THE PEACE TOWER at Brooklyn Paramount in order to make films eligible for Academy Awards.

(b) Screened some fifteen short subjects with considered theatrical release possibilities and arranged for the best of them to be screened by potential US short subject distributors.

(c) Presented Film Board's new commercial representative, Maurice Crompton, to all short subject sales managers.

(d) Arranged for Film Board's trailer technician to visit New York television production facilities.

This verbal smokescreen could not hide the fact that only *one* NFB short was actually released by the American motion picture industry in the United States that year. In spite of all the promises made in 1948, the NFB short was one of only four Canadian-produced short subjects screened in American theatres. Even short films considered by Americans to be of Academy Award stature were not seen in theatres south of the border.

The report was able to list only one picture shot in Canada in 1951, a movie called *The World in His Arms,* which used Nova Scotia locations but had nothing to do with Canada. Only three movies made by Hollywood were listed as having a Canadian background, two of them being Monogram grade C quickies. The production of Canadian content films, in short, was at a new low.

Nonetheless, the annual report talked glibly about "twenty separate feature pictures released during the past year." These, it developed, also included *Border Saddlemates,* a "picture with a Border Background;" *Saturday Island,* a picture in which Linda Darnell plays a Canadian nurse trapped on a desert island; *Bronco Buster,* a picture that contained shots of the Calgary Stampede; and thirteen other movies containing what the report, with its passion for statistics, referred to as "twenty-eight separate dialogue references."

The project's man in Hollywood, Colonel Owensmith, was immensely proud of these dialogue references. His job was to go from studio to studio and try to convince screenwriters and directors to slip a few words about Canada into the scripts.

"The whole idea was to try and get in what we called hidden advertising – in other words to get a plug for Canada without being too obvious,"[39] he told the Canadian Broadcasting Corporation in a 1975 interview. One reference, of which he was apparently very proud, was a line from Universal's *Bend of the River,* in which James Stewart, playing a wagon master, sees some birds and remarks: "Those are red-wing orioles from

Canada." How that comment could in any way reduce the country's dollar deficit, Owensmith did not say; certainly it would not lure any bird-watchers across the border since, as every amateur knows, there isn't any such thing as a red-wing oriole.

The 1951 annual report listed the dialogue references to Canada in that year's crop of movies, a disastrous error not repeated in later reports. I can't resist reproducing these tourist lures just as they were published in the report. In all cases, the italics are those of the CCP:

My Six Convicts
Contains the following dialogue references:
RANDALL: "I married seven years ago, but I been in the *Canadian Army* overseas for four – and I been here for two. I'll kill myself without my wife."
DOC: "Doesn't she come visiting days?"
RANDALL: "She lives in *Canada*."

People Will Talk
Contains the following two dialogue references:
"The first time I was in *Canada*, in 1917. It was Christmas."
"I was walking past a restaurant in Toronto."

Pistol Harvest
Contains the following dialogue reference:
"We figured we would maybe get enough of these cattle to take us to a new country where there's work – *Vancouver*, maybe."

Red Skies of Montana
Contains the following dialogue reference:
"We tie in with the authorities north of the border in *Canada*."

The Tanks are Coming
Contains the following dialogue reference:
COMMENTATOR: "The Canadians were on our left and although taking a terrific pounding were holding magnificently."

This is Dynamite
Contains the following dialogue references:
"I'll refresh your memory. 1932. Peter Manzinates was a produce dealer who refused to pay the organization. He went to *Canada* and never came back. . . ."
"Maybe the guy liked to travel."
"March, 1932. You took a leave of absence from the police force. Gone three weeks. . . ."
"A vacation."
"Did you like *Canada?*"
"Didn't go there."

"You and Jimmy Kchop went to *Canada*. You took Manzinates to *Canada* and murdered him.

"I never went to *Canada*. I don't know Manzinates, I never heard of Jimmy Kchop."

Three Secrets
Contains the following dialogue reference:
"The volunteer climbers will be led by king-pin mountaineer Noel Stephani, expected momentarily from *Winnipeg, Canada.*"

Blake Owensmith failed to see the humour in any of this. To a press agent, after all, a mention is a mention and a plug is a plug. In his CBC interview, only a portion of which was shown on television, Owensmith was still enthusiastic about the long defunct co-operation project. He gave what he termed "a perfect example of what we tried to do over the years" in a dialogue reference from a movie called *New York Confidential:*

> The script read, "They caught Louis Engleday in Detroit." We thought that was a very good chance to put in a plug for Canada, so we changed the dialogue to read, "They caught Louis Engleday on his way to Canada." This was a very good example because it flowed in and it didn't seem forced and it got our plug over.

When the CCP quietly began to fade out of existence and Owensmith was no longer needed he moved on to even greater triumphs, producing the *Sgt. Preston of the Yukon* series for television. "They were quite well received," he told his CBC interviewer. "They sold a lot of shredded wheat or whatever it was. It was interesting to hear people discuss it and say: "Well! I never knew that! Those mounted police, they're really quite something. I mean the small kids, they really went for it in a big way and it was a hell of a good promotional scheme; unwittingly they were selling Canada, which pleased me very much."

It's hard to figure out exactly *when* the CCP came to an end; there was no burial service and certainly there were no mourners. The project was quietly shelved without fanfare or comment. With the dollar balance restored the Canadian government ceased to care how much money Hollywood took out of the country or how many Canadian references were inserted into its pictures. The tourist trade *had* increased in those postwar boom days, boosted no doubt by thousands of Louis Engledays fleeing across the border – but it didn't increase as quickly as it did in some other western countries such as France and England, which somehow managed to outdo Canada in the race for Yankee dollars without any of Blake Owensmith's plugola and without a single reference to those intriguing red-wing orioles.

Most of Hollywood's rare comedies about Canada had to do with snow. Here's Buster Keaton in his Canadian hat. The two-reeler was called The Frozen North.

The Blurred Image

If the world has a confused idea of how Canadians look, dress, and act, these pictures help explain why.

The hardy myth of La Longue Traverse first made its appearance in Cecil B. DeMille's Call of the North in 1914. Here, Graham Stewart, a fur-company employee, takes the death walk. The snow is as ersatz as the scenery; and the temperature, when this scene was filmed, stood at 100°F. When the movie was re-made in 1921 the Hudson's Bay Company sued—and won.

This rare still from the original 1928 version of Rose-Marie *helps explain why* M-G-M *scrapped the entire production and started again with a new cast. This version, which starred Ralph Forbes (being strangled on the bar) and Renée Adorée, dressed here in a Mountie costume, was never seen—in spite of the typically Canadian setting.*

Above: The Hollywood totem pole would make any self-respecting Haida
Indian shudder. It's not only all wrong, it's also in the wrong place—
the Cariboo country of central British Columbia. Randolph Scott, the
star of The Cariboo Trail, *is in the wrong place, too. His dress, gunbelt
and personality belong not to Canada but to Hollywood's wild west.*

Left: The Storm (1922), *based on a Broadway melodrama and starring Matt Moore and
Virginia Valli, perpetuated the myth of northern isolation. It was described
as "an elemental conflict: the love of two men for a girl trapped in a Northwoods
cabin throughout the winter by the great snows."*

197

WELCOME TO TOTEM POLE

*Canadian history buffs will spot a half-dozen major errors in this movie
still from* Klondike Kate *(1944), supposedly set in the Canadian Yukon.
The totem pole, railway train, pine tree, and western cowboy costumes are
among the faux pas. The woman is played by Ann Savage.*

Myrna Loy, Robert Montgomery, and Reginald Owen are waited on by an Eskimo servant in darkest Labrador in Petticoat Fever *(1936). She's the first white woman seen there in a year. Fortunately Montgomery has his dress clothes with him and the post is well supplied with crystal.*

This Canadian small-town street scene from 'Neath Canadian Skies *(1948) bears no relation to any real Canadian small town. Note the costume worn by the heavy on the right. Perfectly acceptable, no doubt, for a Mississippi gambler—but no Canadian has ever dressed in that fashion.*

What would Hollywood do without the birchbark canoe? Here's Kirby Grant as Corporal Rod Webb in Yukon Manhunt *(1953). As usual, this Mountie has never heard of fibreglass or basswood—let alone the outboard motor.*

Yes, it's Buck Jones again, disguised as a typical Canadian, seeking out wrong-doers after having himself drummed out of the Mounties. Will the French-Canadian baddies in their tuques and peaked hats penetrate Buck's cunning disguise? One would think so; he hardly blends into the scenery.

PART FIVE

It Wasn't Like That at All

1: The blurring of the image

"But," said Oliva Dionne, the father of the famous quintuplets as he and his wife emerged, somewhat bewildered, from the New York première of *The Country Doctor*, "it wasn't like that at all! That's crazy!"[1] Flashbulbs pop. Reporters scribble. The desk is going to have fun with *that* quote: funny Papa Dionne with his quaint accent and his store clothes.

It wasn't like that at all from Dionne's point of view; but the world, including the press, had already bought the movie image of the film father as a comic moron, a role in which John Qualen had been typed for years. Qualen had only to look at the camera to get a laugh – the dumb, ineffectual father who doesn't seem to know where babies come from. There are a lot of jokes like that in *The Country Doctor* but Oliva Dionne did not find them funny.

It wasn't like that at all in any of the movies made about Canadian historical events, with the possible exception of a brief four-picture cycle of one-reelers made before the First World War. Vitagraph made one of them, a picture about Cartier and Champlain; Kalem made two of them, one about Father Jogues, the Jesuit martyr, and another about Wolfe and Montcalm; Selig made the fourth, about the Hudson's Bay Company in Lord Selkirk's day. We can't be sure about these one-reelers because they no longer exist. All we have are the critical reviews and the producer's blurbs, which can't be taken as gospel. Certainly nothing made since that time has borne much relationship to Canadian history. The only other film made about the honourable company, *Hudson's Bay*, was called "a script that missed the story by making up its own."[2] That film isn't just wrong; it's also dull. I find that incomprehensible in view of the known historical facts, which are both romantic and bloody.

I don't really know what to make of *Quebec*, a movie which appears to star Corinne Calvet in the role of Louis-Joseph Papineau, the great French-Canadian hero, patriot, and leader of the 1837 rebellion. They didn't actually call her Papineau, of course, but she ran the movie rebellion all right, with the help of her former lover. He wasn't a French-Canadian at all but an Englishman named Charles Douglas who wore a brown beret to distinguish him from all those voyageurs in their colourful tuques. Miss Calvet, who was known in the movie as La Fleur, was described by the flacks as "a blood red rose, history's most tempting spy whose fire enflamed an army of frontiersmen to storm the continent's mightiest fortress."

Paramount had the grace to explain at the opening of the picture that the story was told in terms of fictitious characters, but there must be tens of thousands of moviegoers – many of them Canadians – who still believe the purpose of the revolution of 1837 was to "split Canada from England," to quote the opening commentary. It was nothing of the sort; it was an attempt to achieve responsible government under British rule. Papineau was as far from being a separatist as is Pierre Elliott Trudeau.

No one, of course, expects motion pictures to be historically accurate. American studios have distorted and mythologized their own history and that of other countries just as much as they have twisted the Canadian past. Playwrights do it all the time; Shakespeare, of course, did it – although Shakespeare never went around boasting that his version of history was absolutely authentic.

All the same, it's an unfortunate accident that just as Canada was emerging from the colonial shadows the most powerful educational medium of all was developed by a friendly but alien power. We can't blame Hollywood for ignoring the Canadian character and lifestyle. But there's little doubt that the bludgeoning effect of the motion picture first distorted our image by making us appear as a nation of primitives, and then blurred it by confusing it with the American image. No foreign myth-makers could be expected to reveal to us our own distinctive identity; that must be the task of our own mass media. Hollywood made it hard for us to recognize the Canadian identity because its movies masked it so effectively.

The American producers, of course, were making commercial pictures mainly for US consumption. There was no reason for them to act like Canadians. We ourselves never required them to use any of their Canadian profits to make a different kind of movie or to subsidize a home-grown industry. The idea of government control was seen as a semi-totalitarian measure, and not just by Hollywood lobbyists; Canadian officials such as Donald Gordon, whose successful careers were based entirely on state-controlled enterprises (the Bank of Canada, the CNR), were opposed to state interference in the foreign-controlled motion picture industry. Our leaders, dazzled by the idea of untold publicity in the movies and buttered up by studio heads, were more concerned with paying homage to a free market and a free flow across the border, at least in the entertainment industry. They didn't realize that the flow has always been one way. What the world got was not the publicity that the Canadian

Co-operation Project promised but the Hollywood image of Canada as an American appendage.

The Hollywood attitude to accuracy, as Garth S. Jowett has pointed out in The Journal of Popular Culture,[3] has been to *material* things – to sets, costumes, and props, rather than to interpretive matters. DeMille probably believed his own press releases when they lauded his passion for authenticity. His sets *were* authentic. The backlot replica of Fort Carlton in *North West Mounted Police* was faithful in every detail to the original. So were the mounted police uniforms, except for the hats. He went to considerable trouble to make Walter Hampden, the Broadway actor, actually look like Big Bear, even to the extent of fitting him with brown contact lenses. It didn't occur to him to have Hampden act as Big Bear would have acted; in spite of a superficial resemblance, the noted thespian sounded just like any other Hollywood Indian, grunting away in his deep, mellow voice and carefully trimming all the definite and indefinite articles from his sentences.

In movies about the Canadian frontier – and most of the movies have been about the Canadian frontier – everything is right and everything is wrong. The small-town sets are often works of art – the wood on the false fronts carefully seasoned, the paint peeling to give an impression of age and decay – but they are American sets. The costumes are beautiful and, in the big productions, lovingly made, but they are all wrong because they, too, are American – cowboy outfits in the Canadian north, for instance. The fights are carefully staged, especially the gun-fights. Attention is paid to making the weapons fit the exact historical period – DeMille sent all the way to England in the middle of a war to get 1885 Enfields – but they are American gun-fights; Canadians didn't go around with six-shooters on their hips. The saloons, with their familiar bat-wing doors, their gilded mirrors, their oil paintings, and their long polished bars, are exquisite replicas of American saloons. The saloon is not really part of the Canadian style. For most of its frontier history, Canada has been dry: when the railway was being built, navvies furtively gulped bad whisky in log hovels hidden from the mounted police. That genuinely Canadian institution, the beer parlour of the twenties, thirties, and forties, has never been shown.

What Hollywood did for over half a century was to superimpose its vision of the old west, itself a mythological anachronism, onto the Canadian northwest. Hard-riding posses, men in cowboy outfits, necktie parties, covered wagons, painted Injuns, boot hills, vigilantes, and even tin stars were moved across the border with scarcely a change in the plot except for the presence of the movie Mounties who, all too often, acted like American town marshals.

It didn't occur to Hollywood and it didn't occur to Canadian audiences, either, that the Canadian concept of order imposed from above clashed with the American idea of rough frontier justice administered at grass-roots level by the people's choices. Nor did the moviemakers understand that in Canada the law arrived before the settlers did, in direct contrast to the American experience.

Although Hollywood exaggerated American frontier violence, the western society south of the border was demonstrably less stable than its Canadian counterpart. Shootings on the Canadian frontier were almost unknown. When a Texan on an Alberta ranch shot an adversary in the stomach in 1895, The Fort McLeod Gazette reported that it was only the second such killing since the paper was established in 1882. And, contrary to the impression given by the movies, the Canadian northwest was, to quote Jennings again, "one of the few examples in history of a frontier area settled with comparatively little racial friction."[4]

These contrasts suggest that there *is* a difference between the American and the Canadian approach to frontier problems. Yet, as The Daily Telegraph's critic remarked of *The Canadians*, "Saskatchewan might as well be in Texas, so traditional is the style."[5] Almost two generations before, an American reviewer said much the same thing about a Hoot Gibson picture, *The Calgary Stampede:* "This is a typical Western with all the snap of the best examples of this class. . . . The action take[s] place on a ranch in Western Canada, which seems just like our own ranches. . . ."[6] And why shouldn't it? The gun-play was there along with the ten-gallon hats.

It's a little ironic that the movies with the most Canadian-sounding titles are among the most American in style. (The one exception is *The Canadian*, described in Part One). A good example is a picture called *'Neath Canadian Skies*, produced in 1948, which, if it wasn't for the movie Mounties, could just as easily have been called 'Neath Montana Skies. Everything about it, including the mountains and the trees, is American: the hardrock mine in the wrong place, the villains with gunbelts who shoot strangers on sight, the townspeople all dressed like Mississippi gamblers and, of course, the inevitable saloon. Even the Mounties in this film act like an American posse, thundering along on their horses firing aimless volleys from their smoking pistols; and, when one of them goes undercover and disguises himself as a typical Canadian westerner, *he* wears a gunbelt too.

206

2: How Randolph Scott saved the Northwest

Three postwar movies, each dealing with a piece of frontier history in a different part of Canada, illustrate Hollywood's confusion about Canadian attitudes.

The Cariboo Trail is set in British Columbia in the early 1860's at the time of the gold rush.

Canadian Pacific is set in the Northwest during the building of the railway in 1883.

The Far Country is set in the Yukon Territory in the early days of the 1897-98 stampede.

The plots of these three films turn on the idea of strangers pouring into a lawless land and the tensions that such an influx can bring. The Good settlers – railwaymen, prospectors, and cowboys – are faced with the Bad half-breeds, Indians, scalawags, and crooks who have taken the law into their own hands and who wish to frustrate the advance of civilization. All of these movies could easily have been set in the old west, given the Hollywood mythology. They could never have taken place north of the border because the conditions that existed in the American west simply weren't present anywhere in Canada.

In *The Cariboo Trail* Randolph Scott, in the role of Jim Redfern, a Montana cowboy, is taking cattle into the lawless Cariboo country. Scott literally shoots his way through British Columbia. At a toll bridge scoundrels attempt to charge Scott for passage; he drives on through, guns blazing. Shortly after that he and his partner meet a prospector named Grizzly, played by Gabby Hayes, the perennial comic of the Hopalong Cassidy westerns. "This is the Cariboo Trail, mister," Hayes warns them. "A broken heart for every rock, a dead man for every tree."

That night the scalawags from the toll bridge (those whom Scott hasn't shot full of holes) get their revenge by stampeding the cowboys' cattle. Scott springs into action once again, blasting into the night as men topple in agony from their horses. There is no coroner's inquest.

In the typical British Columbia town of Carson Creek Scott learns that the entire Cariboo country is under the control of a rapscallion named Walsh, played with a sneer by Victor Jory. Walsh owns everything in town except the neighbourhood saloon and gambling hall, identified as a Canadian institution by the presence of three large, if badly carved, totem poles. This environment is the scene of further gun-play: somebody tries to brain Scott with a sledgehammer but Scott, fast as always on the draw, kills him with a single shot.

There is no suggestion, of course, that the law in any form existed in the interior of British Columbia in the 1860's. Law enforcement is an individual matter. As Gabby Hayes tells Randolph Scott: "Up here in the gold country . . . a feller usually shoots first and buries his mistakes later." Life is cheap and nobody seems to be bothered by the corpses lying about in the underbrush, the streets, and the saloons. The Cariboo is the end of the earth: on the other side of the hills, in the mysterious Chilcotin, lies "Injun Country," totally unknown, full of war-whooping braves straight out of Peter Pan.

Hollywood's Cariboo is California in 1849. The real Cariboo was policed from the outset, not by the mounted police who had yet to be invented, but by order of the governor of the colony, James Douglas. This remarkable figure – he was, apparently, a mulatto with West Indian blood – acted decisively as soon as gold was discovered on the Fraser. He sent armed soldiers into the interior and backed them up with all the majesty of British justice, in the person of Judge Matthew Baillie Begbie. This Mephistophelian giant, tough but fair, was known as "the hanging judge of the Cariboo," although hanging was not his style. With this swift move Douglas saved British Columbia from the type of American mass invasion that had lost the empire its Oregon territory.

The last thing that Begbie would have stood for was a Cariboo gun-fight. Lawlessness was quickly stifled. Anybody who came up against the judge got summary treatment. Foreigners who didn't behave were hustled out of the country. The real history of the Cariboo is full of incredible stories and remarkable characters – a tapestry of folly, greed, avarice, eccentricity, profligacy, heroism, and romance. But Nat Holt's shoot-'em-up western might have been made in a foreign country, which of course it was, having been shot entirely in Colorado.

Holt was also the producer of *Canadian Pacific*, the movie that the Americans kept calling the cornerstone of the Canadian Co-operation Project. Early press agentry suggested that Holt was going to do for Canada what DeMille had done for his own country with *Union Pacific,* a prospect designed to flatter both government and railway officials north of the border. Certainly the later picture derived from the earlier one but the technical production was far weaker, the acting more primitive, and the story much thinner. *Canadian Pacific,* too, was just another transplanted western.

The picture's antecedents were obvious. It was the stepson of *Union Pacific,* which was the stepson of John Ford's *The Iron Horse.* Both those movies had similar themes: attempts by renegades, profiteers, and Indians to prevent the transcontinental railway from being finished. "For three valiant years, Indians reddened the rails with the blood of the tracklayers," was the way a DeMille subtitle phrased it. The climax of both

208

pictures was a bloody battle in which painted savages surrounded a work train and fought it out with the railwaymen.

Canadian Pacific borrowed shamelessly from both movies. DeMille's hero was a trouble-shooter played by Joel McCrea. ("You are the law and it's up to you to smash anything that delays us," General Dodge tells him.) Holt's hero was a trouble-shooter played by Randolph Scott. In John Ford's picture the villains try to kill the hero because he has discovered a pass through the mountains. In Holt's picture the villains try to kill the hero because he has discovered a pass through the mountains. In *Union Pacific* the trouble-shooter gets into a fight in a saloon and tears it down so the navvies can get back to work. In *Canadian Pacific* the trouble-shooter gets into a fight in a saloon and closes it up so the navvies can get back to work. In *The Iron Horse* the men rebel because the pay car fails to turn up. In *Canadian Pacific* the men rebel because the pay car fails to turn up. And the Canadian movie, like both of its predecessors, ends with a bloody battle between painted Indians and navvies holed up in a work train.

The violence in this film is remarkable even for a Hollywood western. Scott, in the role of Tom Andrews, surveyor and trouble-shooter (complete with Texas accent), has been given carte blanche by the Canadian Pacific Railway to do anything he wants with those two pearl-handled revolvers in his gunbelt, or with his fists. In an early scene he arrives at End of Track, spots a man he doesn't like, and walks over and punches him in the nose, knocking him to the ground. Then he kicks his prostrate victim and finally throws him out of camp. This action draws an admiring remark from a man identified as William Van Horne, who in real life was the vice-president of the railroad. "He's the best trouble boss in the country," says this Van Horne, overcome with delight at Scott's example of bossmanship. "He has to be quick with his fists." In *Canadian Pacific* Van Horne is a minor figure; it's Randolph Scott who runs things.

In another scene Scott comes across two men he suspects of stealing dynamite for their own nefarious purposes. Without a question or a challenge he pulls both guns from their holsters and opens fire, knocking both of them to the ground. His sidekick, played by J. Carroll Naish, accuses him of being a weakling for shooting them in the arms and not in the head.

There's a subplot in this picture involving a pretty nurse who thinks Scott is far *too* violent. She gets him to hang up his guns and promise her there'll be no more killing because bloodshed never solved anything. She loses out as the result of a gun-fight in a Hollywood-style saloon (known as "the longest bar in the world") which has been set up beside the track. As in *Union Pacific* the railway's enemies have supplied free booze to the saloon to keep the navvies from working. When one of the patrons gets into an argument the bartender solves it by shooting him dead. This is the last straw for Andrews, who clearly believes that bloodshed solves *every-thing*. He eschews pacifism, retrieves his forsaken gunbelt, strides into the saloon, and in his role as surveyor/trouble-shooter/construction-boss/policeman arrests the guilty man behind the bar. When the bartender goes for his gun Scott plugs him and closes up the saloon as the picture moves on to its bloody climax.

Baker Street Irregulars will recall the "singular incident of the dog in the night." "But," said Watson to the great detective, "the dog did nothing in the night." To which Holmes replied that *that* was the singular incident. In *Canadian Pacific* the singular incident was the fact that the mounted police did nothing in the movie. They weren't even shown. The Métis shot up the navvies; the Indians shot up the railway; Randolph Scott shot up everybody; but no movie Mountie appeared to make a report. Men rebelled and threatened violence; people were blasted to death by dynamite; corpses littered the track; but there wasn't a scarlet coat in evidence. This is remarkable when you consider that up to that point Hollywood had made at least two hundred movies about the mounted police.

Actually, the policing of the Canadian Pacific Railway during the construction period was one of the great triumphs of the NWMP. The divided and often opposing jurisdictions that plagued the American peace-keeping forces didn't exist in the Canadian northwest. From the Manitoba border to the Rockies the mounted police were in sole charge. Saloons were illegal; so was gambling; and *nobody* carried a gun. Because of this almost uncanny quiet the railroad was built across the prairies with a dispatch unique in the annals of North American track-laying.

The spectacle of an imported American surveyor in cowboy gear acting as a trouble-shooter for Van Horne, firing his six-guns at the nearest target, and killing men without a by-your-leave is so alien to the Canadian experience that it would be considered ludicrous were it not for the fact that it was believed.

"An authentic story of the vicissitudes of building the famed Canadian railway," wrote The Hollywood Reporter.[7]

"The factual story of the building of the first railroad across the Canadian Rockies," wrote The Showman's Trade Review.[8]

"A virile, outdoor pioneer melodrama ... revolving around the violent opposition encountered by the builders of the Canadian Pacific in the laying of tracks through the Canadian Rockies," wrote Harrison's Reports.[9]

The ultimate seal of approval was supplied by The Motion Picture Herald, which reported that "the program bears outward mark of the co-operation extended by the Dominion government and the Canadian Pacific Railway"[10]– in short, the Canadian Co-operation Project again.[11]

The CPR company probably thought the film really *was* an accurate portrayal since it had demonstrated a remarkable lack of knowledge about its own history when *The Iron Horse* was released in 1925. According to the trade press CPR officials went to see that movie when it opened at the Lyric Theatre in New York and were so impressed that "they immediately began negotiations with the Fox Company to have the story and titles written to fit the building of the first Canadian transcontinental railroad. The conditions . . . were so similar . . . that with just a little changing, the picture could be made to fit the Canadian situation,"[12] it was pointed out.

The conditions were radically different, but nobody seemed to realize that. The necessary historical changes weren't made in *The Iron Horse,* but when the movie was released in Canada it was dedicated to the men who built the CPR. When it had its première in Montreal The Gazette reported that "except for the names applied to the historical participants in the film, it might serve with equal truth as a record of the construction against enormous odds of the Canadian Pacific."[13]

The American idea of an untamed frontier, subdued by individual heroes armed with six-guns, was continued in *The Far Country,* another story about a cowboy from the American west – Wyoming this time – driving his herd of beef cattle into gold country. The picture is a nightmare of geographical impossibilities (a paddlewheel riverboat leaving Skagway for Seattle, for instance), but the real incongruity is the major assumption on which the plot turns – that there was only one mounted policeman in all of the Canadian Yukon at the time of the gold rush and that he could not deal with the lawlessness. When James Stewart and Walter Brennan reach the Yukon border with their cattle (the geographic truth is that they would have had to drive the herd up the side of a mountain), the customs shack is empty.

"Where's the constable?" asks Brennan.

"Up on the Pelly River. Trouble with the Chilkats," someone replies, nicely garbling the geography but preserving the myth of the savage redskins. (The Chilkats in real life were making big money packing supplies over the passes.) "He's got a real tough job, that constable. He patrols some ten or twenty thousand square miles. Sometimes he don't get home for two or three months at a time."

The historical truth is that the Yukon Territory during the gold rush was the closest thing to a police state British North America has ever seen. The NWMP was stationed in the territory in considerable numbers long

211

before the Klondike strike. They controlled every route into the Yukon and they brooked no nonsense. They collected customs duties, often over the wails of the new arrivals, made arbitrary laws on the spot about river navigation, and turned men back if they didn't have enough supplies, or if they simply *looked* bad. In true Canadian fashion, they laid down moral laws for the community. In Dawson the Lord's Day Act was strictly observed; it was a crime punishable by a fine to cut your own wood on Sunday; and plump young women were arrested for what the stern-faced police called "giving a risqué performance in a theatre,"[14] generally nothing more than dancing suggestively on the stage in overly revealing tights.

In such a community, a gunbelt was unthinkable. One notorious bad man from Tombstone who tried to pack a weapon on his hip was personally disarmed by a young constable, who had just ejected him from a saloon for the heinous crime of talking too loudly. The bad man left like a lamb but protested when the policeman, upon discovering he was carrying a gun, told him to hand it over. "No man has yet taken a gun away from me," said the American. "Well, I'm taking it," the constable said mildly and did so, without further resistance. So many revolvers were confiscated in Dawson that they were auctioned off by the police for as little as a dollar and purchased as souvenirs to keep on the mantlepiece.

In 1898, the big year of the stampede, there wasn't a serious crime – let alone a murder – in Dawson. The contrast with Skagway on the American side, which *was* a lawless town run by Soapy Smith, the Denver confidence man, was remarkable. But in *The Far Country* Dawson is seen as a community without any law, which a Soapy Smith character from Skagway – he is called Gannon in the picture – can easily control. (In real life, one of Smith's men who tried to cross the border had all his equipment confiscated and was frogmarched right back again by a mounted police sergeant.)

When Stewart and Brennan hit town, men are being gunned down like rabbits. "Where there's gold there's stealin' and where there's stealin' there's killin'," a bystander remarks. Stewart has hardly dipped his pan into the gravel of a creek before another killing takes place; it's explained that the corpse got into a little argument in a saloon.

Finally Stewart and his sidekick encounter the elusive lone Mountie who enters the Dawson Castle Saloon carrying another corpse over his shoulder. All the shooting and killing is too much for the redcoat. For years Hollywood pictures featured Mounties who cleaned up lawless towns single-handedly in the face of fearful odds, but this one admits defeat in the following dialogue sequence:

212

"Yes, I'm the law. I represent the law in the Yukon Territory. About fifty thousand square miles of it."

"Then why aren't there more of you?"

"Because yesterday this was a wilderness. We didn't expect you to pour in by the thousands. Now that you're here, we'll protect you."

"When?"

"There'll be a post established here in Dawson early in May."

"What happens between now and May? You going to be here to keep order?"

"Part of the time."

"What about the rest of the time?"

"Pick yourselves a good man. Swear him in. Have him act as marshal. . . ."

The movie Mountie leaves and does not appear again in the picture. His astonishing suggestion – that an American town marshal, complete with tin star, be sworn in by a group of townspeople living under British jurisprudence – is accepted. Naturally, they want to make Jimmy Stewart the marshal; he clearly fits the part. But Stewart is playing the role of the Loner who looks after Number One and so another man is elected to get shot. And he does. Others get shot. Even Walter Brennan gets shot. Stewart finally comes to the reluctant conclusion that he must end all the shooting with some shooting of his own. He pins on the tin star and he and the bully, Gannon, blast away at each other in the inevitable western climax.

To anybody with a passing knowledge of the Canadian north, this bald re-telling of the story passes rational belief. Could such a motion picture really have been made? Did people actually believe it? Yes, they did. And reviewers on two continents, including Canada, saw nothing to complain about. It was, in the words of one British periodical, "an enjoyable and exciting western."[15] The New York Times could find no fault with it and in fact praised "the sensible script."[16]

At least two reviewers accepted without question Hollywood's image of a lawless Yukon. The Motion Picture Herald told its readers that the movie was set "in Dawson before the Canadian Mounted Police had law and order firmly established."[17] And in England, C. A. Lejeune, The Observer's highly respected critic, wrote that the scene was laid in "1896 when the gold-rush to the Klondike forced thousands of hard men into a territory hitherto patrolled by a single mounted policeman."[18]

No one really expects foreign critics to have a first-hand knowledge of Canadian history. But I haven't been able to find a Canadian critic who set the record straight, either, even in Vancouver, with its strong Yukon connections. Les Wedman, praising the star's performance in the picture in The Vancouver Province, wrote with approval of how "in a blazing duel . . . Stewart brings law and order to Dawson."[19]

Nothing has changed. Seeing The Far Country again on television took me back to a day in 1960 when a Hollywood movie company decided to make a series about the Klondike, based on my own history of the stampede. I met the executive producer of the series and the following dialogue took place:

ME: Uh. I guess you're going to have some kind of central character to kind of tie the story together, eh?

HIM: Oh, yes; we've figured that out.

ME: I thought maybe a dog driver . . .

HIM: No; we've got it worked out. He's going to be a US marshal.

ME: A US marshal?

HIM: Yes. He brings the law to Dawson City.

ME: But Dawson City is in Canada.

HIM: It is? Really?

ME: Really.

HIM: Well, then, a US marshal-type. He's elected by the miners, see, and –

ME: But they didn't *need* a marshal in Dawson. There wasn't any crime.

HIM: No crime? In Dawson City?

ME: You see they had these mounted police. You know – Mounties –

HIM: Oh yeah. The Mounties.

ME: And two hundred soldiers, all armed. They called that the Yukon Field Force.

HIM: Must have been a few murders, though.

ME: None.

HIM: Hold-ups? A few hold-ups?

ME: No hold-ups.

HIM: No murders? No hold-ups? No crime?

ME: Well, a guy got fined for going down to the Yukon River and chopping a hole in the ice and taking some water back to his cabin. You see it was Sunday, and in Canada we –

HIM: Yeah, yeah. I'm thinking. . . . (HE THINKS) I'm thinking maybe we ought to change the locale. . . .

ME: Well, if you want murders and hold-ups –

HIM: Maybe move it over to the American side. . . .

ME: To Skagway?

HIM: Yeah! Move the whole thing to Skagway! Then it would work!

ME: Yes. It would work all right in Skagway.

HIM: Then that's what we'll do.

And that, so help me, is exactly what they did.

214

3: "Love and Lynch Law where it's 'Five Shirts Cold'"

The idea of a lawless frontier wasn't confined to the three motion pictures that I've just described. These were the end-products of a long process in the Americanization of the Canadian image, which began in the early days of the silent movies and continued until this kind of picture became obsolete.

"The scene of this play is laid in the Canadian lumber wilds . . . where each man is disposed to be a law unto himself."[20] So wrote a reviewer in 1911 describing *A Sin Unpardonable*. From that day on moviegoers were continually shown a lawless, gun-slinging country called Canada, sprinkled with saloons and gambling dens – in spite of the presence of the Mountie who always got his man.

The Wilderness Trail was set in "a region where the law is a remote thing."[21] *The Northern Code* was a story of "that famous district North of '48; where the laws of man do not reach."[22] *The Eternal Struggle* took place in "the vast land of the lawless."[23]

Over and over again in the silent movies Canadians were depicted as a people quick to take the law into their own hands. "Love and Lynch Law where it's 'Five Shirts Cold,'" read one advertising slogan.[24] I've come across nineteen lynching scenes in movies spanning almost three generations. In one picture the villagers storm a prison and attempt to burn the heroine as a witch. In another a group of Canadian lumbermen start to lynch a foreman because they haven't been paid. In a third a mob even tries to lynch a Mountie. The lynchings go back to the very beginning of the movies, as a description of *The Girl of the Northern Woods*, made in 1910, indicates: "Rarely are the courts resorted to in that portion of the North where these events transpired and the rough lumbermen decide to lynch Will."[25]

In all these movies Canadians were shown making up their own laws as they went along, as the Americans of the old west were seen to do. The vigilante movement, however, is not a Canadian phenomenon. It had its birth in California in the early days of political corruption, moved up through the gold-mining states and reached its final explosive moment in the shooting of Alaska's Soapy Smith in 1898. It was an American solution to a peculiarly American political problem. So was the "necktie party," or impromptu hanging which, we are told, was the usual fate of cattle rustlers in the United States. But there were no cattle rustlers in the ranching country of the Alberta foothills; the mounted police saw to that.

During the Klondike stampede there were all sorts of lynchings, floggings, and winter banishments decreed by hurriedly organized min-

215

ers' meetings – another California invention. All of them occurred on the American side of the border. There was no need of them in the Yukon, which was run in an entirely different manner. In fact the NWMP was originally sent to the Yukon because American miners in Fortymile, a Canadian town, were dispensing this form of grass-roots justice. "In 1897, the Klondike was a world unto itself – lawless, gay and bawdy," according to an exhibitor's sheet for *Klondike Kate,* another movie with a lynching scene. Gay, yes; bawdy, sometimes; but lawless *never.*

In the belief that there was no law in the Canadian northwest Hollywood screenwriters invented their own unwritten laws or "codes" ("The code of the Klondike reaps vengeance in full atonement").[26] I have made an attempt below to tabulate these informal but apparently irrevocable decrees:

THE CODE OF THE NORTHWEST (from *Paid in Advance)*	A half-breed floored by a trapper demands the right of the code to fight to the death with a gun on the big lake.
THE OLD CODE (from *The Old Code)*	"A blow has been struck and according to the custom in the wilderness, the men must now fight."[27]
THE NORTHERN CODE (from *The Northern Code)*	"Remember the Northern Code – the survival of the fittest" (hero to wife).
THE LAW OF THE WOODS (also known as The Honor of the Big Snows) (from *Jan of the Big Snows)*	"That the strong must protect the weak – that a man will suffer, starve, die before he takes what belongs to another man. Any man who does not live up to this code cannot live."[28]
THE LAW OF THE KLONDIKE (from *The Call of the Wild)*	"If you can't get something you need take it from the other guy" (Clark Gable to Loretta Young).
THE LAW OF THE NORTH (from *The Law of the North)*	"I don't want your life but remember the law of the North – a broken promise means death up here" (Mountie to Evil Factor).

"ick 'em up everybody~ It's going to be a very merry Christmas"

It's apparently standard practice in Montreal for Santa Claus to wear a gunbelt. This scene from Dangerous Nan McGrew *(1930) stars Frank Morgan as Santa, James Hall as the impotent Mountie, and Victor Moore.*

Transplanted Westerns

Hollywood moved its mythic frontier
into Canada, complete with saloons,
gambling, and six-gun violence.

217

The setting for The Sky Pilot *was supposed to be Alberta but this scene
from the King Vidor production in 1921, with John Bowers (left) and David
Hendricks, is more suggestive of Tombstone, Arizona, or Dodge City.*

*Gun-fights didn't happen in Klondike saloons—only in Klondike movies.
In* Winds of Chance *(1925) Viola Dana, as Rouletta Kirby, tries to
prevent her father, played by Hobart Bosworth, from committing mayhem.*

In order to build the CPR *it was apparently necessary for Randolph Scott
to shoot a lot of people. Actually, both saloons and gunbelts were for-
bidden on the prairies in 1883. Nor did railroad navvies dress as cowboys.*

The western posse above is supposed
to be all-Canadian, even though the style,
the costumes, and the scenery are all-
American. The movie is called North of the
Border and was based on another story by
the ubiquitous James Oliver Curwood.

Here's James Stewart bringing the law to
Dawson City, in The Far Country, another
movie which might just as easily have
been set in the American wild west.

220

In the climactic scene of The Far Country, *Stewart, taking the law into his own hands, blazes away successfully at the villain. Although Dawson was alive with mounted police at the time, they just aren't to be seen.*

The American saloon was unknown in the Canadian Northwest Territories, but that didn't stop Hollywood from using it in movies such as Wilderness Mail *(top) or* Pierre of the Plains *(right).*

Gambling has always been taboo in Canada but not in Hollywood's Athabasca country, as the scene from The Wild North (top) shows. Indians are also taboo in bars but they turned up there in several movies, such as The Yellowback (left) made in 1929.

Believe it or not, this typically Canadian scene is supposed to take place not far from Calgary in 1925. The dude on the left is Hoot Gibson, the great cowboy star of the silent era. The movie is The Calgary Stampede.

Even the movie Mounties acted outside the law, apparently with the approval of their superiors. Charles Bickford is shown running a bloody gauntlet of his fellow police in *River's End*, and Buck Jones emerges, scarred and battered, from a similar gauntlet in *McKenna of the Mounted*.

Gun-fighting, another non-Canadian pastime, goes all the way back to *The Sky Pilot*, made from the Canadian best seller whose author, you'll remember, told Teddy Roosevelt that violence was unknown in the Canadian west. But in the motion picture, Swan Creek in the Canadian Rockies is depicted as a totally lawless community. When the parson-hero tries to hold a Sunday service in the handy neighbourhood saloon, the entire congregation turns up to pray with revolvers strapped to their hips. A fight breaks out and the preacher finds himself rolling about on the floor of his makeshift chapel with one of the local cowhands. His antagonist later befriends him and explains: "You've got a tough job, partner, trying to lay religion on this mob. They won't listen to a parson. You've got to show them you're a man to make 'em listen to you."

In *Pierre of the Plains* a French-Canadian reprobate is shown pushing booze to the Indians on the main street of a Canadian fur-trading settlement, apparently in full view of the mounted police who conveniently turn their backs while John Carroll, who does not care for this sort of corruption, pulls his gun and blasts away at the jugs until they are all smashed. "Now you have no way to put holes in people's stomachs," he tells the liquor-vendor who, maddened at the loss of trade, seizes the pistol by the barrel and whacks Carroll over the head with it. The ensuing tussle is swiftly broken up by a Mountie who makes a magical appearance to enforce the law against street brawls.

Then there's the fight between Blue Blazes Rawden and Lady Fingers Hilgard in William S. Hart's logging picture. "I choose an empty room, guns, and the survivor takes this place, the girl, and the money!" Hart cries, doing his arm-swinging routine and sounding like a man who has just challenged his opponent to a brisk game of squash. One got the impression that this kind of contest was standard fare in the logging camps of British Columbia, circa 1918.

Gun-fights, fisticuffs, and eyeball-scratching brawls generally took place in the saloons, and there was never any dearth of those in Hollywood's Canada. I can't recall ever seeing a Canadian saloon with bat-wing doors, although these are standard fixtures in the Hollywood re-creations; but then I can't recall ever seeing a saloon anywhere in the real Canadian north during the time Hollywood was making movies about Mounties, trappers, and half-breeds, because, of course, they weren't legal. (They have them now, but they're called cocktail bars.)

Even if they had been legal, most of the saloons in the movies would have been closed tight within twenty-four hours by the Liquor Licensing Board because of the rowdiness of the patrons. In *God's Country and the Law* men and women wander about the saloon swilling their booze straight from the bottle. Every Canadian knows *that* isn't allowed, anymore than standing up to drink or singing loudly while knocking back a whisky. Worse things happen: In the Liquid Nugget Bar, far to the north of Edmonton, Jules Vincent, the trapper in *The Wild North*, smashes a man right through a table, picks him up again and then throws him right through the railing of a staircase. So used is the proprietor to this form of amusement that he doesn't even send Vincent a bill.

Hollywood, which has made scores of pictures about its own prohibition period, was never able to understand that Canada has had a much longer and more varied history of public temperance. As we all know, words like bar and saloon are not seen in Canada; but I suppose a typically Canadian phrase like Licensed Premises would remove some of the glamour from a hard-shooting picture. During the thirties and forties the province of Alberta, where so many saloon movies were set, allowed the word DRINKS to appear outside beer parlours. However, women and men were not allowed to mingle, which undoubtedly posed an awkward problem for the scriptwriters, assuming they were aware of it.

The Canadian beer parlour with its linoleum floor slippery with suds, its drab walls, its tiny windows, and its round tables groaning under the weight of a dozen half-finished glasses of stale draft was a far cry from the dazzling saloon-dancehall of the movies, with its winding staircase, its tinkling piano, its mirrored bar, its appetizing array of bottles, its roulette wheels and poker tables, and its buxom songstresses. A poor thing, the beer parlour, but undeniably our own; alas it was never shown in the movies.

What was shown, however, was the presence of natives in the bars, something Canadian law did not tolerate. Chippewa Joe had no trouble buying a drink in a Canadian saloon in *The Law's Lash,* and the Mounties, who moved cheerfully through the guzzling crowd in the Gold Prince in *A Romance of the Northwest,* took no notice of the guzzling Indians.

Bruce Carruthers once had a long squabble with the producers of *Northern Pursuit* who insisted on placing a cocktail bar in wartime Winnipeg. The people at Warner's refused to take Carruthers's word that Winnipeg at the time was as dry as the Gobi so they checked with the Canadian trade commissioner's office in Los Angeles. They didn't believe Carruthers either. The ex-corporal had to write all the way to Winnipeg to get documentation that the producers would believe. As any ex-serviceman knows, a martini was as out of place in Winnipeg during World War Two as a glass of wine was in an Ottawa restaurant in the twenties – an anachronism that appears in *The Happy Time.*

There are other Americanisms scattered through the movies about Canada that only a native would spot. In the typical western town of Maple Rock, Alberta, where the last version of *Rose Marie* is set, an alien characteristic surfaces in the form of a square building on the corner with the single word BANK painted on it. This is *Canada*? Individual and anonymous banks may have existed in pioneer Arizona and Wyoming, but north of the border the western branches of eastern financial institutions proudly proclaim their lineage.

If the buildings bore the stamp of American frontier fashion, so did the people. Hollywood's Northwest Territories – trapping country – and Hollywood's Yukon – prospecting country – have always been populated by American cowboys. These incongruous figures in their broad-brimmed Stetsons stride about, gunbelts hanging low, totally out of tune with their surroundings. The only exceptions to the rule are the French-Canadians in their tuques.

In several of the Monogram quickies made in the fifties, the Mounted hero, Corporal Rod Webb, doffs his scarlet coat and dons a disguise, the better to unmask knavery. In one picture he disguises himself as a prospector. In another he takes on the costume of a northern mail carrier. In a third he cunningly adopts the garb of a backwoods trapper. The disguise, however, is always the same: a mackinaw coat and a familiar white Stetson – the one that won the west.

And then there is the curious instance of Wagon Wheel, typical Canadian western town, somewhere on the outskirts of Montreal, which comes complete with a cowboy sheriff wearing a tin star. The movie, needless to say, is a comedy *(Dangerous Nan McGrew)*, but some of the humour is unintentional.

In the town of Alcana on the Yukon border in the Mountie serial mentioned earlier, everybody dresses like a Montana cowboy or, to be more exact, like Randolph Scott building the CPR. There are plenty of photographs around to show what prospectors and railroad navvies looked like in the last century and in this one. None of them looked like cowboys (and neither, one might add, did the cowboys). The prospectors in the famous photographs that Eric Hegg took during the 1897-98 stampede all wore the standard miner's hat of the day and old, shapeless suits of indiscriminate colour. Today they wear Caribou brand work-clothes. The workmen who built the CPR often wore bowler hats and suits with vests – and even watch chains – because workclothes hadn't been invented. One of the few pictures I've seen in which the extras actually looked the part was *The Trail of '98*, made at the end of the silent era; Clarence Brown, the director, had taken the trouble to examine the Hegg pictures and reproduce them faithfully.

Hollywood's Canada is a place where cougars are called pumas, where

Rock Hudson and Monte Blue shout Haw! at their dogs instead of Mush! (Haw means to turn left; Mush means to travel), and where French-Canadians are referred to as Canucks. Canuck is an American term applied to people of French-Canadian blood living south of the border, and it's considered an insult, as Senator Muskie discovered in the 1968 presidential campaign. But it's never been an insult in Canada; indeed, there was a time when it was used as a generic term for Canadians by cartoonists. Now it's simply obsolete. But in the movie called *The Devil's Brigade,* about the Special Service Force of American and Canadian commandos in World War Two, a Canadian officer is shown telling his American counterpart that "Canuck is a term we consider disparaging." Since when?

In Hollywood's Canada northerners drink coffee. In the real Canada they drink tea – the universal beverage of the trail because it's lighter to pack than coffee and gives more of a lift. Carruthers tried to convince Warner Brothers of that, too, but they wouldn't listen. It was bad enough that Winnipegers couldn't buy anything stronger than beer; but *tea* in the rugged north? Carruthers was told that this was impossible; tea was a sissy drink; no self-respecting French-Canadian trapper would be seen with the stuff. And so Stewart Granger was made to say: "I can take anything this country can offer but I *got* to have my coffee."

Coffee is the beverage of the American plains, drunk by cowboys who, like the Hollywood producers, connected tea with Englishmen at garden parties. Canadians have never thought in those terms but I have never seen a Hollywood movie about the north in which anybody drank tea. And yet, coffee on the trail in the Yukon would be as incongruous as a prospector who referred to a mine instead of a claim, another curious Hollywood blindness. Very few movies were able to sort out the difference between free gold, or placer – the kind that is found in the Yukon – and hardrock gold, which is dug out of a hole in the side of a mountain.* In picture after picture about the gold rush, the plot turns on a stolen deed to a mine. But there are no deeds and no mines in the Klondike; these belong to the world of Tom Mix and of *Northwest Rangers,* another movie in which poor Carruthers, who'd actually patrolled Yukon mining country, was again overruled.

Finally, there is the long-standing American preference for the enlisted man and the NCO over commissioned officers, evident in the various Mountie movies turned out for over half a century. Students of military pictures will know that American enlisted men and top sergeants

---

*Hollywood also apparently believed that all free gold was obtained by panning, which is merely a method of testing ground. Panning, besides being the most arduous of all exercises, is one of the silliest ways of getting any quantity of placer gold out of a riverbed. But that's how Clark Gable got rich in *The Call of the Wild.*

228

are glorified to a far greater extent than their British and Canadian equivalents. This undoubtedly springs again from American attitudes that go back to the War of Independence, to the conviction that one man is as good as another and that a private is every bit the man the colonel is and maybe even better. The majority of Hollywood movies about the US cavalry in the old west or about the US army and marines in World Wars One and Two are told from the point of view of rank. The Irish sergeant, the Jew from Brooklyn, the Negro, the comic Italian – all these stereotyped figures talking about America, Mom, apple pie, and the right to boo the Dodgers are privates and non-coms. The officers are remote and sometimes are even portrayed as martinets.

The Hollywood Mountie movie that shows a commissioned officer performing a deed of valour is rare. Officers are usually seen behind desks, pointing at maps (quite often, in Hollywood's Canada, the *wrong* map) and ordering an underling, usually a sergeant, to head out into the snows and bring back his man. Carruthers, on at least one occasion, had a hard time convincing the studio bosses that sergeants were not placed in charge of large northern detachments. And I have already detailed his struggles with the moviemakers who wanted to turn superior officers into murderous martinets.

Most of the officers I've seen in Mountie movies have clipped British accents to go with their haircuts. The sergeants tend to have Irish brogues like New York policemen. And this, too, is a very American attitude born of revolution and melting pot.

In the real Canada there have been as many heroes among the officers as there have been among the ranks and the non-commissioned officers. Superintendent Samuel B. Steele, the Lion of the Yukon, stands out as the prototype North West Mounted Policeman, but there have been many others: James Walsh, the inspector who more than anyone else was responsible for Sitting Bull's good behaviour in Canada; Charles Constantine, the first officer in the Yukon; Bobby Belcher, the hero of the Chilkoot summit; F. J. Fitzgerald, who starved to death on the Wind River divide; J. D. Moodie, who hacked his way for 1,600 miles from the Peace River to Fort Selkirk; and many, many more. Many of these men were Canadians who rose out of the ranks to earn their commissions. All of them acted above and beyond the call of duty. There isn't one whose story wouldn't make an epic film, crammed with high adventure, sacrifice, and heroism. But in Hollywood's Canada their kind has been portrayed as faceless, paunchy, white-moustached do-nothings, holding down a desk in the fort while the Renfrews, the Kings, and the O'Malleys head out to do their duty in the Great Woods of the Northwest.

4: "Too many deeds of Yankee valor"

Does any of this really matter? Should we care if Canadians are made to drink coffee on the trail instead of tea? If northerners are shown in cowboy hats? If our frontier is ruled by the law of the gun? If the saloons have bat-wing doors? Yes, we should.

Taken individually, no single picture, flawed though it may have been, has posed any grave consequence as far as the Canadian image is concerned. But taken together over half a century, the combined effect of 575 movies has been devastating. It is not so much that they have given the world a false picture of Canada; Hollywood pictures, after all, have given the world a false picture of almost every country, including the United States. What has been damaging is that they have given the world *no* real image of Canada at all, except that of a geographical absurdity – a vast, empty, snowswept land of mountains and pine trees.

Taken together, the Hollywood movies about Canada have carried the implicit message that the Canadian image differs from the American image only in the matter of degree. They have said it to the world and they have said it to Canadians as well. They have said it especially in those motion pictures dealing with the frontier, past and present, and, as we've seen, most of the movies have been about the frontier. The lawmen are American lawmen; the Indians are American Indians; the French-Canadians are more like disguised Mexicans than real French-Canadians. The social customs are depicted as American social customs; the attitudes are American attitudes; the lifestyle is an American lifestyle.

It's simply not true that there is no such thing as a distinctive Canadian identity. As I've tried to show in this book we do differ in some very major ways and in many significant minor ways from our neighbours. From the earliest days we have had our own way of doing things and our own way of looking at life. I don't want to pretend that our way is necessarily better, just that it *is* different. And it is this difference that gives us, for better or for worse, that distinctive identity which eludes so many of the panellists on the CBC's earnest television discussions.

It eludes them, I suggest, because we lack among other things the kind of home-grown mythology that only a Hollywood or a Tin Pan Alley can really provide to a young country in this century. We have had neither. We haven't had (at least until recently) any popular songs to celebrate our own Davey Crocketts or our own Iwo Jimas. We've had no epic films of our own to remind us of the legends of our own Alamos and Gettysburgs. Our triumphs, tragedies, follies, and victories have not been celebrated except by the occasional foreign movie producer who has de-

230

Canadianized them. Television is only now beginning to fill that vacuum.

It's been hard enough to resist the tidal wave of a foreign mass culture that has made our children more conversant with a Daniel Boone than a Jerry Potts, more knowledgeable about a Ben Franklin than an Edward Blake. But when that foreign influence, in the form of a half-thousand movies, has been able to swallow our heritage and water it down to a pale imitation of the American past, then we're in a bad way.

As I indicated at the beginning, this book hasn't been concerned with intentions. I don't suppose many Hollywood producers expected us to take their movies seriously. The effect, however, has nothing to do with the intent. By a process of osmosis that goes back to the days before the First World War the Hollywood image of what we are has been imprinted onto our consciousness, by the cheap serials and the B pictures as much as by the better-produced films. No nation as young as ours can be exposed to as many movies over as many years without being brainwashed to some extent by a message that has never really changed. And that's the remarkable aspect of these movies – the consistency of the message. You Canadians, the message keeps telling us, are really just northern versions of Americans: you have no distinctive personality apart from ours, and no distinctive culture, apart from ours. Your identity is our identity. You're quainter, of course, and less sophisticated; but apart from those quirks you're just like us. This wasn't a concerted propaganda effort by a Yankee cominform; it just happened that way by default and very few of us knew what was happening.

Did no one protest? Yes, at the outset, a few voices were raised, mildly, about some aspects of the Hollywood assault. The earliest complaints, however, had nothing to do with the problems of a Canadian image. English-speaking Canadians thought of themselves as British and it was the lack of British identification that bothered them. Patriotic pictures were all the rage when the movies were young, but it was American patriotic pictures and not British ones that were exposed in the nickelodeons.

There was an outcry in 1911, a sensitive year in American-Canadian relations – the year of the "reciprocity election" in which Sir Wilfrid Laurier's Liberals, advocating free trade with the United States, went down to defeat. The opposition slogan "No truck nor trade with the Yankees" had its effect on the attitude to American movies. Censor boards began to apply the scissors to one-reelers that gratuitously showed the Stars and Stripes. "Canadian Imperialists are complaining about having to witness too many deeds of Yankee valor in moving pictures," Moving Picture World sniffed. "No reciprocity wanted – excepting Yankee dollars."[29]

Several American newspapers were amused over the Canadian attitude and accused Canadians of being super-sensitive and narrow-minded. One charged them with being devoid of a sense of humour, and another referred to the actions of the censor boards as "a piece of petty spite." American patriotic films continued to pour across the border into Canada and provincial censor boards continued to ban them. In 1914, fifty and one-half reels were rejected by the Motion Picture Censor Board of British Columbia for "unnecessary display of US flags."[30]

In the fall of 1915 Moving Picture World quoted an un-named Canadian newspaper that was calling for a distinct government policy which would stipulate that certain attention must be given to Canada by American film makers.

> . . . Let the men who are using the magic of their wonderful art direct their lenses in the direction of a land that is tired of being treated as a second-hand consideration. Let us have a Canadian influence in moving pictures. . . . Let us imitate less and initiate more.[31]

The trade paper's Vancouver correspondent reported, however, that nothing was being done about Canadian production and that American pictures continued to be popular: "Nothing is more sure of a hearty welcome than a story of the great north woods, with perhaps a touch of The Royal Northwest Mounted Police."

In 1918 Bill Gladish, the movie critic of The Toronto Daily News and probably the first regular film critic in Canada, complained that almost every picture shown about the country dealt with "life at a Hudson Bay trading post with players wearing snowshoes and Red River costumes and using firearms and dogsleds freely."[32] He continued to complain without result.

In 1920 Moving Picture World quoted an unnamed Canadian editor on the subject of "American Film Travesties."

> We can bear with fortitude the alleged Canadian soldier wearing chevrons upside-down American fashion and can forgive the fact that what is supposed to be the Rocky Mountains is a California backyard, but, for the love of Mike, are there nothing else in our Dominion but Indians, French Canadian lumberjacks and Northwest Mounted Police?[33]

These stray voices in the Canadian wilderness were supplemented, occasionally, by others calling for a home-grown motion picture industry. At the dawn of the sound era in 1929, a Toronto Star article by a writer using the pseudonym "Celluloid" reported the formation of a British company to make talking pictures "of the British Empire for the Empire"

232

in several Commonwealth countries, including Canada. Two movies mentioned for Canadian production were an historical picture about Wolfe storming Quebec and "a romance of the lumber trade." "Celluloid" commented:

> . . . so far as Canada is concerned it might be as well for the British producer of such pictures to play the game into Canadian hands. We don't want just the average English conception of either the Plains of Abraham or the lumber industry – which are only two of the many romances as yet unfilmed in Canada. What we do want is the story of Canada on the screen for Canadians. It is not merely a matter of sound pictures. The thing should have been done long ago in the silent films.
>
> Canada has never yet had one adequate film about Canada. We have had all sorts of Americanized conceptions of Canada; films supposed to be all Canadian camera'd in California; scenes from Canadian life sequenced into American continuity; half-baked Canadian films made in Canada and getting nowhere because of no direction; fragments of Canadian history and the war reeled into empire films. These and many more we have had to sufficiency . . . it is time for bigger and better things.[34]

The following January the Ontario Board of Censors in its annual report expressed concern about "the Americanization of the screen" and stressed the importance of combatting the educational influence of American-made films "by means of films with a distinct Canadian point of view and outlook."[35]

This touched off a bitter attack by the Canadian Moving Picture Digest, the local trade publication which was, of course, no more than a mouthpiece for the American film industry in Canada. The Digest's editor, Ray Lewis, struck hard at "the threadbare theme of combatting American influence through the filming of pictures which had a decided Canadian point of view." Lewis went on to delineate the party line:

> In respect to the ethics of life, the moral fibre of our Being, I see no difference between the people of the US and Canada! . . . For fifteen years, perhaps twenty, I have viewed Motion Pictures, and I see nothing in them which can make a Canadian, an Italian, or a Frenchman less of what they are . . . . What need most concern us as Canadians is the 'good idea;' which can be made in the US, in England, in Germany, in Canada, without it bearing the label of distinctly belonging to any man's country. . . . No US picture which I have ever seen has taught Canadians sedition, or disloyalty to Canada, nor to the Empire. . . .[36]

With these words, which were the common cant of the day but which fall strangely on the ears of a later generation, the controversy died away.

It was too late, really, for a Canadian motion picture industry, at least in those days of the mass audience. The coming of sound, and later of colour, had made the production of motion pictures too expensive. When the British quota system came in during the mid-thirties Holly-wood actually did some Canadian production in Victoria, BC, with Canadian dummy companies. These quota quickies, as they came to be called, starring such dubious box-office draws as Lyle Talbot and Wendy Barrie,* were produced as cheaply as possible. Few had anything to do with Canada.

With only a few exceptions, in the years that followed, the public and most reviewers accepted uncritically the Hollywood version of their own character, geography, and history. As we have seen even the RCMP liked *Rose Marie* and the newspaper reviewers could not contain themselves when it came to searching for superlatives to praise *North West Mounted Police.*

Why? I think there are several reasons. Those of us who were movie addicts in the thirties and forties have to remember that almost everybody accepted pictures uncritically in those days. We didn't go to see a specific picture: we went to "the movies." We went faithfully and regularly, no matter what was playing, and we didn't mind if we arrived in the middle. In the dark Depression days and in the war and even the postwar years, the movies were the great panacea.

Everybody loved *Rose Marie* when it was first issued because every-body loved Jeanette MacDonald and Nelson Eddy. The idea of a scarlet-coated Mountie carolling his way through the forests in the company of a girl whose brother he is seeking for murder was perfectly acceptable to a nation of moviegoers numbed and dazzled by celluloid make-believe. The joke was only understood years after the event. And everybody loved *North West Mounted Police.* I loved every foot of it: gallons of blood, machine gun rat-tat-tatting, Indian pow-wows, and *our* Mounties, triumphant as always!

While working on this book I screened *The Country Beyond* and realized, about halfway through, that I had seen it long ago at the age of sixteen and forgotten it. Now it all came back – the Vogue Theatre on Yates Street in Victoria, a dark and magic cavern on a Saturday afternoon, and there on the screen was Rochelle Hudson – *Rochelle Hudson!* – in a fabulous fur parka and Paul Kelly in his Mountie suit. It cost a dime and a dime was hard to come by in 1936; it was, in fact, a week's allowance. But sitting alone in the Vogue Theatre, watching the last half of *The Country Beyond* and then the newsreel and the cartoon and the Fitzpatrick

---

*A young and unknown Rita Hayworth appeared in a Victoria-made quota quickie.

travelogue about Samoa and *then* the first half and then the last half again, I counted not the cost.

As for the reviewers, they scarcely existed. In Victoria, where I spent my teens, there weren't any. Movies were big business; the advertisements provided a large and steady source of income for Canadian dailies. When I went to work for a newspaper in 1939 I learned at once that the job of a movie reviewer was to plug the picture, not to pan it. It was not until a decade later, when one or two bolder spirits – such as Clyde Gilmour on The Vancouver Sun – began to buck the system with more honest assessments, that movie criticism in Canada came into its own.

Many reviewers, too, were dazzled by Hollywood and by "production values," were hindered by a basic ignorance of Canadian history and were flattered, as Canadians, when Hollywood deigned to reward the nation with a major movie. How else to explain Herbert Whittaker's review of *Quebec* in The Globe and Mail?

"For those of us (and that means most of us) who have the idea that Canadian history is dull . . . Quebec will provide a pleasant surprise," Whittaker wrote. "For here is an episode of this country's story told with color and excitement, with actual backgrounds to enrich and strengthen the romance."

Was it history? "Well, there you have me," Whittaker admitted. "It is presumably the Papineau rebellion of 1837 which is being used as background but the presentation is that of the popular historical novel. . . . It may be romantic stuff, this Technicolor version of Quebec history but it is fun and it is exciting. . . . We can find something to thrill us in the film called Quebec."[37]

But most reviewers neither burbled nor bled over Hollywood's version of the Canadian past. Like Jack Karr in The Toronto Star, they neither praised nor panned expansively but contented themselves with a straight account of the filmed story. "This is a yarn about the bad old gold-rush days in the Yukon, of claims-jumping and the resultant disregard for human life,"[38] Karr wrote in his review of *The Far Country,* carefully not saying whether or not the bad old days and the disregard for human life were real history or simply the Hollywood version.

"It wasn't like that at all," Oliva Dionne kept saying when he saw himself portrayed on the screen in *The Country Doctor,* but nobody paid any attention. With one notable exception (The Montreal Star), Canadian reviewers praised that movie as enthusiastically as did their British and American counterparts, without any reference to its geographical and cultural gaffes. It *wasn't* like that at all, but nobody really gave a damn.

5: Peace and fishing, billions of pine trees, frozen waste

If there had been no Hollywood, might there have been a home-grown motion picture industry? And if there had been a home-grown industry, would it have projected a more accurate version of Canada to Canadians and to the world?

These are unanswerable questions. We do know that as long as Hollywood made movies about Canada, Canadians made very few movies about themselves. We also know that when Hollywood stopped making movies about Canada, Canadians began to make movies of quite a different kind for the international market – movies such as *Mon Oncle Antoine, Goin' Down the Road, Kamouraska,* and *The Apprenticeship of Duddy Kravitz.* These films spring out of a different kind of Canadian experience, one which has nothing to do with the foreign mythology of the Great Woods. But it is not possible here to suggest a causal relationship between the end of one era and the beginning of another. There are too many complicating factors (such as the Canadian Film Development Corporation).

Hollywood ceased being interested in Canadian subjects because movies changed. The subjects of the films just mentioned became interesting subjects also because movies changed. The movies changed because the audience changed and became fragmented. The backbone of Canadian-subject features was for many years the B picture, and that was killed by television. So was the old-fashioned melodrama, with the Bad Guys easily distinguishable from the Good Guys by speech, mannerisms, and costume.

Hollywood's version of the old west began to change in the 1950's and the Hollywood western reflected this new maturity; but the northerns never changed: the attitudes and the stereotypes were frozen into place in the early silents; the clichés of the twenties were still around in the postwar era. The Canadian myth was never debunked, as the western myth was; it was simply discarded. Except for *The Canadians,* three Walt Disney animal pictures, a soft-core sex movie, *Vixen,* and an excellent film about the Eskimos, *The White Dawn,* Hollywood stopped making movies about Canada after 1960.

Given the theatrical distribution system in Canada and the United States, controlled for most of this period by the major studios, the climate for presenting independently produced Canadian films to the world was certainly unfriendly. The Hollywood film companies weren't interested in helping to fund independent Canadian producers. On the other hand, the old cry that the world market would not accept films with a Canadian setting was so much balderdash. The world market accepted close to six hundred of them over a period of half a century. Some of them could have been vastly superior if they had been made by people with greater knowledge and understanding of the country they were supposed to portray.

I don't think there's much doubt that if Canada had persevered, if the government had insisted that the American film makers use some of their Canadian profits to back Canadian productions, or if we had encouraged a native film industry through public subsidy, the movies coming out of Canada would have matured to become more faithful to the Canadian experience than foreign-made movies. Certainly they could not have been more spurious than the ones Hollywood presented.

But it is fruitless to speculate about what might have been. What we do know is that, for one reason or another, for most of the century this country was blind to the potential of the feature film as a medium of propaganda or education. It was not the National Film Board that gave us our image of ourselves and it was not the National Film Board that gave the rest of the world its image of Canada. It was Hollywood.

The image is still there, as I discovered for myself during the winter of 1969-70 in the course of preparing a nightly interview program for television that took me to various parts of the world. That year I decided to ask some of my better-known guests about their image of Canada and Canadians. Their answers – the answers of literate, well-travelled men and women of above-average intelligence and ability – suggest the extent of Hollywood's influence on the world's view of this country.

Nanette Fabray, American comedienne: "Canada? . . . One vast wonderland of lakes and clear skies and beautiful picturesque small towns that have hanging baskets of flowers on every lamp post, and quaint, lovely old buildings. . . . You don't have smog, you don't have pollution, you don't have any problems. . . ."

Tony Randall, American actor: "I just see billions of pine trees. Am I right?"

Gore Vidal, American novelist: ". . . one thinks of the Queen and cowboys. . . ."

Jack Lemmon, American actor: "Peace and fishing. . . . Peace is being able to get away from the smog, out of the madness, the suicidal drive that makes us all collect like ants in an ant hill. . . . Peace: to be in the woods and to live there where hopefully pollution is not rampant. . . ."

Dyan Cannon, American actress: "My image of Canada? I don't know . . . blinking cold, cold weather . . . [I see] Canadians in a healthy, outdoor way."

237

Ron Moody, British actor: "I think of frozen waste . . . ice, big spaces. I think of tremendous space – freshness. . . . It's not developed yet, is it?"

The Earl of Litchfield, portrait photographer: "I think largely of lakes and I think of trees. . . ."

Arthur Treacher, British actor: "It seems to me you've got to be a pretty virile bloke to live there, don't you?"

Ann Todd, British actress: "You always see Canada with lovely space. I adore space. And *snow.* Snow and dark woods and things against it."

Britt Ekland, European actress: "Mounted police . . . the snow . . . the wilderness and the cold. . . ."

Hermione Gingold, British comedienne: "When I went there I had the image of vast snow everywhere, gorgeous-looking men dressed in furs, riding on sleighs. I got very excited about going. I just saw this wild, virile country – and wolves stalking you and all the rest of it. After I'd been there I found it wasn't like that at all."

Thus did a British musical comedy star, born at the dawn of the motion picture era and exposed for all of her life to the flickering image of a country she had not yet seen, echo the words of Papa Dionne. Like others of her era, her vision of Canada was a confused montage of old plot-lines, scraps of dialogue, screaming advertisements, screen images of snow and pine trees, and marquee posters. How quaint that dialogue seems today; how campy the silent subtitles; how corny the advertising slogans:

THRILL AND THROB AMONG THE SNOW-CLAD MOUNTAINS AND SKIIS AND DOG SLEDS AMONG THE NORTHERN FORESTS, THE HAUNT OF FURRY GAME AND THE TREACHEROUS CHILCOTT INDIAN. . . . "I took an oath when I entered this service. I swore to obey all lawful orders without fear, favour, or affection toward any person." . . . *But who can blame Malloy that the bright eyes of Marie LaFarge had made him forget his quest?* . . . "Looks like war on a big scale, Sir; signal fires are burning and the tribes are gathering from every spot in the West." . . . A MOUNTIE'S ROARING GUNS! A DOG'S VENGEFUL FANGS! . . . *Under the spell of Edith's witchery Annesley throws discretion aside.* . . . "It looks like the whole Cree nation is on the march!". . . NOW . . . AS THE STRANGER WITH A GUN . . . DRIVEN BY RESTLESS LONGINGS, CHALLENGING THE KLONDIKE'S SNOW AND SIN AND GREED. WHERE GOLD WAS THE LURE AND THE FANCIEST WOMAN IN DAWSON HIS FOR THE TAKING! . . . "Some of these thieving Indians can smell liquor for ten miles on a clear night." . . . *and so the rugged spirit of the North locks arms with human kindness.* . . . "The Redcoats have murdered one of my braves and now they must die!" . . . DEATH STRUGGLE WITH THE WOLVES! A FIGHT FOR LIFE AGAINST THE FURY OF FANGS AND CLAWS! . . . "Oh, André, they are feet for a Queen." – "Oui, ma Chérie, that ees who I buy dem for – my Queen." . . . *Never again will Joe La Barge be called the best slugger in Timber Cove.* . . . "W'y all you men want to mak' merry wid me?" . . . THUNDERING TERROR OF THE AVALANCHE! A MOUNTAIN MOVES AND THREATENS TO BURY BEAST AND MEN FOREVER! . . . "The Athabascans won't take this lying down. I wouldn't want to be in your shoes for a minute." . . . *The Far North, where men pit brain and brawn against the cunning of the Silver Fox whose pelts are worth more than their weight in gold.* . . . "Toto, the devil wolf have returned. I weel trap heem." . . . MAD GAMBLE WITH RAGING RAPIDS! A FRAIL CANOE SHOOTS TO THE BRINK OF DESTRUCTION! . . . "White Spirit call all day, all night. Must go!" . . . "My time has come to take the Lone Trail, Joe, and I'm going – Alone." . . . "The Beeg Trapper got me by de t'roat!"

Did we really fall for this hokum? Were we actually glued to our seats when redcoated riders dashed past on the screen? Did we feel a thrill of apprehension when the Blackfoot tied their victims to the stake? Did our eyes mist up when the White Spirit called and the flawed hero hit the Lone Trail and the Beeg Trapper got Akim Tamiroff by the throat? You bet we did. We *all* did. We loved it and the box-office figures prove it. It never occurred to us, or at least not to very many of us, that an entire culture, our own, was being held up to the world to view through a distorted glass. Now it is all over. Hollywood's Canada no longer exists on the silver screen – only on the late, late shows and in the memory boxes of everyone who made their weekly pilgrimage to the movies, in the days before they were called films.

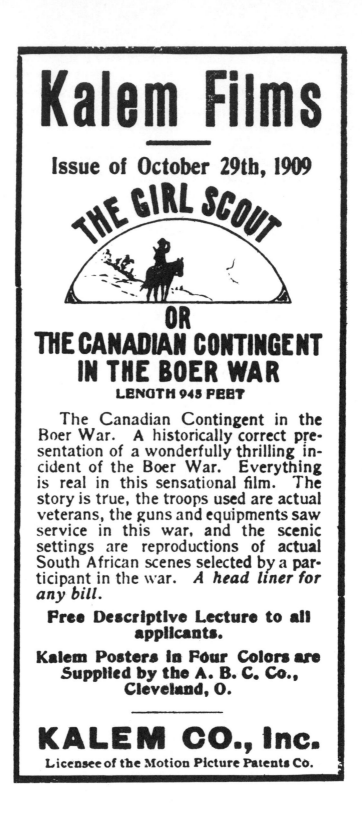

Acknowledgements

In the course of research for this book I was able to search out and view close to one hundred moving pictures made by Hollywood about Canada. Most of the others have disintegrated, been destroyed, or are otherwise unavailable; fortunately I was able in almost every instance to read a plot synopsis. All this was made possible by the indefatigable work of my research assistant, Barbara Sears, a skilled film archivist and movie buff. Without her invaluable contribution this book would not have been possible.

Both Ms. Sears and I want to thank a variety of people who gave so willingly of their time and knowledge, and most especially Stan Horrall, RCMP historian, who opened the force's files to us and cheerfully answered all our questions; and Kevin Smith of Bonded TV sales in Toronto, who searched out dozens of motion pictures from that company's enormous library and projected many of them for us.

We also thank:

In **Ottawa:** Jana Vosikowska, acquisitions co-ordinator, and Peter Morris, curator, of the Canadian Film Institute; and Sam Kula, director, Bill Gallaway, associate director, and Art Middleton, technician, all of the National Film Archive.

In **Toronto:** Ron Tynski, Alan Walker, and Heather McCallum, all of the Metropolitan Toronto Central Library; Gerald Pratley and his staff at the Ontario Film Theatre; and Ann Emin of CBC. Several Toronto distributors helped with the loan of films – Max Sheine of Warner Brothers; Sam Kunitsky of IFD; Linda Mellings and Tony Mitchell of Paramount; Frank Grisbrook at Bellevue Films; Michael Robinson of Astral; and Bill Moreland of Universal.

In **Rochester, New York:** James Card, director, George Pratt, curator, and Marshall Deutelbaum, assistant to the director, all of the Department of Film at George Eastman House.

In **New York City:** Mary Corliss, stills archivist, and Charles Silver, both of the Film Study Centre at the Museum of Modern Art.

In **Los Angeles:** Charles Hopkins of the UCLA Film Archive; Louis George of Metro-Goldwyn-Mayer; and the staff of the Library of the Academy of Motion Picture Arts and Sciences.

In **Washington, DC:** Patrick J. Sheehan, reference librarian of the Motion Picture Section of the Library of Congress; and Tony Slide, assistant archivist of the American Film Institute.

In **London, England:** Clyde Jeavons, deputy curator, Jeremy Boulton, viewings supervisor, John Raisbeck of the stills library, and Pat Coward and Elaine Burrows of the cataloguing department – all at the National Film Archive; and the staff of the British Film Institute's Information Department.

In **Calgary:** Sheilagh S. Jameson, archivist of the Glenbow-Alberta Institute.

In **Winnipeg:** Shirlee Smith, archivist, Hudson's Bay Company.

John Kobal and James Bawden loaned stills from their extensive personal collections. Douglas Wilkinson and George McClellan helped with information about films on which they had worked; and Robert Ramsey, of the Biltmore Hat Company, showed us how the real RCMP hats are made. For their very useful comments on earlier drafts of the book my thanks also to Claire Pratt, Elsa Franklin, and my wife Janet (who, in addition, proofread the manuscript and galleys with her usual eagle eye). Finally my thanks to my secretary, Ennis Armstrong, who typed all the research notes and various drafts with speed and efficiency.

Photo Credits

Abbreviations

AFI American Film Institute
Catalogue of Motion Pictures
Produced in the USA, 1921-1930

BFI British Film Institute

CMPD Canadian Moving Picture Digest

MMA Museum of Modern Art

MPH Motion Picture Herald

MPN Motion Picture News

MPRD Motion Picture Review Digest

MPW Moving Picture World

NFA National Film Archive

PAC Public Archives of Canada

p.33 NFA, London, England
p.34 Academy of Motion Picture Arts &
Sciences, Los Angeles
p.35 J. E. Bawden
p.36 NFA, London
p.37 top – NFA, London
bottom – n.c.
p.38 top – MMA Stills Archive
bottom – NFA, London
p.39 Academy of Motion Picture Arts &
Sciences, Los Angeles
p.40 George Eastman House, Rochester,
New York

p.57 top – George Eastman House
bottom – MMA Stills Archive
p.58 top – MMA Stills Archive
bottom – George Eastman House
p.59 top – J. E. Bawden
bottom – NFA, London
p.60 top – NFA, London
bottom – MMA Stills Archive
p.61 George Eastman House
p.62 top – Academy of Motion Picture
Arts & Sciences, Los Angeles
bottom – NFA, London

p.63 top left – MMA Stills Archive
top right – George Eastman House
bottom – George Eastman House
p.64 left – George Eastman House
right – Academy of Motion Picture
Arts & Sciences, Los Angeles

p.65 George Eastman House
p.66 MMA Stills Archive
p.67 top – NFA, London
bottom – NFA, London
p.68 J. E. Bawden
p.69 top – Academy of Motion Picture
Arts & Sciences, Los Angeles
bottom – NFA, London
p.70 top – George Eastman House
bottom – NFA, London
p.71 top – George Eastman House
bottom – NFA, London
p.72 NFA, London

p.89 MMA, Stills Archive
p.90 NFA, London
p.91 NFA, London
p.92 MMA, Stills Archive
p.93 Kobal Collection
p.94/95 George Eastman House
p.95 MMA, Stills Archive
p.96 J. E. Bawden

p.129 MMA, Stills Archive
p.130 top left – NFA, London
top centre – NFA, London
top right – MMA, Stills Archive
bottom left – Kobal Collection
bottom centre – NFA, London
centre right – NFA, London
bottom right – NFA, London
p.131 top – NFA, London
bottom – Kobal Collection
p.132 top – NFA, London
bottom – NFA, London
centre – NFA, London

p.133   top – National Film Archives, Ottawa
        bottom – NFA, London
p.134   top – Kobal Collection
        bottom – Kobal Collection
p.135   top – George Eastman House
        bottom – George Eastman House
p.136   Kobal Collection

p.153   Kobal Collection
p.154   J. E. Bawden
p.155   n.c.
p.156   top – National Parks of Canada
        bottom – Pierre Berton
p.157   top – National Film Archives, Ottawa
        bottom – © Karsh, Ottawa
p.158   NFA, London
p.159   top – Pierre Berton
        bottom – Pierre Berton
p.160   Royal Canadian Mounted Police

p.193   NFA, London
p.194   Academy of Motion Picture Arts & Sciences, Los Angeles
p.195   Academy of Motion Picture Arts & Sciences, Los Angeles
p.196   NFA, London
p.197   George Eastman House
p.198   NFA, London
p.199   top – NFA, London
        bottom – J. E. Bawden

p.200   top – NFA, London
        bottom – Academy of Motion Picture Arts & Sciences, Los Angeles

p.217   Academy of Motion Picture Arts & Sciences, Los Angeles
p.218   George Eastman House
p.219   top – George Eastman House
        bottom – MMA, Stills Archive
p.220/221   top – J. E. Bawden
p.220   bottom – Kobal Collection
p.221   bottom – MMA, Stills Archive
p.222   top – NFA, London
        bottom – NFA, London
p.223   top – NFA, London
        bottom – J. E. Bawden
p.224   MMA, Stills Archive

Line illustrations

p.23   MPW 3 September 1921
p.24   MPW 20 May 1922
p.28   MPW 3 June 1922
p.43   MPW 24 November 1923
p.49   MPW 15 July 1922
p.50   MPW 3 June 1922 (top)
        MPW 19 July 1924 (bottom)
p.115   MPW 14 October 1922
p.240   MPW 30 October 1909
p.288   MPW 27 September 1913

Appendix

Hollywood Movies About Canada

The following list of films about Canada is as complete as Barbara Sears, my research assistant, and I have been able to make it. Obviously there will be errors of omission. In some cases it has not been possible to view films which, although the title indicates a Canadian setting – may not in fact be set in this country. This is particularly true of movies with the words "Klondike" and "Yukon" in the titles; as the book has pointed out, they are quite often confined to Alaska.

Canadian Content Shorts
1907-1916

1907
An Acadian Elopement (Biograph),
　1 reel.
Chinese Slave Smuggling (Kalem),
　1 reel.

1908
The Discoverers (Vitagraph),
　1 reel.
Evangeline (Kalem), 1 reel.
The Ingrate (Biograph), 1 reel,
　dir: D. W. Griffith.
A Romance in the Fur Country
　(Lubin), 1 reel.
A Woman's Way (Biograph), 1 reel,
　dir: D. W. Griffith.

1909
The Cattle Thieves (Kalem),
　1 reel.
A Cry from the Wilderness
　(Edison), 1 reel.
The Girl Scout (Kalem), 1 reel.
A Priest of the Wilderness
　(Kalem), 1 reel.
Under Northern Skies (Edison),

1910
The Canadian Moonshiners (Kalem),
　1 reel.
The Cowpuncher's Glove (Edison),
　1 reel, dir: J. Searle Dawley.
A Daughter of the Mines (Edison),
　1 reel, dir: J. Searle Dawley.
Fighting the Iroquois in Canada
　(Kalem), 1 reel.
The Girl of the Northern Woods
　(Thanhouser), 1 reel.
Her Indian Mother (Kalem),
　1 reel.
The Indian Girl's Romance
　(Lubin), 1 reel.
In the Great Northwest (Selig),
　1 reel.
Justice in the Far North (Imp),
　1 reel.
A Leap for Life (Kalem), 1 reel.
The Little Station Agent (Edison),
　1 reel, dir: J. Searle Dawley.
More than His Duty (Edison),
　1 reel, dir: J. Searle Dawley.

The Perversity of Fate (Kalem),
1 reel.
Riders of the Plains (Edison),
1 reel, dir: J. Searle Dawley.
The Ship's Husband (Edison),
1 reel, dir: J. Searle Dawley.
The Song That Reached His Heart
(Edison), 1 reel,
dir: J. Searle Dawley.
The Stolen Claim (Edison),
1 reel, dir: J. Searle Dawley.
The Swiss Guide (Edison), 1 reel,
dir: J. Searle Dawley.
True to His Trust, (Kalem), 1 reel.
An Unselfish Love (Edison),
1 reel, dir: J. Searle Dawley.
A Wedding Trip from Montreal
through Canada to Hong Kong
(Edison), 1 reel, dir:
J. Searle Dawley.
White Man's Money, The Indian
Curse (Kalem), 1 reel.

1911
The Empty Shell (Imp), 1 reel.
Evangeline (Selig), 1 reel.
For the Flag (Kalem), 1 reel.
Foraging (Vitagraph), 1 reel.
The Half-Breed's Daughter
(Vitagraph), 1 reel.
In the Arctic Night (Vitagraph),
1 reel.
In the Shadow of the Pines
(Selig), 1 reel.
A Klondike Steal (Vitagraph),
1 reel.
Lost in the Arctic (Selig),
1 reel.
The Modern Dianas (Edison),
1 reel.
Out of the Arctic (Selig),
1 reel.
A Sin Unpardonable (Essanay),
1 reel.
Three Brothers (Vitagraph),
1 reel.

The Trapper's Daughter
(Vitagraph), 1 reel.
The Voyager (Selig), 1 reel.
The Way of the Eskimo (Selig),
1 reel.

1912
The Ace of Spades (Selig),
1 reel.
At the End of the Trail
(Essanay), 1 reel.
The Barrier that was Burned
(Vitagraph), 1 reel.
Blood is Thicker than Water
(Imp), 1 reel.
A Brand for the Burning
(Republic), 1 reel.
A Crucial Test (Selig), 1 reel.
The Darling of the Mounted (Eclair),
1 reel.
In the Aisles of the Wild
(Biograph), 1 reel.
In the Government Service
(Republic), 1 reel.
In the North Woods (Biograph),
1 reel.
In the Northern Woods (Imp),
1 reel.
The Law of the North (Selig),
1 reel.
North of '53 (Reliance), 1 reel.
Northern Hearts (Republic),
1 reel.
One Day (Gem), 1 reel.
The Opium Smugglers (Selig),
1 reel.
The Peculiar Nature of the White
Man's Burden (Selig), 1 reel.
Philip Steele (Reliance), 1 reel.
The Price of a Silver Fox
(Lubin), 1 reel.
The Saint and the Siwash (Selig),
1 reel.
Sergeant Byrne of the NWMP
(Selig), 1 reel.
Silent Jim (Eclair), 2 reels.

248

Sons of the Northwoods (Selig),
    1 reel.
The Stolen Cub (Gaumont), 1 reel.
Two Men (Republic), 1 reel.
The Whiskey Runners (Selig),
    1 reel.

1913
Big Hearted Jim (Eclair),
    2 reels.
Bloodhounds of the North
    (Gold Seal), 2 reels.
Breed of the North (Lubin),
    2 reels.
The Call (Vitagraph), 2 reels.
A Daughter of the Wilderness
    (Edison), 1 reel.
Elise, the Forester's Daughter
    (Edison), 1 reel.
The Final Judgement (Essanay),
    2 reels.
The Good in the Worst of Us
    (Edison), 1 reel.
The Great Unknown (Eclair), 2 reels.
The Greater Call (Eclair), 3 reels.
Hearts of the Northland (Imp),
    1 reel.
Her Nephews from Labrador
    (Thanhouser), 1 reel.
Into the North (Essanay),
    2 reels.
Jacques the Wolf (Eclair),
    2 reels.
The King's Man (Vitagraph),
    1 reel.
The Man Who Dared (Eclair),
    2 reels.
A North Country Romance (Gem),
    1 reel.
Northern Hearts (Selig), 1 reel.
Pierre of the North (Selig),
    1 reel.
The Priest and the Man (Edison),
    1 reel.
A Romance of the Canadian Wilds
    (Kinemacolor), 2 reels.

The Smuggler's Daughter (Lubin),
    1 reel.
The Strength of Men (Vitagraph),
    2 reels.
The Superior Law (Eclair),
    3 reels.
The Trail of the Silver Fox
    (Eclair), 1 reel.
The Translation of a Savage
    (Edison), 1 reel.

1914
Adrift (Eclair), 2 reels.
Aurora of the North (Rex),
    2 reels.
Breed O' the North (Broncho),
    2 reels.
The Devil Fox of the North
    (Eclair), 2 reels.
The First Nugget (Eclair),
    2 reels.
The Going of the White Swan
    (Selig), 2 reels.
The Hero of the North (Sawyer),
    2 reels.
The Honor of the Mounted
    (Gold Seal), 2 reels.
In Defiance of the Law (Selig),
    3 reels.
In the Northland (Lubin), 2 reels.
Jean of the Wilderness
    (Thanhouser), 2 reels.
The Love of Pierre Larose
    (Vitagraph), 1 reel.
The Lure of the Windigo (Selig),
    2 reels.
The Lure of the Yukon
    (Picture Playhouse Film
    Co. Inc.), 3 reels.
North of '53 (Kay Bee), 1 reel.
The Oath of Pierre (American),
    2 reels.
Out of the Night (Domino),
    2 reels, prod: Thomas Ince,
    R. V. Spencer.
A Pack of Cards (Lubin), 2 reels.

The Panther (Broncho), 2 reels.
The Passing of the Beast
    (Nestor), 1 reel.
Pierre of the North (Essanay),
    1 reel.
The Pines of Lory (Edison),
    2 reels.
A Romance of the Northwest
    (Lubin), 1 reel.
The Shanty at Trembling Hill
    (Essanay), 2 reels.
A Tale of the Northwest Mounted
    (Domino), 2 reels.
A Tragedy of the North Woods
    (Domino), 2 reels.
When God Wills (Eclair), 2 reels.
The White Mouse (Selig), 2 reels.
The Wilderness Mail (Selig),
    2 reels.

1915

Alice of Hudson Bay (American),
    2 reels.
Andy of the Royal Mounted
    (Essanay), 1 reel.
A Child of the North (Vitagraph),
    2 reels.
Courage and the Man (Lubin),
    3 reels.
The Cross of Fire (Kay Bee),
    2 reels.
From out of the Big Snows
    (Vitagraph), 3 reels.
Gene of the Northland (Bison),
    2 reels.
The Heart of Sampson (Powers),
    1 reel.
Her Own Blood (Big U), 1 reel.
Hostage of the North (Domino),
    2 reels.
In the Days of Famine
    (Vitagraph), 3 reels.
In the King's Service (Selig),
    2 reels.
In the Land of the Otter
    (Domino), 2 reels.

Jeanne O' the Woods (Victor),
    1 reel.
The Lady of the Snows (Essanay),
    3 reels.
The Man Who Died (Kay Bee),
    1 reel.
The Measure of a Man (Rex), 2 reels.
O'Garry of the Royal Mounted
    (Vitagraph), 3 reels.
The Old Code (Selig), 2 reels.
A Pure Gold Partner (Powers),
    1 reel.
The Trail of the Upper Yukon
    (Rex), 2 reels.
The Trapper's Revenge (Lubin),
    2 reels.
The Wanderers (Vitagraph),
    3 reels.

1916

Beyond the Trail (Bison),
    2 reels.
The Broken Spur (Bison), 2 reels.
The Code of the Mounted
    (Gold Seal), 3 reels.
Darcy of the Northwest Mounted
    (Gold Seal), 3 reels.
Into the Northland (Selig),
    3 reels.
Midwinter Madness (Bison),
    2 reels.
The Primitive Strain (Essanay),
    3 reels.
The Rogue with a Heart
    (Universal), 1 reel.
The Sting of Conscience (Rex),
    3 reels.
The Trail of the Wild Wolf (Imp),
    2 reels.

Canadian Content Features 1914-1930 (Silent)

1914

Call of the North (Jesse Lasky Feature Play Company), dir: Cecil B. DeMille; with Robert Edeson, Theodore Roberts, Winifred Kingston.

God, Man and Devil (Mitten Hall).

An Odyssey of the North (Bosworth), dir: Hobart Bosworth; with Hobart Bosworth, Rhea Haines, Gordon Sackville.

Pierre of the Plains (All Star Feature Corporation), with William Conklin, Joseph Rieder, William Riley Hatch.

The Wolf (Lubin), dir: Barry O'Neil; with Ethel Clayton, George Soule Spencer.

Wolfe, or the Conquest of Quebec (Kalem), dir: Kenean Buel; with Guy Coombes, Helen Lindroth, Alice Hollister.

1915

Bulldogs of the Trail (Interstate Feature Film Company), dir: Kenneth MacDougall; with Kenneth MacDougall, Sydney Shields, Wynne Davidson.

The Darkening Trail (New York Motion Picture Corporation/Thomas H. Ince), dir: William S. Hart; with William S. Hart, Edith Markey, George Fischer.

The Flash of an Emerald (World Film Corporation), dir: Albert Capellani; with Robert Warwick, Dorothy Fairchild, Jean Stuart.

Helene of the North (Famous Players Film Company), dir: J. Searle Dawley; with Marguerite Clark, Conway Tearle, Elliot Dexter.

Jordan is a Hard Road (Fine Art/Triangle), dir: Allan Dwan; with Frank Campeau, Dorothy Gish, Owen Moore.

The Man Trail (Essanay), dir: E. H. Calvert; with Richard C. Travers, June Keith, Thomas McLarnie.

The Right of Way (B. A. Rolfe Company), dir: Jack Noble; with William Faversham, Jane Grey, Edward Brennan.

The Shooting of Dan McGrew (Popular Plays and Players), dir: Herbert Blaché; with Edmund Breese, Dorothy Riggs.

The White Scar (Broadway Universal), dir: Hobart Bosworth; with Hobart Bosworth, Anna Lehr, Norval McGregor.

1916

The End of the Trail (Fox), dir: Oscar Apfel; with William Farnum, Gladys Brockwell, Eleanor Crowe.

Fathers of Men (Vitagraph), dir: William Humphrey; with Robert Edeson, William Humphrey, Naomi Childers.

The Fourth Estate (Fox), dir: Frank Powell; with Sam Ryan, Clifford Bruce, Ruth Blair.

God's Country and the Woman (Vitagraph), dir: Rollin S. Sturgeon; with William Duncan, George Holt, Nell Shipman.

The Lure of Heart's Desire (Popular Plays and Players), dir: Francis J. Grandon; with Edmund Breese, Arthur Hoops, John Mahon.

The Place Beyond the Winds (Universal Pictures), dir: Joseph De Grasse; with Jack Mulhall, Dorothy Phillips, Lon Chaney, Joseph De Grasse.

The Primal Lure (Triangle),
    dir: Reginald Barker; with
    William S. Hart, Margery Wilson,
    Robert McKim.
The Snowbird (B.A. Rolfe Photoplays
    Incorporated), dir: Edwin
    Carewe; with Mabel Taliaferro,
    Edwin Carewe, James Cruze,
    Warren Cook.
The Weakness of Strength (Popular Plays
    and Players), dir: Harry Revier;
    with Edmund Breese,
    Clifford Bruce, Ormi Hawley.

1917
The Best Man (Falcon), dir: Bertram
    Bracken; with William Ehfe,
    Margaret Landis.
The Cook of Canyon Camp (Morosco),
    dir: Donald Crisp; with George
    Beban, Monroe Salisbury,
    Florence Vidor.
The Danger Trail (Selig),
    dir: Frederick A. Thomson;
    with H. B. Warner, Violet
    Heming, W. Lawson Butt.
The Great White Trail (Thunderbird
    Films), dir: Leopold D. Wharton;
    with Thomas Holding, Edgar L.
    Davenport, Doris Kenyon.
The Greater Law (Bluebird Photo-
    plays), dir: Lynn F. Reynolds;
    with Myrtle Gonzalez, Gretchen
    Lederer, Maud Emory.
Her Fighting Chance (A. H. Jacobs
    Photoplays Incorporated), dir:
    Edwin Carewe; with Jane Grey,
    Thomas Holding.
The Jury of Fate (B. A. Rolfe
    Photoplays Incorporated), dir:
    Tod Browning; with Mabel
    Taliaferro, William Sherwood,
    Frank Fisher Bennett.
The Land of Long Shadows (Essanay),
    dir: W. S. Van Dyke; with Jack

Gardner, Ruth King, C. J. Lionel,
    Carl Stockdale.
Land of Promise (Famous Players Film
    Company), dir: Joseph
    Kaufman; with Billie Burke,
    Thomas Meighan.
The Law of the North (Edison), dir:
    Edward H. Griffith; with Charles
    Sutton, Pat O'Malley, Richard
    Tucker, Sally Crute.
The Long Trail (Famous Players Film
    Company), dir: Howard Hansel;
    with Lou Tellegan, Mary Fuller,
    Winifred Allen, Sidney Bracy.
A Man's Law (Overland Film
    Company), dir: Harry La Daven-
    port; with Irvin Cummings,
    Ruth Sinclair, Arthur
    Morrison.
North of '53 (Fox), dir: Richard
    Stanton; with Dustin Farnum,
    Winifred Kingston, William
    Conklin.
Open Places (Essanay), dir: W. S. Van
    Dyke; with Jack Gardner, Ruth
    King, Carl Stockdale.
The Savage (Bluebird), dir: Rupert
    Julian; with Ruth Clifford,
    Colleen Moore, Monroe
    Salisbury.
The Silent Lie (Fox), dir: Raoul Walsh;
    with Miriam Cooper, Ralph
    Lewis, Charles Clary, Monroe
    Salisbury.
Stranded in Arcady (Pathé), dir: Frank
    Crane; with Mrs. Vernon Castle,
    Elliott Dexter.
Tides of Fate (World Film Corpora-
    tion), dir: Marshall Farnum;
    with Alexandra Carlisle,
    Frank Holland, William A. Sheer.
Until They Get Me (Triangle), dir:
    Frank Borzage; with Pauline
    Starke, Joe King, Jack Curtis.
Wild Sumac (Triangle), dir: William

V. Mong; with Margery Wilson, Edwin J. Brady, Frank Brownlee.

1918

Ace High (Fox), dir: Lynn Reynolds; with Tom Mix, Kathleen Connors, Lawrence Peyton, Colin Chase.

Baree, Son of Kazan (Vitagraph), dir: Paul Scardon; with Nell Shipman, Alfred Whitman, Al Garcia.

Beyond the Shadows (Triangle), dir: J. W. McLaughlin; with William Desmond, Graham Pette, Ed Brady, Hugh Sutherland.

Blue Blazes Rawden (Artcraft/William S. Hart Productions Incorporated), dir: William S. Hart and Thomas Ince; with William S. Hart, Maud George, Gertrude Claire, Hart Hoxie.

Closin' In (Triangle), dir: J. W. McLaughlin; with William Desmond, Maud Wayne, George Pearce, Darrell Foss.

The Heart of Humanity (Jewel), dir: Allen Holubar; with Dorothy Phillips, Robert Anderson, Erich von Stroheim.

Heart of the Wilds (Artcraft), dir: Marshall Neilan; with Elsie Ferguson, Joseph Smiley, Matt Moore, Escamilio Fernandez.

Hugon, the Mighty (Bluebird), dir: Rollin S. Sturgeon; with Monroe Salisbury, Margery Bennet, Antrim Short.

Jules of the Strongheart (Jesse Lasky Feature Play Company), dir: Donald Crisp; with George Beban, Helen Eddy, Raymond Hatton, Charles Ogle.

The Law of the Great Northwest (Triangle), dir: Raymond Wells; with Will Jefferies, Eugene Corey, William Dyer, Louis Durham.

The Law of the North (Thomas H. Ince Corporation), dir: Irvin V. Willat; with Charles Ray, Doris Lee, Robert McKim, Gloria Hope.

Nine-Tenths of the Law (Mitchell Lewis), dir: Reaves Eason; with Mitchell Lewis, Jimsey Maye, Reaves Eason, Julius Frankenburg.

Nobody's Wife (Universal Pictures), dir: E. Le Saint; with Hart Hoxie, Alfred Allen, Betty Schade, Louise Lovely.

Prisoner of the Pines (Jesse D. Hampton), dir: Ernest C. Warde; with J. Warren Kerrigan, Lois Wilson, Walter Perry.

The Silent Woman (Metro), dir: Herbert Blaché; with Edith Storey, Frank Mills, Joseph Kilgour.

That Devil, Bateese (Bluebird), dir: William Wolbert; with Monroe Salisbury, Ada Gleason, Lamar Johnstone, Lon Chaney.

Tyrant Fear (Thomas H. Ince Corporation), dir: R. William Neill; with Dorothy Dalton, Thurston Hall, Melbourne MacDowell.

A Woman of Redemption (World Pictures Corporation), dir: Travers Vale; with June Elvidge, Charles H. Martin, John Bowers.

1919

Anne of Green Gables (Realart Pictures Incorporated), dir: William D. Taylor; with Mary Miles Minter, Frederick Burton, Marcia Harris.

The Blinding Trail (Universal
    Pictures), dir: Paul Powell; with
    Monroe Salisbury, Claire
    Anderson, Helen Eddy.
The Clouded Name (World Pictures
    Corporation), dir: Caryl S.
    Fleming; with John Lowell,
    Edgar Keller, Corinne Uzzell,
    Charles Edwards.
Code of the Yukon (Select Pictures
    Corporation), dir: Bertram
    Bracken; with Mitchell Lewis,
    Tom Santschi, Arthur Morrison.
The Confession (Heritage Films),
    dir: Walter Griffin; with Henry
    B. Walthall.
The Devil's Trail (World Pictures
    Corporation), dir: Stuart Paton;
    with Betty Compson, George
    Larkin, William Quinn.
Evangeline (Fox), dir: Raoul Walsh;
    with Miriam Cooper, Albert
    Roscoe.
Forest Rivals (World Pictures
    Corporation), dir: Harry O.
    Hoyt; with Dorothy Green,
    Arthur Ashley, Jack Drumier.
Jacques of the Silver North (Select
    Pictures Corporation), dir:
    Marvel MacGregor; with
    Mitchell Lewis, Fritzi Brunette,
    Capt. C. A. Van Auker.
The Last of His People (Select Pictures
    Corporation), dir: Robert North
    Bradbury; with Mitchell Lewis,
    Harry Lonsdale, Yvette Mitchell.
The Man in the Moonlight (Universal
    Pictures), dir: Paul Powell; with
    Monroe Salisbury, William
    Stowell, Alfred Allen.
The Mints of Hell (Robertson Cole),
    dir: Park Frame; with William
    Desmond, Ed Jobson, Charles
    French.
Paid in Advance (Universal-Jewel),
    dir: Allen Holubar; with Dorothy
    Phillips, Joseph Girard,
    Lon Chaney.
Rose of the West (Fox), dir: Harry
    Millarde; with Madlaine
    Traverse, Frank Leigh, Beatrice
    La Plante.
The Wilderness Trail (Fox), dir:
    Edward J. Le Saint; with Tom
    Mix, Colleen Moore, Sid Jordan,
    Frank Clark.
The Wolf (Vitagraph), dir: James
    Young; with Earle Williams,
    Brinsley Shaw, George Nichols,
    Jane Novak.

1920
Behold My Wife (Famous
    Players-Lasky Corporation),
    dir: George Melford; with Mabel
    Julienne Scott, Milton Sills,
    Ann Forest.
The Challenge of the Law (Fox), dir:
    Scott Dunlap; with William
    Russell, Helen Ferguson, Arthur
    Morrison.
The Courage of Marge O'Doone
    (Vitagraph), dir: David Smith;
    with Pauline Starke, Niles Welch,
    George Stanley, Jack Curtis.
The Cyclone (Fox), dir: Cliff Smith;
    with Tom Mix, Colleen Moore,
    Henry Herbert, William
    Ellingford.
Isobel, or The Trail's End (George H.
    Davis), dir: Edwin Carewe; with
    House Peters, Jane Novak,
    Edward Pell, Tom Wilson.
King Spruce (Mitchell Lewis), dir: Roy
    Clements; with Mitchell Lewis,
    Melbourne MacDowell, Mignon
    Anderson.
The Law of the Yukon (Mayflower
    Photoplay Corporation), dir:
    Charles Miller; with Edward

254

Earle, Joseph Smiley, Nancy
Deever, Tom Velmar.

Nomads of the North (James Oliver
Curwood Productions),
dir: David M. Hartford; with
Betty Blythe, Lon Chaney,
Lewis Stone.

The One Way Trail (Republic),
dir: Fred Kelsey; with Edythe
Sterling, Gordon Sackville,
Jack Connelly.

Out of the Snows (Selznick Pictures),
dir: Ralph Ince; with Ralph Ince,
Zena Keefe, Patrick Hartigan,
Gladys Coburn.

The Right of Way (Metro),
dir: Jack Dillon; with Bert Lytell,
H. Gibson Cowland, Laetrice Joy.

River's End (Marshall Neilan);
dir: Marshall Neilan; with Lewis
Stone, Jane Novak, Yama Mata,
Marjorie Daw.

The Sin That Was His (Selznick
Pictures), dir: Hobart Henley;
with William Faversham, Lucy
Cotton, Pedro de Cordoba.

Under Northern Lights (Universal
Pictures), dir: Jacques Jaccard;
with William Buckley, Leonard
Chapham, Virginia Faire.

The Valley of Doubt (Selznick Pictures),
dir: Burton George; with
Thurston Hall, Arline Pretty,
Anna Lehr, William Davidson.

1921

The Barbarian (Monroe Salisbury),
dir: Donald Crisp; with Monroe
Salisbury, George Burrell,
Barney Sherry.

Big Game (Metro Pictures),
dir: Dallas M. Fitzgerald; with
May Allison, Forrest Stanley,
Edward Cecil.

Bring Him In (Vitagraph), dir: Earle

Williams; with Earle Williams,
Fritzi Ridgeway, Elmer Dewey.

The Broken Spur (Ben Wilson
Productions), dir: Ben Wilson;
with Jack Hoxie, Evelyn Nelson,
Jim Welch.

The Call of the North (Famous
Players-Lasky Corporation),
dir: Joseph Henabery; with Jack
Holt, Madge Bellamy, Noah
Beery, Francis McDonald.

Conceit (Selznick Pictures),
dir: Burton George; with
William D. Davidson, Hedda
Hopper, Charles Gerard.

Flower of the North (Vitagraph),
dir: David Smith; with Henry B.
Walthall, Pauline Starke, Harry
Northrup.

Get Your Man (Fox), dir: George W.
Hill; with Buck Jones, William
Lawrence, Beatrice Burnham.

The Girl from God's Country (Nell
Shipman Productions), dir: Nell
Shipman, Bert Van Tuyle; with
Nell Shipman, Edward Burns,
Al Filson.

Go Get Him (Western Feature
Productions), with William
Fairbanks.

God's Country and the Law (Pine Tree
Pictures), dir: Sidney Olcott;
with Fred C. Jones, Gladys Leslie,
William H. Tooker.

The Golden Snare (David Hartford
Productions), dir: David M.
Hartford; with Lewis Stone,
Wallace Beery, Melbourne
MacDowell.

The Heart of the North (Quality Film
Productions), dir: Harry Revier;
with Roy Stewart, George
Morrell, Harry von Meter,
Roy Justi.

The Idol of the North (Famous

Players-Lasky Corporation),
dir: R. William Neill; with
Dorothy Dalton, Edwin August,
E. J. Ratcliffe.

Kazan (Col. William N. Selig),
dir: Bertram Bracken; with Jane
Novak, Ben Deeley, William Ryno,
Benjamin Haggerty.

Life's Greatest Question (Quality Film
Productions), dir: Harry Revier;
with Roy Stewart, Louise Lovely,
Harry von Meter.

Lying Lips (Thomas H. Ince
Productions), dir: John Griffith
Wray; with House Peters,
Florence Vidor, Joseph Kilgour.

The Magnificent Brute (Universal),
dir: Robert Thornby; with
Frank Mayo, Dorothy Devore,
Percy Challenger, Alberta Lee.

The Man Trackers (Universal),
dir: Edward Kull; with George
Larkin, Josephine Hill, Al Smith,
Barney Furey.

The Man Worthwhile (Romaine
Fielding Productions),
dir: Romaine Fielding; with
Joan Arliss, Lawrence Johnson,
Eugene Acker,
Margaret Seddon.

O'Malley of the Mounted (William S.
Hart Company), dir: Lambert
Hillyer; with William S. Hart, Eva
Novak, Leo Willis.

Playthings of Destiny (Anita Stewart
Productions), dir: Edwin Carewe;
with Anita Stewart, Herbert
Rawlinson, Walter McGrail.

The Raiders (William N. Selig
Productions), dir: Nate Watt; with
Franklyn Farnum, Bud Osborne,
Vester Pegg, Claire Windsor.

The Recoil (Milburn Morante), with
George Chesebro, Evelyn Nelson,
Virginia Morante.

Silent Years (R-C Pictures),

dir: Louis J. Gasnier; with
Rose Dione, Tully Marshall,
George McDaniel.

The Sky Pilot (Cathrine Curtis
Corporation), dir: King Vidor;
with John Bowers, Colleen
Moore, David Butler.

Skyfire (Pinnacle), dir: Neal Hart;
with Artie Ortego, Leo Bates,
Neal Hart.

Snowblind (Goldwyn Pictures),
dir: Reginald Barker; with
Russell Simpson, Mary Alden,
Cullen Landis.

Tangled Trails (Neal Hart Produc-
tions), dir: Charles Bartlett; with
Neal Hart, Violet Palmer, Gladys
Hampton, Jean Bary.

A Wise Fool (Famous Players-Lasky
Corporation), dir: George
Melford; with James Kirkwood,
Alice Hollister, Ann Forrest.

Wolves of the North (Universal),
dir: Norman Dawn;
with Herbert Hayes, Percy
Challenger, Eva Novak.

1922

Blind Circumstances (Morante
Productions), dir: Milburn
Morante: with George Chesebro,
Alfred Hewston, Harry Arras.

The Broken Silence (Pine Tree
Pictures), dir: Del Henderson;
with Zena Keefe, Robert Elliott,
Barney Sherry, Jack Hopkins.

Channing of the Northwest (Selznick
Pictures), dir: Ralph Ince; with
Eugene O'Brien, Gladden
James, Norma Shearer.

Colleen of the Pines (Chester Bennett
Productions), dir: Chester
Bennett; with Jane Novak,
Edward Hearn, Alfred Allen.

Diamond Carlisle (Milburn Morante),
dir: Milburn Morante; with

George Chesebro, Iva Brown,
Virginia Morante.

Duty First (Sanford Productions), dir:
Marcel Perez; with
Pete Morrison.

The Fighting Guide (Vitagraph), dir:
William Duncan, Don Clark;
with William Duncan, Edith
Johnson, Harry Lonsdale.

For Love of Service (Milburn
Morante), with George Chesebro.

Gleam O' Dawn (Fox), dir: Jack
Dillon; with John Gilbert,
Barbara Bedford, James Farley.

Guilty (Bill Miller Productions), with
Bill Miller, May Carson.

The Hate Trail (Milburn Morante),
dir: Milburn Morante; with
George Chesebro, Frank Caffray,
Alfred Hewston.

I Am the Law (Edwin Carewe
Productions), dir: Edwin Carewe;
with Alice Lake, Kenneth Harlan,
Rosemary Theby.

Jan of the Big Snows (Charles M. Seay),
dir: Charles M. Seay; with
Warner Richmond, Louise
Prussing, William Peavy.

The Lane that Had No Turning (Famous
Players-Lasky Corporation),
dir: Victor Fleming; with Agnes
Ayres, Theodore Kosloff,
Mahlon Hamilton.

The Lonely Trail (Credit-Canada
Productions), with Fred K.
Beauvais, Christina McNulty,
W. L. Tremaine.

The Man from Hell's River (Irving
Cummings Productions),
dir: Irving Cummings; with
Irving Cummings, Eva Novak,
Wallace Beery.

The Man She Brought Back (Charles
Miller Productions), dir: Charles
Miller; with Earle Foxe, Doris
Miller, Frank Losee.

Man's Law and God's (Finis Fox
Productions), dir: Finis Fox; with
Jack Livingston, Ethel Shannon,
Kate Anderson.

The Man Who Paid, dir: Oscar Apfel;
with Wilfred Lytell, Norma
Shearer, Florence Rogan.

My Dad (R-C Pictures), dir: Cliff
Smith; with Johnnie Walker,
Wilbur Higby, Mary Redmond.

Out of the Silent North (Universal),
dir: William Worthington; with
Frank Mayo, Barbara Bedford,
Frank Leigh.

Over the Border (Famous
Players-Lasky Corporation),
dir: Penrhyn Stanlaws; with
Betty Compson, Tom Moore,
J. Farrell MacDonald.

The Silent Vow (Vitagraph),
dir: William Duncan; with
William Duncan, Edith Johnson,
Dorothy Dwan.

South of Northern Lights (William
Steiner Productions), dir: Neal
Hart; with Neal Hart, James
McLaughlin, Ben Corbett.

The Storm (Universal),
dir: Reginald Barker; with
Matt Moore, House Peters,
Josef Swickard.

The Trap (Universal),
dir: Robert Thornby; with
Lon Chaney, Alan Hale,
Dagmar Godowsky.

Trooper O'Neil (Fox), dir: Scott
Dunlap; with Charles Jones,
C. R. Wallace, Beatrice
Burnham, Francis McDonald.

Up and Going (Fox), dir: Lynn
Reynolds; with Tom Mix, Eva
Novak, William Conklin.

The Valley of Silent Men (Cosmo-
politan Productions), dir: Frank
Borzage; with Alma Rubens,
Lew Cody, Joseph King.

A Virgin's Sacrifice (Vitagraph), dir: Webster Campbell; with Corinne Griffith, Curtis Cooksey, David Torrence.

White Hell (Charles E. Bartlett Productions), dir: Bernard Feikel; with Richard Travers, Muriel Kingston, J. Thornton Baston.

Wolf Pack (World Film Corporation), dir: William J. Craft; with Joe Moore, Eileen Sedgwick, S. W. Williams.

The Wolf's Fangs (Apfel Productions), dir: Oscar Apfel; with Wilfred Lytell, Nancy Deaver, Manilla Martans.

The Woman Conquers (Preferred Pictures), dir: Tom Forman; with Katherine MacDonald, Bryant Washburn, Mitchell Lewis.

1923

Below the Rio Grande (William Steiner Productions), dir: Neal Hart; with Neal Hart.

Burning Words (Universal Pictures), dir: Stuart Paton; with Roy Stewart, Laura La Plante, Harold Goodwin.

The Call of the Wild (Hal Roach Studios), dir: Fred Jackman; with Jack Mulhall, Walter Long, Sidney D'Albrook, Buck.

Dangerous Trails (Rocky Mountain Productions), dir: Alvin J. Neitz; with Irene Rich, Tully Marshall, Noah Beery.

The Devil's Partner (Iroquois Productions), dir: Caryl S. Fleming; with Norma Shearer, Charles Delaney, Henry Sedley.

The Eternal Struggle (Louis B. Mayer Productions), dir: Reginald Barker; with Renée Adorée, Earle Williams, Barbara La Marr.

The Fighting Strain (William Steiner Productions), dir: Neal Hart; with Neal Hart, Beth Mitchell, William Quinn.

The Grub Stake (Nell Shipman Productions), dir: Bert Van Tuyle; with Nell Shipman, Hugh Thompson, Alfred Allen.

Jacqueline, or Blazing Barriers (Pine Tree Pictures), dir: Dell Henderson; with Marguerite Courtot, Lew Cody, Russell Griffin.

McGuire of the Mounted (Universal Pictures), dir: Richard Stanton; with William Desmond, Louise Lorraine, Willard Louis.

The Man Between (Finis Fox Productions), dir: Finis Fox; with Allan Forest, Edna Murphy, Fred Malatesta.

Man's Size (Fox), dir: Howard M. Mitchell; with William Russell, Alma Bennett, Stanton Heck.

North of Hudson Bay (Fox), dir: John Ford; with Tom Mix, Kathleen Key, Jennie Lee, Frank Campeau.

Shadows of the North (Universal Pictures), dir: Robert F. Hill; with William Desmond, Virginia Brown Faire, Fred Kohler.

Slander the Woman (Allen Holubar Pictures), dir: Allen Holubar; with Dorothy Phillips, Lewis Dayton, Robert Anderson.

The Snow Bride (Famous Players-Lasky Productions), dir: Henry Kolker; with Alice Brady, Maurice B. Flynn, Mario Majeroni.

Soul of the Beast (Thomas H. Ince Corporation), dir: John Griffith Wray; with Madge Bellamy, Cullen Landis, Noah Beery, Oscar.

Tiger Rose (Warner Brothers Pictures), dir: Sidney A.

Franklin; with Lenore Ulric,
Forrest Stanley, Joseph Dowling.

Unseeing Eyes (Cosmopolitan
Productions), dir: E. H. Griffith;
with Lionel Barrymore, Seena
Owen, Louis Wolheim

The Valley of Lost Souls (Iroquois
Productions), dir: Caryl S.
Fleming; with Muriel Kingston,
Victor Sutherland, Anne
Hamilton.

Where the North Begins (Warner
Brothers Pictures), dir: Chester
M. Franklin, with Claire Adams,
Walter McGrail, Part Hartigan,
Rin-Tin-Tin.

1924

Empty Hands (Famous Players-
Lasky Corporation), dir: Victor
Fleming; with Jack Holt, Norma
Shearer, Charles Clary.

For Another Woman (Rayart Pictures),
dir: David Kirkland; with
Kenneth Harlan, Florence
Billings, Henry Sedley.

Getting Her Man (Paul Gerson
Pictures), dir: Tom Gibson;
with Ora Carew, Jay Morley,
Hal Stephens.

The Love Master (Trimble-Murfin
Productions), dir: Laurence
Trimble; with Strongheart,
Lady Julie, Lillian Rich,
Harold Austin.

Love's Wilderness (Corinne Griffith
Productions), dir: Robert Z.
Leonard; with Corinne Griffith,
Holmes E. Herbert, Ian Keith.

Playthings of Desire (Jans Produc-
tions), dir: Burton King; with
Estelle Taylor, Mahlon Hamilton,
Dagmar Godowsky.

The Rejected Woman (Distinctive
Pictures), dir: Albert Parker;
with Alma Rubens, Bela Lugosi,

George MacQuarrie.

The Shooting of Dan McGrew
(S-L Productions), dir: Clarence
Badger; with Barbara La Marr,
Lew Cody, Mae Busch.

The Trail of Vengeance (J. J. Fleming
Productions), dir: Al Ferguson;
with Al Ferguson, Pauline
Curley.

The Wolf Man (Fox), dir: Edmund
Mortimer; with John Gilbert,
Norma Shearer, Alma Francis.

1925

The Ancient Highway (Famous
Players-Lasky Corporation),
dir: Irvin Willat; with Jack Holt,
Billie Dove, Montagu Love,
Stanley Taylor.

Baree, Son of Kazan (Vitagraph), dir:
David Smith; with Anita Stewart,
Donald Keith, Jack Curtis.

The Bloodhound (Independent
Pictures), dir: William James
Craft; with Bob Custer, David
Dunbar, Ralph McCullough.

The Calgary Stampede (Universal
Pictures), dir: Herbert Blaché;
with Hoot Gibson, Virginia
Brown Faire, Clark Comstock.

The Gold Hunters (Guaranteed
Pictures), dir: Paul Hurst; with
David Butler, Hedda Nova,
Mary Carr.

Kivalina of the Ice Lands
(BCR Productions), dir: Earl
Rossman; with Kivalina,
Aguvaluk, Nashulik, Tokatoo.

The Knockout (First National),
dir: Lambert Hillyer; with
Milton Sills, Lorna Duveen,
John Philip Kolb.

The Lure of the Wild (Columbia
Pictures), dir: Frank R. Strayer;
with Jane Novak, Alan Roscoe,
Billie Jean.

North Star (Howard Estabrook Productions), dir: Paul Powell; with Virginia Lee Corbin, Stuart Holmes, Ken Maynard.

Northern Code (Gotham Productions), dir: Leon De La Mothe; with Robert Ellis, Eva Novak, Francis McDonald.

Scarlet and Gold (J. J. Fleming Productions), dir: Frank Grandon; with Al Ferguson, Lucille Du Bois, Frank Granville.

Ship of Souls (Encore Pictures), dir: Charles Miller; with Bert Lytell, Lillian Rich, Gertrude Astor, Earl Metcalf.

Steele of the Royal Mounted (Vitagraph), dir: David Smith; with Bert Lytell, Stuart Holmes, Charlotte Merriam.

The Storm Breaker (Universal Pictures), dir: Edward Sloman; with House Peters, Ruth Clifford, Nina Romano.

Tides of Passion (Vitagraph), dir: J. Stuart Blackton; with Mae Marsh, Ben Hendricks, Laska Winter, Earl Schenck.

Tracked in the Snow Country (Warner Brothers), dir: Herman C. Raymaker; with Rin-Tin-Tin, June Marlowe, David Butler.

When the Door Opened (Fox), dir: Reginald Barker; with Jacqueline Logan, Walter McGrail, Margaret Livingston.

Winds of Chance (First National Pictures), dir: Frank Lloyd; with Anna Q. Nilsson, Ben Lyon, Viola Dana, Hobart Bosworth.

A Woman's Faith (Universal Pictures), dir: Edward Laemmle; with Alma Rubens, Percy Marmont, Jean Hersholt.

1926

The Call of the Klondike (Paul Gerson Pictures), dir: Oscar Apfel; with Gaston Glass, Dorothy Dwan, Earl Metcalfe.

The Canadian (Famous Players-Lasky Corporation), dir: William Beaudine; with Thomas Meighan, Mona Palmer, Wyndham Standing.

Code of the Northwest (Chesterfield Motion Pictures), dir: Frank S. Mattison; with Sandow, Richard Lang, Tom London.

The Country Beyond (Fox), dir: Irving Cummings; with Olive Borden, Ralph Graves, Gertrude Astor.

The Flaming Forest (Cosmopolitan Productions), dir: Reginald Barker; with Antonio Moreno, Renée Adorée, Gardner James.

Forest Havoc (Elbee Pictures), dir: Stuart Paton; with Forrest Stanley, Peggy Montgomery, Martha Mattox.

Glenister of the Mounted (Harry Garson Productions), dir: Harry Garson; with Lefty Flynn, Bess Flowers, Lee Shumway.

A Hero of the Big Snows (Warner Brothers Pictures), dir: Herman C. Raymaker; with Rin-Tin-Tin, Alice Calhoun, Don Alvarado.

Law of the Snow Country (Bud Barsky Corporation), dir: Paul Hurst; with Kenneth McDonald, Jane Thomas, Noble Johnson.

Law or Loyalty, dir: Lawson Harris; with Lawson Harris, Delores Dorian, Robert Walker.

The Lodge in the Wilderness (Tiffany Productions), dir: Henry McCarthy; with Anita Stewart, Edmund Burns, Duane Thompson.

Mantrap (Famous Players-Lasky
Corporation), dir: Victor
Fleming; with Ernest Torrence,
Clara Bow, Eugene Pallette.

Moran of the Mounted (Harry J.
Brown Productions), dir: Harry
J. Brown; with Reed Howes,
Sheldon Lewis, J. P. McGowan.

Phantom of the Forest (Gotham
Productions), dir: Henry
McCarthy; with Betty Francisco,
Eddie Phillips, James Mason.

Prisoners of the Storm (Universal
Pictures), dir. Lynn Reynolds,
with House Peters, Peggy
Montgomery, Walter McGrail.

The Test of Donald Norton (Chadwick
Pictures), dir: B. Reeves Eason;
with George Walsh, Tyrone
Power, Robert Graves.

The Wolf Hunters (Ben Wilson
Productions), dir: Stuart Paton;
with Robert McKim, Virginia
Browne Faire, Alan Roscoe.

1927

Back to God's Country (Universal
Pictures), dir: Irvin Willat; with
Renée Adorée, Robert Frazer,
Walter Long, Mitchell Lewis.

Border Blackbirds (Leo Maloney
Productions), dir: Leo Maloney;
with Leo Maloney, Eugenia
Gilbert, Nelson McDowell.

The Coward (R-C Pictures), dir: Alfred
Raboch; with Warner Baxter,
Sharon Lynn, Freeman Wood.

The Devil's Masterpiece (Sanford F.
Arnold), dir: John P. McCarthy;
with Virginia Browne Faire,
Gordon Brinkley, Fred Kohler.

Pajamas (Fox), dir: J. G. Blystone;
with Olive Borden, John J. Clark,
Lawrence Gray.

Ranger of the North (FBO Pictures),

dir: Jerome Storm; with Ranger,
Hugh Trevor, Lina Basquette,
Bernard Siegel.

Rubber Heels (Paramount Famous
Lasky Corporation), dir: Victor
Heerman; with Ed Wynn,
Chester Conklin, Thelma Todd.

Where the North Holds Sway (Morris R.
Schlank), dir: Bennett Cohn;
with Jack Perrin.

Winners of the Wilderness (Metro-
Goldwyn-Mayer), dir: W. S. Van
Dyke; with Tim McCoy, Joan
Crawford, Edward Connelly.

Woman's Law (Dallas M. Fitzgerald
Productions), dir: Dallas M.
Fitzgerald; with Pat O'Malley,
Lillian Rich, Ernest Wood.

1928

The Code of the Scarlet (Charles R.
Rogers Productions), dir: Harry
J. Brown; with Ken Maynard,
Gladys McConnell, Ed Brady,
J. P. McGowan.

Danger Patrol (Duke Worne Produc-
tions), dir: Duke Worne; with
William Russell, Virginia Browne
Faire, Wheeler Oakman.

Dog Justice (FBO Pictures), dir: Jerome
Storm; with Ranger, Edward
Hearn, Nita Martan, James
Welsh.

Fashion Madness (Columbia Pictures),
dir: Louis J. Gasnier; with Claire
Windsor, Reed Howes, Laska
Winters.

Hoofbeats of Vengeance (Universal
Pictures), dir: Henry MacRae;
with Rex, Jack Perrin, Helen
Foster, Al Ferguson.

The Land of the Silver Fox (Warner
Brothers), dir: Ray Enright; with
Rin-Tin-Tin, Leila Hyams, John
Miljan, Carroll Nye.

Law of the Mounted (El Dorado
    Productions), dir: J. P.
    McGowan; with Bob Custer,
    J. P. McGowan, Sally Winters.
The Law's Lash (Fred J. McConnell
    Productions), dir: Noel Mason
    Smith; with Klondike, Robert
    Ellis, Mary Mayberry, Jack
    Marsh.
The Little Wild Girl (Hercules Film
    Productions), dir: Frank S.
    Mattison; with Lila Lee, Cullen
    Landis, Frank Merrill.
The Lone Patrol (Major Pictures), with
    William Bailey, Jean Dolores.
The Old Code (Morris R. Schlank
    Productions), dir: Benjamin
    Franklin Wilson; with Walter
    McGrail, Lillian Rich,
    Cliff Lyons.
Red Riders of Canada (FBO Pictures),
    dir: Robert De Lacy; with Patsy
    Ruth Miller, Charles Byer, Harry
    Woods.
Rose-Marie (Metro-Goldwyn-Mayer),
    dir: Lucien Hubbard; with Joan
    Crawford, James Murray, House
    Peters, Creighton Hale.

1929
Evangeline (Edwin Carewe Produc-
    tions-Feature Productions),
    dir: Edwin Carewe; with
    Dolores del Rio, Roland Drew,
    Alec B. Francis.
The One Man Dog (FBO Pictures),
    dir: Leon D'Usseau; with
    Ranger, Sam Nelson, Edward
    Hearne, Virginia Bradford.
Smoke Bellew (Big 4 Productions),
    dir: Scott Dunlap; with Conway
    Tearle, Barbara Bedford, Mark
    Hamilton.
The Trail of '98
    (Metro-Goldwyn-Mayer),

dir: Clarence Brown; with
    Dolores del Rio, Ralph Forbes,
    Karl Dane.
The Wilderness (Fox),
    dir: J. P. McGowan; with Lotus
    Thompson, Shannon Day,
    William Cody.
Wolf Song (Paramount Famous Lasky
    Corporation), dir: Victor
    Fleming; with Gary Cooper,
    Lupe Velez, Louis Wolheim.
The Yellowback (FBO Pictures), dir:
    Jerome Storm; with Tom Moore,
    Irma Harrison, Tom Santschi.

1930
Brought to Justice, dir: Jerome Storm;
    with Tom Moore, Irma
    Harrison, Lionel Belmore.
O'Malley Rides Alone, dir: J. P.
    McGowan; with Bob Custer,
    Phyllis Bainbridge, Martin Cichy.

Canadian Content Features Made by Hollywood 1929-1974 (Sound)

1929

Frozen Justice (Fox), dir: Allan Dwan; with Lenore Ulric, Robert Frazer, Louis Wolheim.

Tiger Rose (Warner Brothers Pictures), dir: George Fitzmaurice; with Monte Blue, Lupe Velez, H. B. Warner, Tully Marshall.

1930

The Dancers (Fox), dir: Chandler Sprague; with Lois Moran, Phillips Holmes, Walter Byron, Mae Clarke.

Dangerous Nan McGrew (Paramount Publix Corporation), dir: Malcolm St. Clair; with Helen Kane, Victor Moore, James Hall.

Men of the North (Metro-Goldwyn-Mayer), dir: Hal Roach; with Gilbert Roland, Barbara Leonard, Arnold Korff.

River's End (Warner Brothers Pictures), dir: Michael Curtiz; with Charles Bickford, Evelyn Kapp, J. Farrell MacDonald.

Rough Romance (Fox), dir: A. F. Erickson; with George O'Brien, Helen Chandler, Antonio Moreno.

The Silent Enemy (Burden-Chanler Productions), with Chief Yellow Robe, Chief Long Lance, Chief Akawanush.

The Storm (Universal Pictures), dir: William Wyler; with Lupe Velez, Paul Cavanagh, William Boyd.

Under Suspicion (Fox), dir: A. F. Erickson; with J. Harold Murray, Lois Moran, J. N. Kerrigan.

1931

Mounted Fury (Sono Art World Wide), dir: Stuart Paton; with John Bowers, Blanche Mehaffey, Robert Ellis.

Riders of the North (Syndicate), dir: J. P. McGowan; with Bob Custer, Blanche Mehaffey, Eddie Dunn.

The Right of Way (First National), dir: Frank Lloyd; with Conrad Nagel, Loretta Young, Fred Kohler.

The Viking (Newfoundland-Labrador Film Company Incorporated), dir: George Melford; with Louise Huntington, Charles Starrett, Capt. Bob Bartlett.

1932

The Drifter (Willis Kent), dir: William O'Connor; with William Farnum, Noah Beery, Phyllis Barrington.

Honor of the Mounted (Monogram), dir: Harry Frazer; with Stanley Brystone, Francis McDonald, G. D. Wood.

Igloo (Universal Pictures), dir: Ewing Scott; with Chee-ak, Kyatuk, Toyuk, Lanak.

Klondike (Monogram), dir: Phil Rosen; with Lyle Talbot, Capt. Frank Hawks, Thelma Todd.

Law of the North (Monogram), dir: Harry Frazer; with Nadine Dore, W. L. Thorne, A. St. John.

McKenna of the Mounted (Columbia), dir: D. Ross Lederman; with James Flavin, Walter McGrail, Ralph Lewis.

Mason of the Mounted (Monogram), dir: Harry Frazer; with Nancy Drexel, Jack Carlyle, LeRoy Mason.

1933

Eskimo/Mala the Magnificent
(Metro-Goldwyn-Mayer),
dir: W. S. Van Dyke; with an all
native cast.

Trailing North (Monogram), dir: J. P.
McCarthy; with Doris Hill,
Arthur Rankin, George Hayes,
Fred Burns.

1934

Anne of Green Gables (RKO),
dir: George Nicholls Jr.; with
Anne Shirley, Tom Brown,
O. P. Heggie.

1935

Call of the Wild (20th Century/Darryl
Zanuck), dir: William Wellman;
with Clark Gable, Loretta Young,
Jack Oakie.

The Fighting Trooper (Ambassador),
dir: Ray Taylor; with Kermit
Maynard, Barbara Worth,
LeRoy Mason.

Jalna (RKO), dir: John Cromwell;
with Kay Johnson, Ian Hunter,
C. Aubrey Smith.

Northern Frontier (Ambassador), dir:
Sam Newfield; with Kermit
Maynard, Eleanor Hunt, Russell
Hopton.

Red Blood of Courage (Ambassador),
dir: Jack English; with Kermit
Maynard, Ann Sheridan,
Reginald Barlow.

Trails of the Wild (Ambassador), dir:
Sam Newfield; with Kermit
Maynard, Billie Seward, Fuzzy
Knight.

Wilderness Mail (Ambassador), dir:
Forrest Sheldon; with Kermit
Maynard, Doris Brook.

1936

Code of the Mounted (Guaranteed),
dir: Sam Newfield; with Kermit
Maynard, Lilian Miles.

The Country Beyond (20th Century-Fox),
dir: Eugene Ford; with Rochelle
Hudson, Paul Kelly, Robert
Kent.

The Country Doctor (20th
Century-Fox), dir: Henry King;
with Jean Hersholt, June Lang,
Slim Summerville, Dorothy
Peterson.

I Conquer the Sea (Academy), dir:
Victor Halperin; with Steffi
Duna, Stanley Morner, Douglas
Walton.

King of the Royal Mounted (20th
Century-Fox), dir: Howard
Bretherton; with Robert Kent,
Rosalind Keith, Alan Dinehart.

Klondike Annie (Paramount), dir:
Raoul Walsh; with Mae West,
Victor McLaglen, Phillip Reed.

O'Malley of the Mounted (20th
Century-Fox), dir: David
Howard; with George O'Brien,
Irene Ware, Stanley Fields.

Petticoat Fever
(Metro-Goldwyn-Mayer), dir:
George Fitzmaurice; with Robert
Montgomery, Myrna Loy,
Reginald Owen.

Reunion (20th Century-Fox),
dir: Norman Taurog; with the
Dionne Quintuplets, Jean
Hersholt, Rochelle Hudson.

Rose Marie (Metro-Goldwyn-Mayer),
dir: W. S. Van Dyke; with
Jeanette MacDonald, Nelson
Eddy, James Stewart.

Trapped (Republic), dir: Bernard B.
Ray; with Grant Withers, Monte
Blue, Rin-Tin-Tin, Jr.

1937

God's Country and the Man
(Monogram), dir: R. N.
Bradbury; with Tom Keene,
Betty Compson, Charlotte
Henry.

God's Country and the Woman (Warner
Brothers), dir: William Keighley;
with George Brent, Beverly
Roberts, Barton MacLane.

Phantom Patrol (Ambassador), dir:
Charles Hutchison; with Kermit
Maynard, Joan Barclay, Harry
Worth.

Renfrew of the Royal Mounted (Grand
National), dir: Al Herman; with
James Newill, Caroll Hughes,
William Royle.

Wildcat Trooper (Syndicate), dir:
Elmer Clifton; with Kermit
Maynard, Hobart Bosworth,
Fuzzy Knight.

1938

Clipped Wings (National), dir: Stuart
Paton; with Lloyd Hughes,
Rosalind Keith, William Janney.

Five of a Kind (20th Century-Fox),
dir: Herbert I. Leeds; with Jean
Hersholt, Claire Trevor, Cesar
Romero, the Dionne
Quintuplets.

Heart of the North (Warner Brothers),
dir: Lewis Seiler; with Dick
Foran, Gloria Dickson, Gale
Page, Allen Jenkins.

On the Great White Trail (Renfrew
series: Grand National), dir: Al
Herman; with James Newill,
Terry Walker, Robert Fraser.

1939

Crashing Thru (Renfrew series:
Monogram), dir: Elmer Clifton;
with James Newill, Warren Hull,
Jean Carmen.

Fighting Mad (Renfrew series:
Criterion Pictures for
Monogram), dir: Sam Newfield;
with James Newill, Sally Blanc.

North of the Yukon (Columbia), dir:
Sam Nelson; with Charles
Starrett, Linda Winters, Bob
Nolan.

Outpost of the Mounties (Columbia),
dir: C. C. Coleman; with Charles
Starrett, Iris Meredith, Stanley
Brown.

Susannah of the Mounties (20th
Century-Fox), dir: William A.
Seiter; with Shirley Temple,
Randolph Scott, Margaret
Lockwood.

Wolf Call (Monogram), dir; George
Waggner; with John Carroll,
Movita, Peter George Lynn.

1940

Anne of Windy Poplars (RKO), dir: Jack
Hively; with Anne Shirley, James
Ellison, Henry Travers.

Danger Ahead (Renfrew series:
Monogram), dir: Ralph Staub;
with James Newill, Dorothy
Kent, Guy Usher.

The Girl from God's Country (Warner
Brothers), dir: Herbert Mason;
with Clifford Evans, Leonora
Corbett.

Hudson's Bay (20th Century-Fox),
dir: Irving Pichel; with Paul
Muni, Gene Tierney, Laird
Cregar.

Man from Montreal (Universal
Pictures), dir: Christy Cabanne;
with Richard Arlen, Andy
Devine, Kay Sutton.

Morton of the Mounted (Stage and

Screen Productions), dir: Robert
Emmet; with John Preston,
William Desmond.

Murder on the Yukon (Renfrew series:
Criterion Pictures for
Monogram), dir: Louis Gasnier;
with James Newill, Polly Ann
Young, Dave O'Brien.

North West Mounted Police
(Paramount), dir: Cecil B.
DeMille; with Gary Cooper,
Madeleine Carroll, Paulette
Goddard, Preston Foster, Robert
Preston, George Bancroft, Akim
Tamiroff, Lynne Overman.

Queen of the Yukon (Monogram), dir:
Phil Rosen; with Charles
Bickford, Irene Rich, Melvin
Long.

River's End (Warner Brothers), dir:
Ray Enright; with Dennis
Morgan, George Tobias,
Elizabeth Earl.

Sky Bandits (Criterion Pictures for
Monogram), dir: Ralph Staub;
with James Newill, Louise
Stanley, Dewey Robinson.

Untamed (Paramount), dir: George
Archainbaud, with Ray Milland,
Patricia Morison, Akim
Tamiroff.

Yukon Flight (Criterion Pictures for
Monogram), dir: Ralph Staub;
with James Newill, Dave O'Brien.

1941

Mutiny in the Arctic (Universal
Pictures), dir: John Rawlins; with
Richard Arlen, Andy Devine,
Anne Nagel.

Niagara Falls (Hal Roach Studios),
dir: Gordon Douglas; with
Marjorie Woodworth, Tom
Brown, Zasu Pitts.

Royal Mounted Patrol (Columbia), dir:

Lambert Hillyer; with Charles
Starrett, Russell Hayden, Lloyd
Bridges.

Sign of the Wolf (Monogram), dir:
Howard Bretherton; with
Michael Whalen, Grace Bradley,
Darryl Hickman.

1942

Captains of the Clouds (Warner
Brothers), dir: Michael Curtiz;
with James Cagney, Dennis
Morgan, Brenda Marshall, Air
Marshall W. A. Bishop (as
himself).

Klondike Fury (Monogram), dir:
William K. Howard; with
Edmund Lowe, Leslie Fairbanks,
Bill Henry.

North to the Klondike (Universal
Pictures), dir: Erle C. Kenton;
with Brod Crawford, Evelyn
Ankers, Andy Devine, Lon
Chaney.

Northwest Rangers
(Metro-Goldwyn-Mayer), dir:
Joe Newman; with James Craig,
William Lundigan, Patricia
Dane.

Northwest Trail (Action Pictures
Incorporated), dir: Derwin
Abrahams; with John Litel, Joan
Woodbury, Bob Steele, Madge
Bellamy.

Pierre of the Plains
(Metro-Goldwyn-Mayer), dir:
George B. Seitz; with John
Carroll, Ruth Hussey, Bruce
Cabot.

Springtime in the Rockies
(20th Century-Fox), dir:
Irving Cummings; with
Betty Grable, John Payne,
Carmen Miranda.

Unseen Enemy (Universal Pictures), dir: John Rawlins; with Don Terry, Irene Hervey.

1943

Corvett K-225 [released in UK as *The Nelson Touch*] (Universal Pictures), dir: Richard Rosson; with Randolph Scott, Ella Raines, James Brown.

False Clues (Columbia), dir: Lambert Hillyer; with Bill Elliott, Tex Ritter, Frank Mitchell.

Law of the Northwest (Columbia), dir: William Berke, with Charles Starrett, Shirley Patterson, Arthur Hunnicutt.

Northern Pursuit (Warner Brothers), dir: Raoul Walsh; with Errol Flynn, Julie Bishop.

Riders of the Northwest Mounted (Columbia), dir: William Berke; with Russell Hayden, Bob Wills.

1944

Jack London (Samuel Bronston), dir: Alfred Santell; with Michael O'Shea, Susan Hayward.

Klondike Kate Columbia), dir: William Castle; with Ann Savage, Tom Neal.

The Scarlet Claw (Universal Pictures), dir: Roy William Neill; with Basil Rathbone, Nigel Bruce, Gerald Hamer.

1947

Where the North Begins (Screen Guild), dir: Howard Bretherton; with Russell Hayden, Jennifer Holt, Denver Pyle.

1948

The Iron Curtain (20th Century-Fox), dir: William A. Wellman; with Dana Andrews, Gene Tierney, June Havoc.

Johnny Belinda (Warners), dir: Jean Negulesco; with Jane Wyman, Lew Ayres.

'Neath Canadian Skies (Screen Guild), dir: B. Reeves Eason; with Russell Hayden, Inez Cooper, Cliff Nazarro.

North of the Border (Screen Guild), dir: B. Reeves Eason; with Russell Hayden, Lyle Talbot, Inez Cooper.

Northwest Stampede (Eagle-Lion), dir: Albert S. Rogell; with Joan Leslie, James Craig, Jack Oakie.

Trail of the Mounties (Screen Guild), dir: Howard Bretherton; with Russell Hayden, Emmett Lynn, Jennifer Holt.

1949

Canadian Pacific (20th Century-Fox), dir: Edwin L. Marin; with Randolph Scott, Jane Wyatt, J. Carroll Naish, Victor Jory.

Mrs. Mike (Nassour Studio), dir: Louis King; with Dick Powell, Evelyn Keyes, J. M. Kerrigan, Angela Clarke.

Trail of the Yukon (Monogram), dir: William X. Crowley; with Kirby Grant, Chinook, Suzanne Dalbert.

Valley of Hunted Men (Republic), dir: John English; with Bob Steele, Tom Tyler, Jimmie Dodd.

The Wolf Hunters (Monogram), dir: Oscar Boetticher; with Kirby Grant, Jan Clayton, Edward Norris.

1950

Call of the Klondike (Monogram), dir: Frank McDonald; with Kirby Grant, Chinook, Anne Gwynne, Lynne Roberts.

The Cariboo Trail (20th Century-Fox), dir: Edwin L. Marin; with Randolph Scott, George Gabby Hayes, Bill Williams.

North of the Great Divide (Republic), dir: William Witney; with Roy Rogers, Trigger, Penny Edwards, Gordon Jones.

Snow Dog (Monogram), dir: Frank McDonald; with Kirby Grant, Elena Verdugo, Rick Vallin, Milburn Stone.

1951

Gene Autry and the Mounties (Columbia), dir: John English; with Gene Autry, Pat Buttram, Elena Verdugo.

Northwest Territory (Monogram), dir: Frank McDonald; with Kirby Grant, Gloria Saunders, Warren Douglas.

Quebec (Paramount), dir: George Templeton; with John Barrymore, Jr., Corinne Calvet, Barbara Rush.

The 13th Letter (20th Century-Fox), dir: Otto Preminger; with Linda Darnell, Charles Boyer, Michael Rennie.

The Wild North (Metro-Goldwyn-Mayer), dir: Andrew Marton; with Stewart Granger, Wendell Corey, Cyd Charisse.

Yukon Manhunt (Monogram), dir: Lindsay Parsons; with Kirby Grant.

1952

Blue Canadian Rockies (Columbia), dir: George Archainbaud, with Gene Autry, Pat Buttram, Gail Davis, Carolina Cotton.

Border Saddlemates (Republic), dir: William Witney; with Rex Allen, Koko, Mary Allen Kay, Slim Pickens.

The Happy Time (Columbia/A Stanley Kramer Company Production), dir: Richard Fleischer; with Charles Boyer, Louis Jordan, Marsha Hunt, Bobby Driscoll.

Yukon Gold (Monogram), dir: Frank McDonald; with Kirby Grant, Martha Hyer, Harry Lauter.

1953

Back to God's Country (Universal-International), dir: Joseph Pevney; with Rock Hudson, Marcia Henderson, Steve Cochran.

Fangs of the Arctic (Monogram), dir: Rex Bailey; with Kirby Grant, Lorna Hansen, Warren Douglas.

Fort Vengeance (Allied Artists), dir: Lesley Selander; with James Craig, Rita Moreno, Keith Larsen.

I Confess (Warner/An Alfred Hitchcock Production), dir: Alfred Hitchcock; with Montgomery Clift, Anne Baxter, Karl Malden.

Niagara (20th Century-Fox), dir: Henry Hathaway; with Marilyn Monroe, Joseph Cotten, Jean Peters, Casey Adams.

Northern Patrol (Allied Artists), dir: Rex Bailey; with Kirby Grant, Marian Carr, Bill Phipps, Claudia Drake.

Pony Soldier [released in UK as *MacDonald of the Canadian Mounties*] (20th Century-Fox), dir: Joseph M. Newman; with Tyrone Power, Cameron Mitchell, Thomas Gomez.

Scandal at Scourie
(Metro-Goldwyn-Mayer), dir:
Jean Negulesco; with Greer
Garson, Walter Pidgeon, Donna
Corcoran, Agnes Moorehead.

1954

The Far Country
(Universal-International), dir:
Anthony Mann; with James
Stewart, Ruth Roman, Corinne
Calvet, Walter Brennan.

Operation Manhunt (United Artists),
dir: Jack Alexander: with Harry
Townes, Irja Jensen, Jacques
Aubuchon.

Rose Marie (Metro-Goldwyn-Mayer),
dir: Mervyn LeRoy; dir: dance
sequence Busby Berkeley; with
Ann Blyth, Howard Keel,
Fernando Lamas.

Saskatchewan [released in UK as
O'Rourke of the Royal Mounted]
(Universal-International), dir:
Raoul Walsh; with Alan Ladd,
Shelley Winters, J. Carroll Naish,
Hugh O'Brien.

Yukon Vengeance (Allied Artists), dir:
William Beaudine; with Kirby
Grant, Monte Hale, Mary Ellen
Kay, Henry Kulky.

1958

The Challenge of Rin-Tin-Tin,
(Columbia), dir: Robert G.
Walker; with Jim L. Brown,
Lee Aaker, Rin-Tin-Tin.

The Lost Missile (William Berke
Productions), dir: Lester William
Berke; with Robert Loggia, Ellen
Parker, Philip Pine.

1959

Frontier Rangers
(Metro-Goldwyn-Mayer), dir:

Jacques Tourneur; with Keith
Larsen, Buddy Ebsen, Don
Burnett.

Mission of Danger
(Metro-Goldwyn-Mayer), dir:
George Waggner; with Keith
Larsen, Buddy Ebsen, Don
Burnett.

Woman Obsessed (20th Century-Fox),
dir: Henry Hathaway; with
Susan Hayward, Stephen Boyd,
Dennis Holmes.

1960

Nikki, Wild Dog of the North (Walt
Disney/Cangary/Westminster),
dir: Don Haldane, Jack Couffer;
with Jean Coutu, Emile Genest,
Vriel Luft.

1961

The Canadians (20th Century-Fox),
dir: Burt Kennedy; with Robert
Ryan, John Dehner, Torin
Thatcher, Burt Metcalfe.

1962

Big Red (Walt Disney), dir: Norman
Tokar; with Walter Pidgeon,
Gilles Payant, Emile Genest.

1963

The Incredible Journey (Walt
Disney/Cangary), dir: Fletcher
Markle; with Emile Genest, John
Drainie, Tommy Tweed.

1968

Vixen (Eve-Coldstream), dir: Russ
Meyer; with Erica Gavin,
Harrison Page, Garth Pillsbury.

1974

The White Dawn (Paramount),
dir: Philip Kaufman; with
Warren Oates, Timothy Bottoms,
Lou Gosset.

Canadian Content Serials
1917-1956

1917
The Red Ace (Universal Pictures), dir: Jacques Jaccard; with Marie Walcamp, Bobby Mack, Larry Peyton.

1922
Nan of the North (Ben Wilson), dir: Duke Worne; with Ann Little, Joseph Girard, Hal Wilson.

1924
Wolves of the North (Universal), dir: William Duncan; with William Duncan, Edith Johnson, Esther Ralston, Edward Cecil.

1929
Queen of the Northwoods (Pathé Exchange), dir: Spencer Gordon Bennet, Thomas L. Storey; with Ethlyne Clair, Jean Diamond, Walter Miller.

1932 (approx. date)
Trail of the Royal Mounted (Guaranteed Pictures Incorporated), dir: Stuart Paton; with Robert Frazer, Blanche Mehaffey, Buzz Barton.

1933
Clancy of the Mounted (Universal Pictures), dir: Ray Taylor; with Tom Tyler, Jaqueline Wells, Earl McCarthy.

1940
King of the Royal Mounted (Republic), dir: William Witney, John English; with Allan Lane, Robert Strange, Robert Kellard.

1942
King of the Mounties (Republic), dir: William Witney; with Allan Lane, Gilbert Emery, Russell Hicks.

Perils of the Royal Mounted (Columbia), dir: James W. Horne; with Robert Stevens, Kenneth MacDonald, Herbert Rawlinson.

1945
The Royal Mounted Rides Again (Universal), dir: Lewis D. Collins, Ray Taylor; with Bill Kennedy, Milburn Stone, Daun Kennedy.

1948
Dangers of the Canadian Mounted (Republic), dir: Fred Brannon, Yakima Canutt; with Jim Bannon, Virginia Belmont, Anthony Warde.

1953
Canadian Mounties Versus the Atomic Invaders (Republic), dir: Franklin Andreon; with Bill Henry, Susan Morrow, Arthur Space.

1954
Gunfighters of the Northwest (Columbia), dir: Spencer Bennet; with Jack Mahoney, Clayton Moore, Phyllis Coates.

1956
Perils of the Wilderness (Columbia), dir: Spencer Bennet; with Dennis Moore, Richard Emory, Eve Anderson.

Notes

Abbreviations

AFI   American Film Institute Catalogue of Motion Pictures Produced in
        the USA, 1921-1930
BFI   British Film Institute
CMPD   Canadian Moving Picture Digest
MMA   Museum of Modern Art
MPH   Motion Picture Herald
MPN   Motion Picture News
MPRD   Motion Picture Review Digest
MPW   Moving Picture World
PAC   Public Archives of Canada

Quotations for which no source is given come directly from the soundtrack or
subtitles of the motion pictures.

PART ONE: **The Great Woods and the Big Snows**

1   New York Mail *quoted* MPW, May 25, 1921.
2   Unidentified review *quoted* MPW, May 7, 1921.
3   D. W. Griffith advertised his *A Woman's Way* as "A Romance of the
    Canadian Woods." The Kalem company went on location in Canada
    for several films before World War One, including *The Girl Scout*, a
    story of the Lord Strathcona Horse in the Boer War (which used
    actual members of that famous Canadian group of roughriders);
    The Cattle Thieves, featuring real, live Mounties; *The Canadian Moon-
    shiners;* and *Fighting the Iroquois in Canada.* Vitagraph made *Foraging*,
    also billed as a story of Canadian action in the Boer War. Canada's
    part in the Boer War got as much attention from the pioneer
    moviemakers as her much larger contribution to the two world wars
    that followed.
4   Man to Man Magazine, Vols. 6 and 7, Jan.-June 1911, pp. 935-940.
5   MPW, Oct. 1, 1910.
6   *Ibid.,* Dec. 12, 1914.
7   "Northwoods" became a popular phrase in movie vernacular as

273

early as 1912. Moving Picture World that year referred to "The Royal Mounted Police of the Northwest woods" (carefully omitting the word Canadian) and two one-reelers used the phrase that year in their titles. In *The Man Who Died* (1915), the action was described as centring around the village of Grand Pierre "in the Northwest woods." The locale did not need to be identified. Twenty-one years later The Hollywood Reporter, reviewing *The Country Beyond*, simply described it as a story of "the Mounties in the great north-woods," never once mentioning Canada.

8   Robert C. McElravy, reviewing *Nine Tenths of the Law*, May 4, 1918.

9   *The Old Code*, MPW, Jan. 9, 1915.

10 MMA Photoplay clipping file re: *Paid in Advance, n.d.*

11 In *Gene of the Northland*, the heroine and her brother are described as living alone "in the great Northwestern country" (MPW, May 1, 1915). It was not thought necessary to identify the locale further. In *Blood Is Thicker Than Water* (1912) the Northwest was western ranch country but in *A Leap for Life* (1910) it was clearly French Canada. In *Mounted Fury*, made twenty-one years later, the code word was still being used. Because the Northwest was mentioned, Variety's reviewer explained that the "audience is supposed to guess it is Canada."

12 Advertisements for *A Hero of the Big Snows* (1926) merely said the story took place among trappers "in the snow country." *The Law of the North* was described as "a dramatic story of hearty, red-blooded life in the snow-clad North" (MPW, April 20, 1912). Again it wasn't necessary to identify the locale.

13 MPW, Sept. 18, 1915.

14 *quoted*, James S. McQuade, MPW, Sept. 5, 1919.

15 *quoted* 20th Century Authors' Index, New York, 1942.

16 Curwood, James Oliver, *Son of the Forests* (New York, 1930), pp. 200-201.

17 CMPD, Oct. 18, 1925.

18 MPW, May 20, 1916.

19 *Ibid.*

20 *quoted* MPRD, March 29, 1937.

21 *Ibid.*

22 *Ibid.*

23 MMA, Photoplay clipping file, Film Daily, Dec. 5, 1926. The New York Times, Mirror, and Graphic were among those who praised the picture. The Herald Tribune wrote: "There is nothing colorful in . . . 'The Canadian'. . . . The story is dull and the people in it are rude types, the sort who never have time to bathe. Yet there is something in the production which makes it all ring true. We like the way the scenarist and the director have not tried to glorify the hero or the heroine."

274

24 CMPD, July 19, 1927.

25 MPW, July 8, 1911.

26 In *North West Mounted Police*, set entirely in Saskatchewan, DeMille could not resist showing the Rockies behind his main title; the same error occurs in *Hudson's Bay*. *North of Hudson Bay* also has snow-capped mountains; the geography here was so interchangeable that the picture was re-titled *North of the Yukon* for British circulation. Rock Hudson never left the mountains in his dogteam trip from the Mackenzie's mouth to Fort Simpson in *Back to God's Country*, although the obvious route is by river. *The Heart of Humanity*, set in the St. Lawrence valley, was another movie that showed snow-capped peaks (as well as gigantic redwoods). And *The Country Doctor*, which supposedly takes place north of Montreal, had a similar mountain background – Sierras, not Laurentians.

27 The tune is played behind the main titles of *Northern Pursuit, Susannah of the Mounties*, and *Dangers of the Canadian Mounted*, among others. O Canada is heard in both *Hudson's Bay* and *Johnny Belinda*.

28 Of *Conceit*, one of the first pictures to use a Canadian Rockies setting: "The picture should be booked for its scenery if for no other reason . . ." (MPN, Feb. 17, 1921). Of *Pajamas*, shot near Lake Louise: "There has never been anything half so beautiful photographed for the screen . . ." (New York American, July 7, 1927). Of *Saskatchewan*, filmed near Banff: "Too much cannot be said about the sheer, breathtaking beauty against which the film was produced" (MPH, Feb. 27, 1954).

29 Of *Mantrap*, the Clara Bow picture based on a Sinclair Lewis story supposedly set in Manitoba, Moving Picture World wrote (July 24, 1926): "The locations are beautiful, scenically and photographically, carrying the real atmosphere of the woods and lakes." It might have added "American" woods and lakes. The trees were far too gigantic for Manitoba. Boxoffice magazine praised "the backgrounds of arresting beauty" in the 1937 version of *God's Country and the Woman*, (MPRD, March 29, 1937) but those backgrounds were shot in Washington State. Another trade reviewer, S. M. Weller, extolling *Heart of the Wilds* (Hollywood Reporter *quoted* MPRD, March 29, 1937) wrote that "the scenic background with its immensity of space, and the photographic effects would make the feature interesting, even with a weaker story." The picture, however, was shot in Yellowstone National Park.

30 *Nomads of the North* (1920).

31 The Montreal Star, March 16, 1936.

32 There are several startling geographical twists in the early movies. In *The Confession* (1919) Henry B. Walthall travels from Northwest Canada to Montana by way of Montreal on a lake boat! In *River's End* (1930), Charles Bickford manages to go from the Arctic coast to

275

a town apparently not too far from Vancouver by dogteam and horseback in only a few months. An even more arduous journey is made by Renée Adorée in *The Eternal Struggle* (1923). She travels from the eastern slope of the Rockies to Herschel Island off the tip of the Yukon Territory by way of Fort Churchill, Manitoba, and Rankin Inlet on Hudson Bay. All movie heroes and heroines made their way to their goals by following the most difficult route. It's a matter of geographical fact as well as plain common sense that Klondike gold-seekers waited for the ice to break in order to reach the gold-fields by river. Almost every movie, however, shows them going overland by dogteam in the dead of winter – a journey that killed half the handful of men who attempted it in the early days. That's the way Clark Gable travelled in *The Call of the Wild.* And in the 1953 serial *Canadian Mounties versus Atomic Invaders,* a group of green homesteaders were shown mushing into the heart of the Yukon in the dead of winter, bringing in their farm equipment by dogteam.

33   Edmund Breese, Bioscope, Sept. 28, 1916.

34   MPW, March 22, 1924.

35   *Carmen of the Klondike* was set in Seward, Alaska; *Belle of the Yukon* in the interior of Alaska; and *The Call of the Yukon* on the Arctic coast of Alaska.

36   Spectator, May 22, 1936, *quoted* in Greene, G., "The Pleasure Dome" (London, 1972).

37   Mix, Paul E., "The Life and Legend of Tom Mix" (New York, 1972), p. 121.

38   Bioscope, Nov. 8, 1923.

39   MPW, Aug. 6, 1921.

40   Bioscope, April 25, 1918.

41   MPW, July 12, 1919.

42   *Ibid.,* May 4, 1918.

43   In *The Sting of Conscience* (1916), the key figure is a boy known as Johnny o' the Mountains, who has grown to manhood among the trappers of the Rockies without ever having seen a female face. His first view of a woman is in the pages of a magazine. In *The Barbarian* (1921), set north of Winnipeg, the hero, Eric Straive, "a simple child of nature," has never met a white woman until he encounters the daughter of the man who is trying to cheat him out of his inheritance.

44   Spectator, July 12, 1936, *quoted* in Greene, *op. cit.* Kine Weekly, April 4, 1936, said: "The North Country atmosphere is flawless." The Boston Transcript's critic, March 7, 1936, declared the picture never lost touch with reality. By that time the most sophisticated foreign critics believed in the isolation of northern Canada, having had it drummed into them by the movies for years. In *Empty Hands,*

276

for instance, Jack Holt and Norma Shearer lived a desert-island existence after being marooned in a valley in the rockies. In *Nomads of the North,* Lon Chaney was able to find shelter from the Mounties for three years "in the far forests of the Yellowknife, hidden from the eyes of men." In *The Eternal Struggle,* two Mounties and a girl travel for months through the Canadian north without encountering a soul. A similar theme appears in *The Storm,* a Broadway play twice made into a movie.

45 In *Closin' In,* Jack Brandon takes the rap for his girlfriend's father, who has been embezzling bank funds, and flees to the Northwest, joins the mounted police, and is finally cleared by a deathbed confession. In *South of the Northern Lights,* Jack Hampton, falsely accused of murder by a villain who wants to steal his gold mine, flees to Canada and is exonerated by a last-minute confession. In *When the Door Opened* Clive Grenfal, who had surprised his wife in the arms of a lover and believes he has killed him in a jealous passion, runs for cover and becomes a hermit in the Canadian woods. In *The Love Master,* David, believing he has killed the legal master of the hero dog, Strongheart, flees with the animal to Canada. In *Bring Him In,* Dr. John Hood, believing that he has killed a gambler, is persuaded by his butler to flee to the Canadian north. There were many similar films.

46 *Philip Steele* and *Channing of the Northwest* are both about men who become Mounties to forget the women who betrayed them.

47 MPW, Dec. 16, 1911.

48 *Ibid.,* Nov. 10, 1917. Other curative powers were ascribed to the north in *Into the Northland,* in which the hero, George Collins, losing all to gamblers, heads for British Columbia and makes a fortune in gold; and in *The Call,* in which Ned Wilson loses his job through drink, makes his way to the forests of Canada, and becomes sober and wealthy.

49 *Empty Hands,* AFI.

50 *The Woman Conquers, Ibid.*

51 MPW, Feb. 22, 1913.

52 *Ibid.,* April 20, 1918.

53 Similarily, in *Sgt. Byrne of the NWMP,* a young rancher, disgusted with himself for gambling and drinking, is "determined to seek the company of real men and brace up" (MPW, Sept. 7, 1912). And in *Big Game* the wife of a pampered aristocrat lures him north into the Canadian woods so he can prove that he is a man.

54 In *The Valley of Doubt* Tommy Hilgrade is sent away by his father, who hopes to improve the boy's morals by giving him a taste of rugged life in the Canadian woods. And in *A Woman of Redemption* the owner of a lumber camp maroons his worthless son in the woods in the hope of reforming him.

1   *Nine Tenths of the Law* was "a story of primitive life far out in the wilds and of corresponding passion" (Bioscope, Oct. 17, 1918). The hero of *Hugon, the Mighty* was "a blend of childish charm and primitive passions" (*Ibid.*, Aug. 28, 1919). *The Devil's Partner* was about "two young lovers in a primitive Canadian village" (Motion Picture News Booking Guide, Oct. 1923). The opening subtitle for *The Sky Pilot* described the Rocky Mountains locale as "primitive and lawless." A review of *The Savage* explained that "Northwestern Canada is where the action is placed and the various types of primitive humanity to be found in that region supply most of the characters" (MPW, Nov. 10, 1917). An advertisement for *Slander the Woman* hailed "the rough, red-blooded characters of the vast snow wastes, where primitive instincts come into play" (*Ibid.*, May 19, 1923). Almost thirty years later an advertisement for a Stewart Granger movie, *The Wild North,* called it "M-G-M's big drama of primitive love in the wildest north."

2   "French-Canadians and North West Mounted Police make picturesque screen characters. They have been tried and proven many times," Matthew Taylor wrote in 1921 (MMA Photoplay file, unidentified, Oct. 1921). "The atmosphere of Canadian border life is . . . very picturesque" wrote Moving Picture World of *Breed o' the North* (Oct. 11, 1913). Canadians were also seen as childlike: Dupré, the French-Canadian in *The Cross of Fire,* "has a childlike faith in the efficacy of prayer" (*Ibid.*, Jan. 23, 1915). Priscilla Glenn in *The Place Beyond the Winds* is "a product of the woods, a wild, impulsive, nature loving child" (*Ibid.,* Nov. 11, 1916). For these children the mandatory father-figure was the Roman Catholic priest, in his ankle-length cassock and flat black hat. He turns up in *The Heart of Humanity,* kindly and silver-haired, "sowing the seeds of love and faith in the hearts of his children."

3   MPW, Aug. 14, 1920.

4   The sophisticated American seducer was a stock Hollywood character. He turned up again as a New York theatrical producer attempting to rape the heroine of *The Little Wild Girl* and again in *The Wolf,* seducing a young French-Canadian girl.

5   "Biograph Bulletins: 1896-1908" (Los Angeles, 1971), p. 306.

6   The only exception I've discovered is in the 1938 version of *Heart of the North,* which had a former mounted policeman as technical adviser.

7   In *For Another Woman* the villagers try to drive a woman from the town because they believe (wrongly) that she is an unwed mother. In *The Little Wild Girl* the villagers try to drive the heroine from their midst because they believe (again wrongly) that she has committed

murder. *Johnny Belinda* has a somewhat similar incident in which the villagers drive the young doctor from the community because they believe (wrongly as usual) that he has seduced one of their own.

8   MPW, July 26, 1919. The ads were for *That Devil, Bateese, Closin' In,* and *The Shooting of Dan McGrew,* respectively. Passions also ran untrammelled in *O'Garry of the Royal Mounted,* a story of "strong passions and fiercer jealousies" (MPW, Jan. 23, 1915); and in *Fathers of Men,* which dealt with "the primitive passions of humanity" (*Ibid.,* July 22, 1916).

9   MPW, Jan. 23, 1915. Another picture praised for its realism was *Sons of the Northwoods* in which, the reviewer claimed, "we are given an accurate true to life portrayal of the romantic incident in the lives of an isolated group of these danger-daring, big-hearted though rough people of the last great west" (*Ibid.,* March 30, 1912).

10 For example: *Tiger Rose, God's Country and the Woman, Men of the North, Pierre of the Plains, Untamed,* and even *The Thirteenth Letter,* all of which carried into the sound era the well-established themes that the silents had launched: pastoral village life, untamed northern passion, and rough frontier justice.

11 Variety, May 27, 1959.

12 The stereotype was imprinted early on American minds: in reviewing *The Wolf* Margaret I. MacDonald wrote, "George Nichols as Andrew MacTavish, the cruel father of the girl, typifies well the traditional Scottish male parent" (MPW, Aug. 16, 1919). The domineering factor characterization had a ten-year run in the silent films before it finally petered out. There was Angus Fitzpatrick, the factor of *The Wilderness Trail,* "domineering, vindictive, jealous and cunning" (Paul Mix, *op. cit.,* p. 122); Duncan McDougall of *Nomads of the North,* "a tiger of the old regime still ruling his domain with a hand of iron and a heart of stone;" and Cameron MacDonald in *North of Hudson Bay,* who holds court in his trading post and sends his enemies on the dreaded Journey of Death.

13 Bioscope, May 29, 1919.

14 MPW, April 20, 1918.

15 MMA, Photoplay file, unidentified clipping.

16 Bioscope, Feb. 14, 1924.

17 CMPD, Dec. 15, 1922.

18 Factors were also shown as seducers. Chad Galloway, villain of *Where the North Begins* "has long cast a covetous eye on Felice, the daughter of McTavish, his storekeeper." The strangest of these Romeos was the Right Honourable Reginald Annesley (an Englishman for once) who ran the Keewatin post in *The Law of the North* and was shown dressing for dinner every night, being served by a turbanned East Indian, and ordering fresh flowers sent up all the way from Winnipeg to lavish upon the heroine.

19 St. Paul Pioneer Press, *quoted* in Quirk, J., "The Films of Joan Crawford", (Toronto, 1968), p. 57.

20 AFI, p. 813.

21 Paramount press sheet.

22 Larue in *One Day* was "a typical ignorant man of the brute type and his treatment of his wife is such that one would accord to a dog (MPW, Dec. 14, 1912). Raoul LaFane of *The Northern Code* was "a drunken Canadian trapper [who] attacks his young wife" (AFI Catalogue, p. 553). Francois LeFevre in *Out of the Night* is "fickle as well as faithless" (MPW, May 9, 1914).

23 The one exception to the stereotype was Monroe Salisbury's portrayal of Rossignol, the mysterious outlaw in *The Man in the Moonlight* who is dressed as a South American gaucho in a flat black hat, black poncho, open shirt, and beads. To complete the characterization Salisbury kept a cigarette dangling constantly from his lips.

24 *In the Northland* told of "the intense love and wonderful heroism of a stout-hearted French-Canadian, whose wife is on the point of deserting him for a cowardly city weakling" (MPW, May 16, 1914). The hero of *Hugon, the Mighty* was "a vigorous woodsman respected for his physical strength and moral courage" (*Ibid.*, Oct. 26, 1918). 'Poleon Dufresne in *The Lure of the Wild* "loved the wild things of the forest too much to ever become rich as a trapper."

25 For example: Baptiste, the "jovial, hearty, light-hearted woodsman" of *Sons of the Northwoods* (*Ibid.*, March 30, 1912); Jacques, the "happy-go-lucky Canuk trapper" of *Jacques of the Silver North* (*Ibid.*, June 14, 1919); Hilair Latour, the "impulsive, warm-hearted trapper" of *Prisoner of the Pines* (*Ibid.*, Sept. 14, 1918); Jules, the "high-spirited, laughing, whole-souled woodsman" of *Jules of the Strongheart* (MMA Photoplay file, unidentified); and another Jacques of *Wild Sumac,* "a happy-go-lucky French adventurer running over with the wine of life, with zest, humour and complete fidelity" (MPW, Oct. 17, 1917).

26 MPW, May 13, 1922.

27 Friar, Ralph E. and Natasha A., "The Only Good Indian . . . The Hollywood Gospel" (New York, 1972), p. 81. *"The Cattle Rustlers* used that classic character of the dime novel: the dirty, no-good, half-breed. . . ."

28 *Ibid.*, p. 243.

29 MPW, Nov. 6, 1909.

30 Bioscope, Feb. 7, 1918.

31 MPW, Nov. 2, 1912.

32 *Ibid.*, Feb. 22, 1913.

33 *Ibid.*, March 21, 1908.

34 *Ibid.*, May 2, 1914.

35 *Ibid.*, Sept. 27, 1913.

36   MMA Photoplay files, New York Journal, undated clipping.

37   MPW, Feb. 6, 1915.

38   DeMille, C. B. and Hayne, Donald, ed., "The Autobiography of Cecil B. DeMille" (New York, 1959), p. 369.

39   BFI files, The Spectator, Dec. 6, 1940.

40   Jennings, John, "The Plains Indians and the Law," in Dempsey, Hugh, ed., "Men in Scarlet" (Calgary, 1974), p. 11.

41   The Canadian Historical Review, March, 1942, p. 65.

42   Eagle Blanket, a good Indian in *Unseeing Eyes,* kills the half-breed villain. In *A Romance in the Fur Country,* a good Indian helps the hero, Pierre, by knifing a drunken half-breed. In *The Hero of the North,* an Indian named Long-Arm, a half-breed, and a Mountie are all in love with the same girl. The Indian kills the violently jealous half-breed, but the Mountie gets the girl. The Indian is described as "a good loser" (MPW, Oct. 24, 1914).

43   MPW, May 1, 1915.

44   Jennings, *op. cit.,* p. 54.

45   *Ibid.,* p. 57.

PART THREE: Perils of the Royal Mounted

1   Agnes Smith, MMA Photoplay file, unidentified clipping.

2   MPW, Nov. 6, 1909.

3   *Ibid.,* Nov. 2, 1912.

4   *Ibid.,* July 23, 1921.

5   *Ibid.,* April 15, 1922.

6   *Ibid.,* June 17, 1922.

7   MMA Photoplay file, unidentified clipping.

8   The New York Times, Oct. 16, 1923.

9   Variety, March 11, 1931.

10   The Toronto Daily Star, March 14, 1936.

11   Greene, *op. cit.,* Spectator, May 22, 1936.

12   MPW, Oct. 4, 1924.

13   RCMP File G 517-47, H. Bruce C. Carruthers to Insp. C. E. Rivett-Carnac, Nov. 4, 1936.

14   MMA Photoplay file, unidentified clipping, Oct. 1921. As far as is known, the get-your-man mythology had its genesis in a newspaper story in the Fort Benton, Montana, Record of April 12, 1877: "Thanks to the vigilance of Major Irving and the energy of Captain Windsor of the NW Mounted Police, another attempt to smuggle whisky into Indian country has been frustrated by the arrest of three men, who were tried, found guilty and then sentenced to pay a fine of $5,000.00. The MPs are worse than bloodhounds when they scent the track of a smuggler, and they fetch their man every time."

15 MPW, Sept. 18, 1926.

16 *Ibid.,*   Nov. 29, 1913.

17 AFI, p. 914.

18 MPW, July 11, 1925.

19 Atkin, Ronald, "Maintain The Right" (Toronto, 1973), p. 358.

20 Barbour, Alan J., "Days of Thrill and Adventure" (New York, 1970), p. 111.

21 Connor, Ralph, "Postcript to Adventure" (Toronto, 1975), p. 157.

22 Film Daily, July 14, 1936, *quoted* in MPRD, p. 132.

23 RCMP File G 556-2, L. du Plessis to Commissioner RCMP, Oct. 22, 1919.

24 *Ibid.*

25 RCMP File G 563-1, H. P. Carver to Perry, telegram, March 26, 1922.

26 *Ibid.,* handwritten memorandum attached to telegram, Perry to Carver, March 27, 1922.

27 *Ibid.,* Starnes to Frank E. Smith, Vitagraph Studios, March 30, 1925.

28 *Ibid.,* Starnes to G. L. McDonell, May 7, 1926.

29 *Ibid.,* McDonell to Starnes, May 7, 1926.

30 *Ibid.,* McDonell to Starnes, May 28, 1926.

31 *Ibid.,* Peck to Starnes, June 4, 1926.

32 *Ibid.*

33 MMA Photoplay clipping file, New York Journal American, *n.d.*

34 RCMP File G 563-1, Starnes to Lt. Col. J. K. Gordon McGee, Feb. 17, 1931.

35 RCMP File G 563-15, Mayer to Elliott, Aug. 28, 1935, copy.

36 *Ibid.,* Elliott to Mayer, Aug. 31, 1935, copy.

37 *Ibid.,* Mayer to MacBrien, Aug. 31, 1935.

38 *Ibid.,* MacBrien to Mayer, telegram, Sept. 4, 1935.

39 *Ibid.,* Grady to MacBrien, Sept. 16, 1935.

40 *Ibid.,* Grady to MacBrien, telegram, Sept. 20, 1935.

41 Bennett papers, PAC MG 26K, Vol. 453, Bennett to Geary, telegram, Oct. 2, 1935; Bennett to MacBrien, telegram, Oct. 3, 1935.

42 RCMP file G 563-15, MacBrien to Bennett, telegram, Oct. 5, 1935.

43 *Ibid.,* Badgley to MacBrien, Oct. 21, 1935.

44 *Ibid.,* MacBrien to Badgley, Oct. 23, 1935.

45 *Ibid.,* Park B. Rohrbaugh to Commissioner, RCMP, April 20, 1936. MacBrien had wired William A. Orr at M-G-M on Feb. 1 that he and twenty officers had seen the picture at a special screening "and all are of the opinion that it is a first class film. We are quite satisfied that the reputation of the Mounted Police will be upheld due to the high standard of acting and production. . . ."

46 *Ibid.,* J. W. Spalding to Rohrbaugh, April 23, 1936.

47 Nov. 22, 1969.

48 RCMP File G 563-1, W. J. Reid to Wood, Oct. 25, 1938.

49 *Ibid.,* Wood to Reid, Oct. 27, 1938.

50 RCMP File G 517-47, Carruthers to chairman, Censorship Co-ordinating Committee, June 5, 1940, copy.

51 *Ibid.*, Carruthers to Wood, Nov. 3, 1938.

52 RCMP File G 786-17, Carruthers to Virginia Wright, Los Angeles News, May 5, 1940, copy.

53 RCMP File G 517-47, Carruthers to Rivett-Carnac, Nov. 4, 1938; Carruthers to Wood, Aug. 29, 1938.

54 *Ibid.*, Carruthers to chairman, Censorship Co-ordinating Committee, June 5, 1940, copy.

55 *Ibid.*, Carruthers to Wood, Nov. 3, 1958.

56 *Ibid.*, Carruthers, "The No-Men of Hollywood," *ms.* p. 8.

57 *Ibid.*, Carruthers to chairman, Censorship Co-ordinating Committee, June 5, 1940, copy.

58 *Ibid.*, Carruthers to Wood, Aug. 20, 1938.

59 *Ibid.*, Carruthers to MacBrien, July 17, 1937.

60 *Ibid.*

61 *Ibid.*

62 *Ibid.*, Carruthers to Wood, Dec. 4, 1938.

63 *Ibid.*

64 RCMP File G 563-1, Winchell, "Things I Never Knew 'Til Now About the Mounties," *ms.* copy *n.d.*

65 *Ibid.*, clipping Halifax Daily Star, Sept. 6, 1938.

66 RCMP File G 517-47, Carruthers to Wood, Nov. 3, 1938.

67 *Ibid.*

68 *Ibid.*, Carruthers to Kenneth Macgowan, producer. Memo re: suggested script changes, Dec. 7, 1938, copy.

69 *Ibid.*

70 *Ibid.*, Carruthers to Wood, June 24, 1939.

71 *Ibid.*, Suggestions made by Carruthers on *Gambler's Choice* (release title *Northwest Rangers*), *ms.* copy, p. 4, 1942.

72 RCMP File G 563-8, Carruthers script suggestions on *To The Last Man* (re-titled *Northern Pursuit*) *ms.* copy p. 19 *n.d.*

73 *Ibid.*, Carruthers to Wood, Dec. 17, 1947.

74 MPW, Aug. 29, 1914, "DeMille 'Talks Shop.'"

75 *Ibid.*, Aug. 18, 1914.

76 The Canadian Historical Review, March 1942, p. 65.

77 *quoted* RCMP File G 786-17, Milligan to Wood, May 17, 1939.

78 RCMP File G 517-47, Carruthers to Wood, Feb. 9, 1952. The director who made the remark was Joseph M. Newman *(Pony Soldier)*.

79 RCMP File G 786-17, Regina Leader Post, July 24, 1939, clipping.

80 *Ibid.*, Wood to Pine, July 15, 1939.

81 *Ibid.*

82 *Ibid.*, Pine to Wood, July 19, 1939.

83 *Ibid.*, Hann to Pine, July 28, 1939.

84 *Ibid.*, Calgary Herald, Canadian Press dispatch, July 26, 1939, clipping.

85 *Ibid.*, unidentified clipping: "C. B. DeMille to pretend there isn't any war," *n.d.*
86 *Ibid.*, Carruthers to Wood, Nov. 27, 1939.
87 *Ibid.*, Wood to Carruthers, Dec. 5, 1939.
88 *Ibid.*, Ottawa Citizen, Dec. 22, 1939, clipping.
89 *Ibid.*, Carruthers to Wood, April 10, 1940.
90 *Ibid.*, Hann to Wood, memorandum, April 15, 1940.
91 *Ibid.*, Regina Leader Post, April 20, 1940, clipping.
92 *Ibid.*, Los Angeles Times, May 2, 1940, clipping.
93 *Ibid.*, Moriarty to Thompson, May 14, 1940, copy.
94 *Ibid.*, Wood to Thompson, June 8, 1940.
95 *Ibid.*, Lash to Thompson, June 10, 1940.
96 *Ibid.*, Regina Leader Post, June 11, 1940, clipping.
97 *Ibid.*
98 *Ibid.*, Regina Leader Post, Oct. 22, 1940, clipping.
99 *Ibid.*
100 Globe and Mail, Toronto, Oct. 26, 1940.
101 Toronto Daily Star, Oct. 24, 1940.
102 Variety, Oct. 23, 1940.
103 MMA Photoplay File, clipping, *n.d.*
104 Motion Picture Herald, Oct. 26, 1940.
105 Jefferys, Charles W., "History in Motion Pictures," The Canadian Historical Review, Dec. 9, 1941, p. 11.

PART FOUR: Canadian Co-operation, Hollywood Style

1 PAC, Trade and Commerce Department records, RG 20 B1, Vol. 575, McLean to McCann, Dec. 1, 1947.
2 *Ibid.*, Eric Johnston to J. J. Fitzgibbons, Jan. 21, 1948.
3 *Ibid.*
4 CMPD, April 10, 1948.
5 PAC, Trade and Commerce Department records, *op. cit.*, Fitzgibbons to Skouras, March 4, 1948, copy.
6 *quoted* CMPD July 10, 1948.
7 *Ibid.*, June 26, 1948.
8 PAC, Trade and Commerce Department records, *op. cit.*, Gordon to Mackenzie, June 19, 1948.
9 Hansard, June 25, 1948, pp. 5844-55.
10 PAC, Trade and Commerce Department records, *op. cit.*, McLean to Francis S. Harmon, May 31, 1948, copy.
11 *Ibid.*, Gordon to Howe, June 24, 1948.
12 *Ibid.*, Scott to Newman, Aug. 19, 1948.
13 *Ibid.*, Fitzgibbons to Skouras, March 4, 1948.
14 *Ibid.*, Newman to Jay Bonafield of RKO-Pathé, March 16, 1950.

Newman wrote: "Please accept our sincere thanks for the references to Canada. . . ."

15 *Ibid.*, Dolan to Newman, April 4, 1950.
16 *Ibid.*, Mills to Blake Owensmith, March 29, 1950; Newman to Don Henshaw, April 6, 1950.
17 *Ibid.*, Newman to Henshaw, April 12, 1950.
18 *Ibid.*, Ade to Newman, April 13, 1950.
19 *Ibid.*, Gray to Newman.
20 Canada: Sessional Papers, 1906, Annual Report of the Commissioner of the NWMP, p. 3.
21 *Ibid.*
22 RCMP File G 563-57, Carruthers to Wood, Oct. 7, 1950.
23 New Liberty, Dec., 1950.
24 RCMP File G 563-57, Knowlton to Wood, Dec. 27, 1950.
25 *Ibid.*, The Monitor, Jan. 18, 1951, clipping.
26 *Ibid.*, Owensmith to C. K. Gray, Jan. 10, 1951, *encl.* R. Monta, Loew's, Inc., to Owensmith, Jan. 4, 1951.
27 *Ibid.*, Memorandum for Secretary of State for External Affairs, March 9, 1951, copy.
28 *Ibid.*, Garson to Pearson, May 21, 1951.
29 RCMP File G 563-1, Minutes of Interdepartmental Committee on Canadian Information Abroad, April 29, 1952, copy.
30 *Ibid.*, Nicholson to Johnston, May 9, 1952.
31 *Ibid.*, MacNeil to Nicholson, memorandum, Nov. 6, 1952. Nicholson's comment, dated Nov. 18, is handwritten on the report.
32 RCMP File G 563-12, Wood to Harvison, Aug. 11, 1960.
33 *Ibid.*, Harvison to Wood, Oct. 6, 1960.
34 McClellan to author, personal memo.
35 RCMP File G 563-12, Kennedy to Harvison, Feb. 22, 1961.
36 *Ibid.*, Harvison to Kennedy, March 17, 1961.
37 The reports have vanished from the Trade and Commerce Department files but the RCMP files have copies.
38 It's instructive to see exactly what the newsreels showed in their so-called "Canadian sequences" that year. The largest number – thirty-eight – dealt with the Royal Tour of Canada by Princess Elizabeth and Prince Philip. The CCP report included five newsreel stories about the couple's visit to Washington as "Canadian sequences." The second largest category – thirty – dealt with sports. Of these, thirteen were sports sequences of events in the United States in which Canada as one of many entrants got a passing mention. The remainder took place in Canada and included wrestling, barrel jumping, and judo, as well as one Stanley Cup sequence. The third category – twenty-seven sequences – consisted of news about NATO and the Korean War with some passing references to Canada as a NATO member and a contributor to the UN forces. (President Tru-

man's White House greeting to eight NATO trainees, representing the member nations, was a "Canadian sequence.") The fourth category – twenty-five sequences – dealt with such disasters as floods, fires, bridge collapses, and the death of a stunt man at Niagara Falls. The smallest category – twenty-four sequences – had to do with specific Canadian events, running all the way from a NATO meeting in Ottawa to an Eskimo nun taking the veil.

39 The interview was carried on the program "Prime Time," Feb. 4, 1975. The quotations used here are from the unedited transcript.

PART FIVE: It Wasn't Like That at All

1 New York World Telegram, March 21, 1936.
2 Otis Ferguson, The New Republic, May 4, 1941 *quoted* in "The Film Criticism of Otis Ferguson," Philadelphia, 1971.
3 Jowett, Garth S., "The Concept of History in American Produced Films," The Journal of Popular Culture, Spring, 1970.
4 Jennings, *op. cit.*, p. 50.
5 BFI Files, Daily Telegraph, Feb. 25, 1961, clipping.
6 MPW, Oct. 10, 1925.
7 MMA Photoplay file, Hollywood Reporter, March 9, 1949, clipping.
8 *Ibid.*, Showman's Trade Review, March 12, 1949, clipping.
9 *Ibid.*, Harrison's Reports, March 9, 1949.
10 MPH, March 12, 1949.
11 Some of the non-trade reviews in the more sophisticated dailies were more realistic. Howard Barnes in The New York Herald Tribune tagged the movie as "merely a sprawling horse opera" and The Christian Science Monitor called it "a pseudo-documentary . . . whose resemblance to history is probably only coincidental" (MMA Photoplay clipping file).
12 MPW, May 30, 1925.
13 Montreal Gazette, June 1, 1925.
14 For a detailed description of law and order in Dawson, including the no-gun rule and the Sabbath laws, see the author's "Klondike," revised edition, (Toronto, 1972), pp. 306-311.
15 MFB, Sept. 1954.
16 New York Times, Feb. 14, 1955.
17 MPH Jan. 22, 1955.
18 Observer, Aug. 1, 1954.
19 Vancouver Province, Feb. 17, 1955.
20 MPW, Feb. 4, 1911.
21 Paul Mix, *op. cit.*, p. 121.
22 MPW, Feb. 13, 1926.

23 Subtitle. Other references include *Isobel* ("Cupid's law alone holds sway 'North of Fifty-three'" said MPW, April 12, 1920); and *The Broken Spur,* in which Jacques Durand fights the intrusion of a railway into the north country, fearing it will bring law and order.

24 For *The Law of the North,* 1918.

25 MPW, June 4, 1910. The movies referred to are *Wild Sumac, Jules of the Strongheart,* and *I Am the Law,* respectively. Lynching scenes also occurred in *A Woman of Redemption, The Valley of Doubt, The Cowpuncher's Glove, The Heart of the North, Klondike Kate,* and many others.

26 *The Old Code,* MPW, Jan. 9, 1915.

27 *Ibid.*

28 MMA Photoplay file, unidentified clipping, Jan. 6, 1922.

29 MPW, Oct. 28, 1911.

30 MPW, Nov. 27, 1915.

31 MPW, Oct. 9, 1915.

32 Toronto Daily Star, Sept. 16, 1918.

33 MPW, Oct. 9, 1920.

34 Toronto Daily Star, June 22, 1929.

35 CMPD, Jan. 25, 1930.

36 *Ibid.*

37 Globe and Mail, Toronto, May 14, 1951.

38 Toronto Daily Star, Feb. 4, 1955.

"Breed of the North"

Two Reel

Released Thursday, October 9th

"The Breed of the North" is a very picturesque story of the Northwest lumber and trapper region. Two twin brothers, Jim and John, love the same girl; the former wins her, and the latter joins the Northwest Mounted, and it becomes his duty to track a man who is wanted, really for a crime he did not commit, and he discovers it to be his brother. The fugitive being caught, they exchange clothes, and John gives himself up. The real murderer is, however, caught, and Jim returns to his wife, while John returns to his police duty.

Index

A.D.C., The see *For Another Woman*
Abel, Walter 173
Acadian Elopement, An 15, 76, 247
Ace High 253
Ace of Spades, The 45, 248
Adams, Claire *94-95*
Ade, Sergeant H.J.F. 178
Adirondack Mountains 55
Adorée, Renée 15, *57, 59,* 83, 128, *195,* 276
Adrift 249
African Queen, The 16
Alaska 29, 30, 45, 46, 142, 215, 276
Alaskan, The 29
Alberta 16, 30, 99, 206, 215, 226, 227
Alice of Hudson Bay 249
American Mutoscope and Biograph
   Company 15 *see also* Biograph Company
Ancient Highway, The 80, 259
Andy of the Royal Mounted 250
Anne of Green Gables (novel) 20
Anne of Green Gables (1919) 253
Anne of Green Gables (1934) 20, 264
Anne of Windy Poplars 20, 265
Apache Indians 103, 105, 107
Apprenticeship of Duddy Kravitz, The 236
Arizona 32, *34*
Assiniboia 100
Assiniboine Indians 127
At the End of the Trail 248
Athabasca, Alberta 31
Aurora of the North 249
Autry, Gene 15, *60*
Ayres, Lew 77

Back to God's Country (1927) *38, 59,* 261
Back to God's Country (1953) 30, *38,* 47, 268,
   275
Badgley, Frank C. 138
Bancroft, George *93*
Banff, Alberta 22, 41, 124, 148, 171, 275
Banff Springs Hotel 175

Bank of Canada 170, 183, 204
Bank of Commerce 45
Barbarian, The 75, 255, 276
Barbour, Alan J. *quoted* 191
Baree, Son of Kazan (1918) 253
Baree, Son of Kazan (1925) *63,* 259
Barrie, Wendy 234
Barrier 142
Barrier that was Burned, The 248
Barrymore, Lionel 15
Batoche 152
Baxter, Anne 16
Baxter, Warner 15
Bear Mountain, California 42
Bear Valley, California 29
Beau Geste 16
Beery, Noah *61*
Beery, Wallace 15
Begbie, Matthew Baillie 208
Behold My Wife 254
Belaney, Archie 102-103, *156*
Belcher, Inspector Bobby 229
Bellamy, Madge *61*
Belle of the Yukon 276
Below the Rio Grande 258
Bend of the River 189
Bennett, Richard Bedford 137-138
Beregi, Oscar 88
Berkeley, Busby 102
Best Man, The 55, 252
Beyond the Shadows 253
Beyond the Trail 250
Bickford, Charles 77, 225, 275
Big Bear 152, 162, 163, 205
Big Game 253, 277
Big Hearted Jim 117, 119, 249
Big Red 269
Biltmore Company 120
Biograph Company 76 *see also* American
   Mutoscope and Biograph Company
Birth of a Nation, The 87

291

Bison Film Company 51
Blackfoot Indians 31, *65, 68,* 101, 104-105, 106, 107, 126, 145
Blaisdel, G. F. *quoted* 112
Blind Circumstances 83, 256
Blinding Trail, The 254
Blood is Thicker Than Water 248, 274
Bloodhound, The 118, 259
Bloodhounds of the North 249
Blue, Monte *33,* 97, 228
Blue Blazes Rawden 29, 80, 98, 225, 253
Blue Canadian Rockies 268
Blyth, Ann 138
Boer War 273
Border Blackbirds 261
Border Saddlemates 189, 268
Borzage, Frank 16
Bosworth, Hobart *219*
Bow, Clara 15, *35,* 275
Bowers, John *218,* 225
Boyd, Stephen 79
Boyd, William 16
Boyer, Charles 16, 85, 111
Brand for the Burning, A 248
Brandon, Manitoba 179
Breed O' the North, The 249, 278
Brennan, Walter 211, 212, 213
Brent, George 16, *39,* 80
Bring Him In 255, 277
British Columbia 21, 32, 77, 79, 207, 208, 225, 277
Broken Silence, The 28, 256
Broken Spur, The (1916) 250
Broken Spur, The (1921) 255, 287
Bronco Buster 189
Brought to Justice 262
Brown, Clarence 227
Bruce, Nigel 86
Bulldogs of the Trail 104, 251
Buntline, Ned 100
Burning Words 258
Busch, Mae 15
Bushnell, Ernest 170
Byer, Charles *90*

Cagney, James 16
Calgary, Alberta 45, 77
Calgary Stampede, The 47, 189
Calgary Stampede, The 83-84, 97, 206, *224,* 259
California 29, 46, 108, 142, 208, 215, 232, 233
Call, The 249, 277
Call of the Klondike, The (1926) 260

Call of the Klondike (1950) 267
Call of the North, The (1914) 81, 147, *194,* 251
Call of the North, The (1921) 81, 255
Call of the Wild, The (1923) 258
Call of the Wild, The (1935) 48, 79, 216, 228, 264, 276
Call of the Yukon, The 276
Calvet, Corinne 83, 203
Calvin, Frank 148, 149
Canadian, The 31, 206, 260, 274
Canadian Broadcasting Corporation 170, 189
Canadian Co-operation Project 169-191 *passim,* 204-205, 208, 211
Canadian Film Development Corporation 236
Canadian Government Motion Picture Bureau 126, 138
Canadian Government Travel Bureau 177, 187
Canadian Moonshiners, The 247, 273
Canadian Mounties versus the Atomic Invaders 123, *130,* 270, 276
Canadian National Railways 29, 163, 204
Canadian Pacific 11, 18, *69,* 106, 107, 175, 207, 208-211, *219,* 267
Canadian Pacific Irrigation Colonization Company 20-22 *passim*
Canadian Pacific Railway 11, 18, 20-22, 27, 29, 106, 152, 175, 208-211 *passim,* 227
Canadians, The 107, *133,* 184-186, 206, 236, 269
Cannon, Dyan *quoted* 237
Capra, Frank 47
Captains of the Clouds 266
Cariboo country, British Columbia 207, 208
Cariboo Trail, The 80, 104, 106, 176, *197,* 207-208, 267
Carmen of the Klondike 276
Carroll, John 31, *62,* 82, 85, 225
Carroll, Madelaine 16, 99, 164
Carruthers, Bruce 115, 139-146 *passim,* 148, 150, 151, *160,* 180-181, 226, 228, 229
Cartier, Jacques 203
Casablanca 16
Castle, Mrs. Vernon 16
Cattle Thieves, The 87, 112, 247, 273
Caulfield, Joan 171
Censor boards: British 124; Ontario 124, 233; Quebec 124; British Columbia 232
Challenge of Rin-Tin-Tin, The 269
Challenge of the Law, The 254

Chambers, Col. E. J. 124
Champlain, Samuel de 203
Chaney, Lon 15, 82, 84-85, 277
Chaney, Lon, Jr. 161
Channing of the Northwest 130, 256, 277
Charisse, Cyd *158*
Charlesworth, Hector *quoted* 29
Charlottetown, Prince Edward Island 20
Cheyenne Autumn 157
Chilcotin country, British Columbia 101,
   104, 106, 208
Child of the North, A 98, 250
Chilkoot Pass 20, *37*
Chinese Slave Smuggling 247
Chipewyan Indians *72,* 101
Churchill, Winston 186
Clancy of the Mounted 97, 270
Clifford, Ruth *89*
Clift, Montgomery 16
Clipped Wings 265
Closin' In 253, 277, 279
Clouded Name, The 254
Code of the Mounted, The (1916) 250
Code of the Mounted (1936) *130,* 264
Code of the Northwest 260
Code of the Scarlet, The 261
Code of the Yukon 254
Cole, Florence 98
Colleen of the Pines 49, 256
Colorado (State) 208
Columbia Pictures 178
Columbia Valley, British Columbia 21
Comanche Indians 105
Conceit 255, 275
Confession, The 25, 83, 123, *131,* 254, 275
Connor, Ralph 19, 122
Constable's Manual 123
Constantine, Inspector Charles 229
Cook of Canyon Camp, The 252
Cooper, Gary 16, *133,* 151
Cooper, Col. John 137
Corey, Wendell 123, *135,* 179, 187
Corrado, Geno *58*
Corvette K-225 267
Cosmopolitan Productions 124, 127
Country Beyond, The (1926) 76, 260
Country Beyond, The (1936) 234, 264, 274
Country Doctor, The (1936) 41, 45, 53, 86,
   203, 235, 264, 275
Courage and the Man 250
Courage of Marge O'Doone, The 25, 254
Coward, The 261
Cowpuncher's Glove, The 247, 287
Craig, James 30

Crashin' Thru 265
Crawford, Joan 15, *60,* 83, 128, *134*
Cree Indians *69,* 101, 105, 107, 116, 152,
   162
Criminal Code of Canada 123
Crompton, Maurice 189
Cronjager, Henry 22
Cross of Fire, The 250, 278
Crowfoot 104, 106, 107
Crozier, Inspector Leif 152
Crucial Test, A 248
Cry from the Wilderness, A 247
Curtiz, Michael 16
Curwood, James Oliver 24, 26-29, 30, 44,
   52, 124-125, 127
Custer, General George Armstrong 107,
   108
Cyclone, The 121, *130,* 254
Cypress Hills, Saskatchewan 79
Cypress Hills Massacre of 1873 127, 185

Dalio, Marcel *59*
Dana, Viola *219*
Dancers, The 263
Danger Ahead 265
Danger Patrol, The 261
Danger Trail, The 252
Dangers of the Canadian Mounted 46, 121,
   270, 275
Dangerous Nan McGrew 111, *132, 217,* 227,
   263
Dangerous Trails 258
Darcy of the Northwest Mounted 250
Darkening Trail, The 251
Darling of the Mounted, The 248
Darnell, Linda 16, 189
Daughter of the Mines, A 247
Daughter of the Wilderness, A 249
Dawson City, Yukon Territory 45, 47, 77,
   83, 85, 142, *155,* 212, 213, 214
Days of Thrill and Adventure *quoted* 121
de la Roche, Mazo 19, 20
del Rio, Dolores 15
DeMille, Cecil B. 11, 16, 81, 98-99, 119,
   121, 146-152 *passim, 153,* 161-166 *passim,*
   175, 205, 208, 209, 275
Denison, Muriel 144
Devil Fox of the North, The 249
Devil's Brigade, The 228
Devil's Masterpiece, The 261
Devil's Partner, The 258, 278
Devil's Trail, The 254
Diamond Carlisle 256-257
Dionne, Elzire 25, 203

Dionne, Oliva 203, 235, 238
Dionne Quintuplets 25, 86, 203
Discoverers, The 247
Disney, Walt 236
Doctor Zhivago 41
Dog Justice 261
Dolan, Leo 177
Douglas, Sir James 208
Dove, Billie 15
Drifter, The 263
Driscoll, Bobby *59*
Duck Lake 150
Duck Lake Massacre 98, 150, 152, 162-163
Dumont, Gabriel 99-100
Duty First 257

Eddy, Nelson 16, 25, 32, *91*. 102, 119, 128, 137, 138, 139, 234
Edison Film Company 20-22, 124
Edmonton, Alberta 32, 45, 47, 143, 226
Ekland, Britt *quoted* 238
Elise, the Forester's Daughter 249
Elliott, C. Fraser 128
Empty Hands 258, 276-277
Empty Shell, The 248
End of the Trail, The 251
Eskimo (1933) 108, 137, 264
Eskimo people 31, 108, 236
Eternal Struggle, The 57, 83, 118, 123, 215, 258, 276, 277
Evangeline (1908) 247
Evangeline (1911) 248
Evangeline (1919) 254
Evangeline (1929) 262
External Affairs, Department of 170, 182, 187

Fabray, Nanette *quoted* 237
False Clues 130, 267
Famous Players Canadian Corporation 164, 169
Famous Players Film Service 124
Famous Players-Lasky Corporation 81
Fangs of the Arctic 46, 104, 268
Far Country, The 11, *37*, 80, 82-83, 207, 211-214, *220*, *221*, 235, 269
Farnum, Dustin 15
Fashion Madness 71, 261
Fathers of Men 251, 279
Fenton, Frank 181
Fidler, Jimmy 144
Fighting Guide, The 257
Fighting Mad 265
Fighting Strain, The 258

Fighting the Iroquois in Canada 247, 273
Fighting Trooper, The 264
Final Judgement, The 249
Find Your Man 113
First Nugget, The 249
Fitzgerald, F. J. 229
Fitzgibbons, J. J. 169, 170, 171, 172, 188
Five of a Kind 265
Flagstaff, Arizona 42
Flaherty, Robert 108
Flaming Forest, The 88, 104, 126, 260
Flash of an Emerald, The 251
Flower of the North 255
Flynn, Errol 16, 32, 54
For Another Woman 55, 258, 278
For Love of Service 257
For the Flag 104, 248
Foraging 248, 273
Foran, Dick 32, 41
Forbes, Ralph 128, *195*
Ford, John 16, 18, 42, 43, 208, 209
Forest Havoc 80, 260
Forest Rivals 254
Fort Carlton *153,* 205
Fort Chipewyan, N.W.T. 178
Fort Churchill, Manitoba 276
Fort McKay 178
Fort Macpherson, N.W.T. 53
Fort Saskatchewan, Alberta 31, 178, 179
Fort Simpson, N.W.T. 30, 275
Fort Smith, N.W.T. 47
Fort Vengeance 30, 107, 268
Fort Walsh, Saskatchewan 31
Fortymile, Yukon Territory 77, 142, 216
Forty-Ninth Parallel, The 31
Foster, Preston 133, 151
Fourth Estate, The 251
Fox Film Company 78, 211 *see also* 20th Century-Fox
Foxe, Earle *115*
Fraser River 44, 208
French, George 117
French, John 117
Freuchen, Peter 108
Friar, Ralph and Natasha *quoted* 87, *quoted* 101
Friml, Rudolph 128
From Out of the Big Snows 26, 250
Frontier Rangers 269
Frozen Justice 263
Frozen North 193

Gable, Clark 15, 30, 79, 150, 151, 216, 228, 276

Garson, Greer 16, 17
Garson, Stuart 182-183
Garwood, William *64*
Gaspard, the Wolf see *Man from Hell's River, The*
Gatling gun 11, 152, 161, 162, 166
Geary, Hon. G. R. 137
Gene Autry and the Mounties *60,* 178, 268
Gene of the Northland 250, 274
George Eastman House, Rochester, N.Y. 147
Get Your Man 255
Getting Her Man 258
Gibson, Hoot 15, 84, 206, *224*
Gilbert, John 15
Gilmour, Clyde 235
Gingold, Hermione *quoted* 238
Girl from God's Country, The (1921) 255
Girl from God's Country, The (1940) 265
Girl of the Northern Woods, The 215, 247
Girl Scout, The 247, 273
Gladish, William 232
Gleam o' Dawn 257
Glenister of the Mounted 260
Go Get Him 255
God, Man and Devil 251
God's Country and the Law 25, 84, 88, *92,* 104, 129, 226, 255
God's Country and the Man 265
God's Country and the Woman (1916) 29-30, 251
God's Country and the Woman (1937) 30, *39,* 80, 265, 275, 279
Goddard, Paulette 16, *95,* 98-99
Goin' Down the Road 236
Going of the White Swan, The 249
Gold Hunters, The 259
Golden Snare, The 52, 255
Gomez, Thomas *96,* 97
Good in the Worst of Us, The 249
Gordon, Reverend Charles see Connor, Ralph
Gordon, Donald 170, 172-175 *passim,* 204
Gordon Leon 188
Grady, William 137-138
Granger, Stewart 82, 85, *135,* 179, 228, 278
Grant, Kirby *200*
Gray, Deputy Commissioner C. K. 178
Great Unknown, The 249
Great White Trail, The 252
Greater Call, The 249
Greater Law, The 252
Greene, Graham *quoted* 46, *quoted* 53, *quoted* 113

Grennan, Inspector William 137
Grey Owl see Belaney, Archie
Griffin, Sergeant Major G. F. 151
Griffith, David Wark 16, 18, 77, 82, 87, 273
Group of Seven 42 see also Jackson, A. Y. and Thomson, Tom
Grub Stake, The 258
Guilty 257
Gulf of Georgia, British Columbia 21
Gunfighters of the Northwest 270
Gunga Din 16
Gwynne, Edmund 177

Hackett, Jeff 181 see also Hirshberg, Jack
Hale, Alan 85
Half Breed's Daughter, The 248
Halifax, Nova Scotia 76-77
Hall, James *132, 217*
Hampden, Walter 205
Hann G. T. 149, 151
Happy Time, The *59,* 85, 86, 111, 226, 268
Harmon, Francis 169, 170, 172, 173
Hart, William S. 15, 29, 32, 65, 80, 104, 113, 120, 225
Harvison, Commissioner Clifford 184-186
Hate Trail, The 257
Hawks, Howard 47
Hayes, Gabby 106, 207, 208
Hayworth, Rita 234
Hearst, William Randolph 127
Heart of Humanity, The 77, 86, 253, 275, 278
Heart of Sampson, The 250
Heart of the North, The (1921) *23,* 51, 255
Heart of the North, The (1938) 32, 41, 113, 115, 116, 143, 144, 265, 278, 287
Heart of the Wilds 253, 275
Hearts in Reunion see *Reunion*
Hearts of the Northland 249
Heeney, Arnold 182
Hegg, Eric A. *quoted 37, quoted 155,* 227
Helene of the North 251
Hendricks, David *218*
Henshaw, Don 177, 183, 186-191 *passim*
Her Fighting Chance 52, 252
Her Indian Mother 247
Her Nephews from Labrador 47, 249
Her Own Blood 250
Herman, Al 142
Hero of the Big Snows, A 260, 274
Hero of the North, The 249, 281
Herschel Island, Yukon Territory 118, 276
Hersholt, Jean 86
High Noon 16

Hirshberg, Jack 181-182 *see also* Hackett, Jeff
Hitchcock, Alfred 16, 86
Holt, Jack 15, 277
Holt, Nat 208, 209
Honor of the Mounted (1914) 249
Honor of the Mounted (1932) 263
Hoofbeats of Vengeance 261
Hostage of the North 250
Howard, Lieutenant Arthur L. 152
Howard, Marion *quoted* 29
Howe, C. D. 169-173
Hudson, Rochelle 234
Hudson, Rock 16, 30, *38*, 47, 48, 228, 275
Hudson Bay 32, 55, 104, 276
Hudson's Bay 57, 85, 101, 203, 275
Hudson's Bay Company 17, 75, 79, 80-81, 83, 101, 147, 188, 203, 232, 265
Hugon, the Mighty 253, 278, 280
Hussey, Ruth 62

I Am the Law 52, 257, 287
I Confess 86, 111, 268
I Conquer the Sea 264
Idaho (State) 42
Idol of the North, The 255-256
Igloo 263
In Defiance of the Law 249
In the Aisles of the Wild 248
In the Arctic Night 31, 248
In the Days of Famine 250
In the Government Service 248
In the Great Northwest 247
In the King's Service 250
In the Land of the Otter 249
In the North Woods 248
In the Northern Woods 248
In the Northland 249
In the Shadow of the Pines 54, 248
Incredible Journey, The 269
Indian Girl's Romance, The 247
Ingrate, The 247
Interdepartmental Committee for Information Abroad 182-183
Into the North 249
Into the Northland 250, 277, 280
Iron Curtain, The 267
Iron Horse, The 18, 208, 209, 211
Iroquois Indians 101
Island of Orleans, Quebec 22
Isobel, or the Trail's End 254, 287

Jack London 267
Jackson, A. Y. 41 *see also* Group of Seven

Jacqueline, or Blazing Barriers 258
Jacques of the Silver North 254, 280
Jacques, the Wolf 88, 249
Jalna (novel) 20
Jalna 20, 264
Jan of the Big Snows 24, 216, 257
Jasper Park, Alberta 22, 32, 41, 76
Jean of the Wilderness 249
Jeanne of the Woods 250
Jefferys, Charles *quoted* 166
Jennings, John *quoted* 100, *quoted* 105, *quoted* 206
Jest of God, A (novel) 20
Jogues, Father 203
Johnny Belinda 76, 146, 267, 275, 279
Johnson, Albert 53
Johnson, Erskine 144
Johnston, Eric 169, 171, 181, 183
Jones, Buck *130, 136, 200,* 225
Jordan is a Hard Road *131,* 251
Jory, Victor 107, *157,* 207
Jourdan, Louis *59*
Jowett, Garth S. *quoted* 205
Jules of the Stronghart 63, 253, 280, 287
Jury of Fate, The 252
Justice, Department of 182-183
Justice in the Far North 247

Kalem Company 22, 25, 112, 124, 203, 273
Kamouraska 236
Karr, Jack *quoted* 165, *quoted* 235
Kaszner, Kurt *59*
Kazan 256
Keaton, Buster *193*
Keel, Howard 32, 138
Kelly, Mary *quoted* 75
Kelly, Paul 234
Kennedy, Burt 184, 185
King, W. L. Mackenzie 31
King of the Mounties 270
King of the Royal Mounted (1936) 264
King of the Royal Mounted (1940) 141, 270
King Spruce 254
King's Man, The 249
Kivalina of the Ice Lands 108, 259
Klondike 45, 46, 119, 228
Klondike 263
Klondike Annie 46, 113, 264
Klondike Days 47
Klondike Fury 266
Klondike Gold Rush 11, 20, *37, 119,* 142, 146, *155,* 211-214 *passim,* 215-216, 228, 235, 276
Klondike Kate *198,* 216, 267, 287

Klondike Steal, A 248
Knockout, The 80, 259
Knowlton, Keith 181

Labrador 47, 53, 85, 108
Lac La Biche, Alberta 178, 179
Ladd, Alan 16, 31, 36, 105, 107, 184
Lady of the Snows, The 250
Lake Louise, Alberta 171, 275
Lake Tahoe, California 32, 42
Lamas, Fernando 82, 138
Land of Long Shadows, The 252
Land of Promise 252
Land of the Silver Fox 261
Lane that Had No Turning, The 257
Larkin, Charles quoted 112, quoted 113
Lash, G. H. 163
Last of His People, The 254
Laurence, Margaret 20
Laurentian Mountains 171, 275
Laurentian Shield 42
Laurier, Sir Wilfred 231
Law of the Great Northwest, The 81, 253
Law of the Mounted 262
Law of the North, The (1912) 248, 274
Law of the North, The (1917) 54, 81, 97, 120,
    123, 216, 252, 279
Law of the North, The (1918) 70, 253
Law of the North (1932) 263
Law of the Northwest 267
Law of the Snow Country 260
Law of the Yukon, The 254-255
Law or Loyalty 260
Law's Lash, The 226, 262
Lawrence of Arabia 16
Leacock, Stephen 19
Leap for Life, A 247, 274
Lejeune, C. A. quoted 213
Lemmon, Jack quoted 237
Leroy, Mervyn 16
Leslie, Gladys 92
Lest We Forget 137
Lewis, Mitchell 59
Lewis, Ray quoted 233
Lewis, Sinclair 275
Library of Congress, Washington, D.C. 82
Life's Greatest Question 256
Litchfield, Earl of quoted 238
Little Big Horn 107
Little Station Agent, The 247
Little Wild Girl, The 262, 278, 279
Lives of a Bengal Lancer, The 16
Lodge in the Wilderness, The 260
Lone Patrol, The 262

Lonely Trail, The 257
Long, Ray quoted 27
Longfellow, Henry Wadsworth 29
Long Trail, The 252
Lord Strathcona Horse 273
Losee, Frank 115
Lost in the Arctic 108, 248
Lost Missile, The 269
Louisa 177
Love, Montagu 86
Love Happy 177
Love Master, The 50, 51, 257, 277
Love of Pierre Larose, The 249
Love's Wilderness 258
Lovely, Louise 23
Loy, Myrna 16, 199
Lugosi, Bela 16
Lure of Heart's Desire, The 103, 251
Lure of the Wild, The 55, 259, 280
Lure of the Windigo, The 249
Lure of the Yukon, The 249
Lying Lips 256
Lyon, Ben 15

MacBrien, Sir James 127, 128, 137-138,
    139, 141, 142, 146
McCann, J. J. 170, 174
McClellan, George B. 184-186
McCrea, Joel 151, 209
MacDonald, Jeannette 16, 91, 97, 102, 119,
    127-128, 234
MacDonald, Margaret quoted 279
McDonnell, G. L. 125-126
McGuire of the Mounted 258
McKenna of the Mounted 130, 136, 200, 225,
    263
MacKenzie, J. Alex 164
MacKenzie M. W. 173
Mackenzie River 30, 32, 42, 44, 47, 143,
    275
McLaglen, Victor 15
MacLane, Barton 80
MacLaren Advertising Agency 177
McLean, Ross 170, 173-175
MacNeil, Inspector R. S. 183-184

M-G-M see Metro-Goldwyn-Mayer
Mad Trapper of Rat River see Johnson,
    Albert
Magnificent Brute, The 256
Maine (State) 20, 42
Mala the Magnificent see Eskimo
Man Between, The 258
Man from Glengarry, The (novel) 19

Man from God's Country, The 30
Man from Hell's River, The 257
Man from Montreal, The 265
Man in the Moonlight, The 77, 123, 254, 280
Man in the Peace Tower 189
Man She Brought Back, The 115, 116, 257
Man Trackers, The 112, 256
Man Trail, The 251
Man Who Dared, The 249
Man Who Died, The 250, 274
Man Who Paid, The 257
Man Worthwhile, The 256
Man's Law, A 252
Man's Law and God's 112, 257
Man's Size 258
Manitoba 20, 32, 46, 79, 210, 275
Mantrap 35, 261, 275
Maple Leaf Forever, The (song) 41
Marsh, Mae 15
Marx Brothers 177-178
Mason of the Mounted 263
Mayer, Louis B. 127, 128, 137-138
Maynard, Ken 15, 122
Measure of a Man, The 78, 250
Men of the North 64, 77, 82, 97, 122, 132,
    263, 279
Métis 11, 86-101 passim, 105, 126, 152,
    161-166, 175, 210
Metro-Golwyn-Mayer 108, 125-128 passim,
    137-139, 142, 145, 178-182 passim 188,
    278
Midwinter Madness 51, 250
Milland, Ray 16, 55
Miller, Doris 115
Milligan, M. A. 147, 148
Mills, Taylor 177, 188
Mints of Hell, The 254
Mission of Danger 269
Mrs. Mike 267
Mix, Tom 15, 43, 48, 81, 130, 120, 121, 228
Modern Dianas, The 248
Mon Oncle Antoine 236
Monogram Pictures 46, 173, 176, 177, 189,
    227
Montana (State) 25, 30
Montcalm, Louis Joseph, Marquis de 203
Monte Carlo Saloon, Dawson City 155
Montgomery, L. M. 19, 20
Montgomery, Robert 15, 53, 199
Montreal 19, 20, 41, 42, 44, 45, 53, 86, 227,
    275
Monument Valley, Utah/Arizona 42
Moodie, J. D. 229
Moody, Ron quoted 238

Moore, Colleen 15
Moore, Matt 196
Moore, Victor 217
Moran of the Mounted 261
More than His Duty 247
Morgan Dennis 16
Morgan, Frank 217
Moriarty R. C. 163
Morriss, Frank quoted 165
Morton of the Mounted 265-266
Motion Picture Association of
    America 169-191 passim
Motion Picture Distributor and Exhibitors
    Association 137
Mount Baker, Washington State 142
Mount Shasta, California 42
Mounted Fury 263, 274
Muni, Paul 16, 17, 57, 82, 85
Murder on the Yukon 70, 266
Muskie, Edmund 228
Mutiny in the Arctic 266
My Dad 257
My Six Convicts 190

Naish, J. Carroll 58, 69, 85, 91, 97, 106, 107,
    209
Nan of the North 270
Nanook of the North 17, 108
National Council of Jewish Women quoted
    30
National Education Association,
    U.S.A. 166
National Film Archives, Ottawa 76
National Film Board 11, 170, 171, 174-175,
    187, 188-189, 237
National Parks 103
'Neath Canadian Skies 199, 206, 267
Neeka of the Northlands see Girl from God's
    Country, The
Neighbour to the North 173
Neill, A. W. 126
Nelson Touch, The see Corvette K-225
New York City 55
New York State 56
New York Confidential 191
Newman, Archibald 175-180 passim, 186
Niagara 268
Niagara Falls 266
Nichols, George 279
Nicholson, Commissioner L. H. 182-183,
    184
Nikki, Wild Dog of the North 269
Nine-Tenths of the Law 253, 278
Nobody's Wife 253

Nomads of the North 27, 84, 119, 255, 277, 279
Nome, Alaska 46, 47, 113
North Bay, Ontario 45
North Country Romance, A 249
North of 53 (1912) 248
North of 53 (1914) 249
North of 53 (1917) 252
North of Hudson Bay 43, 81, 83, 111, 258, 275, 279
North of the Border 220-221, 267
North of the Great Divide 268
North of the Yukon see North of Hudson Bay
North of the Yukon (1939) 83, 265
North Star 260
North to the Klondike 266
North West Company 147
North West Mounted Police 11, 93, 95, 97, 98-99, 119, 121, 133, 146-152 passim, 153, 161-166 passim, 205, 234, 266, 275
North West Rebellion see Saskatchewan Rebellion of 1885
Northern Code, The 78, 215, 216, 260, 280
Northern Frontier 264
Northern Hearts (1912) 248
Northern Hearts (1913) 117, 249
Northern Patrol 268
Northern Pursuit 32, 54, 97, 146, 226, 267, 275
Northwest Rangers 145, 154, 228, 266
Northwest Stampede 267
Northwest Territories 47, 101, 105, 227
Northwest Territory 84, 268
Northwest Trail 266
Nova Scotia 55, 76-77, 99, 189
Novak, Jane 49

Oath of Pierre, The 64, 249
O'Brien, Eugene 130
O'Brien, George 118
Odyssey of the North, An 251
Of Mice and Men 162
O'Garry of the Royal Mounted 250, 279
Ojibway Indians 103
Okanagan Valley, Brittish Columbia 32
Old Code, The (1915) 216, 250
Old Code, The (1928) 262
O'Malley of the Mounted (1921) 32, 113, 120, 256
O'Malley of the Mounted (1936) 264
O'Malley Rides Alone 262
On the Great White Trail 265
One Day 248, 280
One Man Dog, The 262

One Way Trail, The 255
Only Good Indian, The (non-fiction) quoted 87
Ontario 17, 86, 100, 111
Open Places 252
Operation Manhunt 269
Opium Smugglers, The 248
Oregon Territory 208
Orr, William 138
Ottawa, Ontario 86, 137, 142, 150, 226
Out of the Arctic 248
Out of the Night 249, 280
Out of the Silent North 257
Out of the Snows 51, 255
Outpost of the Mounties 265
Over the Border 50, 52, 257
Owen, Myrtle 94-95
Owen, Reginald 199
Owensmith, Colonel Blake W. 180-181, 182, 183, 188, 189-191
Owosso, Michigan 26

Pack of Cards, A 83, 249
Paid in Advance 53, 97, 216, 254
Pajamas 261, 273
Panther, The 250
Papineau, Louis Joseph 203-204
Paramount Pictures 121, 147, 148, 150, 151, 163-166 passim, 204
Parsons, Louella quoted 88, quoted 127
Passing of the Beast, The 250
Pearson, Lester B. 170, 182-183
Peck, Ray 126, 127, 138
Peculiar Nature of the White Man's Burden, The 248
Pedley, Constable A. 178-182 passim
People Will Talk 190
Perils of the Royal Mounted 104, 270
Perils of the Wilderness 270
Perry, Commissioner A. Bowen 124
Perversity of Fate, The 248
Peters, House 134
Petticoat Fever 53, 199, 264
Phantom of the Forest 261
Phantom Patrol 265
Philip Steele 248, 277
Piapot 106
Pidgeon, Walter 17
Pierre of the North (1913) 88, 249
Pierre of the North (1914) 250
Pierre of the Plains (1914) 31, 88, 251
Pierre of the Plains (1942) 31, 62, 82, 85, 222, 225, 266, 279
Pine, William 148, 149, 150, 164

Pine-Thomas Productions 188
Pines of Lory, The 250
Pistol Harvest 190
Place Beyond the Winds, The 251, 278
Plains of Abraham 233
Playthings of Desire 258
Playthings of Destiny 256
Pony Soldier 32, *34, 69, 96,* 97, 104, 105, 116, 268
Poundmaker 152
Powell, Dick 16
Power, Tyrone 16, 32, *96,* 105, 116
Preminger, Otto 16, 85
Price of a Silver Fox, The 248
Priest and the Man, The 249
Priest of the Wilderness, A 247
Primal Lure, The 63, 65, 104, 252
Primitive Strain, The 250
Prince Albert, Saskatchewan 31
Prince Edward Island 20
Prisoner of the Pines 253, 280
Prisoners of the Storm 117, 261
Pure Gold Partner, A 250

Quaint Quebec 173
Qualen, John 86, 203
Quebec, Province of 32, 41, 53, 79, 85-86, 101, 102, 128, 233, 235
Quebec 83, 203-204, 235, 268
Quebec City 86, 233
Queen of the Northwoods 270
Queen of the Yukon 266

RCMP Band 151
RKO 176-177
Rachel, Rachel 20
Radisson, Pierre 17, 85
Raiders, The 256
Randall, Tony *quoted* 237
Ranger of the North 261
Rankin Inlet, Hudson Bay 276
Rathbone, Basil 86
Rebellion of 1837 203-204, 235
Recoil, The 256
Red Ace, The 270
Red Blood of Courage, The 264
Red Riders of Canada 90, 262
Red River Rebellion 1869-70 88, 126-127, 149
Red Skies of Montana 190
Regina, Saskatchewan 125, 148, 149, 164
Regina Board of Trade 164
Rejected Woman, The 258

Renfrew of the Royal Mounted 97, 120, 121, *130,* 142, 265
Republic Studios 142, 178
Reunion 264
Rex the Wonder Horse 16
Richardson, C. H. 183
Riders of the North 263
Riders of the Northwest Mounted 267
Riders of the Plains 248
Riel, Louis 88, 152, 161-166 *passim*
Riel Rebellion *see* Red River Rebellion 1869-70
  Saskatchewan Rebellion of 1885
Right of Way, The (1915) 251
Right of Way, The (1920) 255
Right of Way, The (1931) 263
Rin-Tin-Tin 16, 113
River's End (1920) *135,* 255
River's End (1930) 113, 120, 225, 263, 275-276
River's End (1940) 266
Roach, Hal 17
Roberts, Beverly *39*
Rocky Mountains 17, 19, 21, 31, 41, 42, 80, 85, 102, 106, 128, 148, 161, 171, 210, 225, 232, 275, 276, 278
Rogers, Roy 15
Rogue with a Heart, The 250
Roland, Gilbert *64,* 77, 82, 85, *132*
Romance in the Fur Country, A 88, 247, 281
Romance of the Canadian Wilds, A 87, 249
Romance of the Northwest, A 226, 250
Roosevelt, Theodore 122, 225
Rose Marie (1928, un-released version) 62, 128, *195*
Rose-Marie (1928) 60, 83, 119, 128, *134,* 262
Rose Marie (1936) 16, 25, 32, 42, *66, 91,* 97, 102, 119, 127-128, 137-139, 142, 184, 234, 264
Rose Marie (1954) 32, *67,* 119, 138-139, 227, 269
Rose of the West 78, 254
Rosenberg, Aaron 183, 184
Rossman, Earl 108
Rough Romance 263
Royal Journey 189
Royal Mounted Patrol 266
Royal Mounted Rides Again, The 46, 270
Rubber Heels 261
Ryan, Robert *133*

Saint and the Siwash, The 248
St. Laurent 99-100, 152
St. Laurent, Louis 176

St. Lawrence River 22, 44
St. Lawrence Valley 25, 75, 77, 275
Salisbury, Monroe 87, *89*, 280
San Fernando Valley, California 42, 48
Sandow the Strong Man 16
Saskatchewan, Province of 31, 32, 44, 105, 183, 184, 206, 275
Saskatchewan 16, 31, *36, 58,* 105, 107-108, 183-184, 269, 275
Saskatchewan Rebellion of 1885 11, 98, 100, 105, 149, 152, 161-166 *passim,* 175
Saskatchewan River 42, 44, 100, 152
Saturday Island 189
Savage, Ann *198*
Savage, The 87, *89,* 252, 278
Savage Innocents, The 108
Scandal at Scourie 17, 111, 268
Scarlet and Gold 260
Scarlet Claw, The 86, 267
Schary, Doré 188
Scott, Randolph 11, 16, *68,* 80, 104, 106-107, 175, 176, *197,* 207, 208, 209, *219,* 227
Scott, Thomas 127
Seattle, Washington 30, 211
Selig Company 203
Selkirk, Lord 203
Sennett, Mack 17
Sergeant Byrne of the NWMP 248, 277
Sergeant Preston of the Yukon (TV series) 191
Service, Robert W. 19, 20, 45, 47
Sewell, C. S. *quoted* 117
Shadows of the North 258
Shakespeare, William 204
Shane 16
Shanty at Trembling Hill, The 250
Shearer, Norma 277
Sheridan, Ann 16
Sherlock Holmes film series 86
Ship of Souls 260
Ship's Husband, The 248
Shooting of Dan McGrew, The (1915) 251, 279
Shooting of Dan McGrew, The (1924) 45, 258
Sidney, L. K. 188
Sign of the Wolf 266
Silent Enemy 263
Silent Jim 56, 88, 112, 248
Silent Lie, The 252
Silent Vow, The 112, 257
Silent Woman, The 253
Silent Years 75, 256
Sin that was His, The 255
Sin Unpardonable, The 215, 248
Sioux Indians 102, 107, 108, 185
Sitting Bull 107, 108, 185, 229

Skagway, Alaska 83, 211, 212, 214
Skouras, Spyros P. 172
Sky Bandits 266
Sky Pilot, The (novel) 19
Sky Pilot, The 218, 225, 256, 278
Skyfire 256
Slander the Woman 40, *58, 71,* 258, 278
Smith, Capt. Jefferson Randolph (Soapy) 212, 215
Smoke Bellew 262
Smuggler's Daughter, The 249
Snow Bride, The 258
Snow Capers 171
Snow Dog 268
Snowbird, The 56, 82, 252
Snowblind 51, 256
Son of the Forests (Curwood's autobiography) 27
Sons of the Northwoods 249, 279, 280
Song that Reached His Heart, The 248
Soul of the Beast 54, *61,* 258
South of Northern Lights 257, 277
Spell of the Yukon, The (poem) 45
Springtime in the Rockies 266
Square Dance Kate 176
Stagecoach 16
Stanley, Forrest *134*
Starnes, Commissioner Cortland 125-126, 127
Steele, Supt. Samuel Benfield 229
Steele of the Royal Mounted 125, 260
Stewart, James 11, 16, 80, 119, 189, 211, 212, 213, *220, 221*
Stewart, Roy *23*
Sting of Conscience, The 250, 276
Stolen Claim, The 248
Stolen Cub, The 249
Stone, Lewis 15, 119, *135*
Storm, The (1922) 257, 277
Storm, The (1930) *196,* 262, 277
Storm Breaker, The 260
Stranded in Arcady 252
Strathmore, Alberta 21-22
Strength of Men, The 82, 249
Strongheart 50, 277
Sturges, Preston 47
Summerville, Slim 86
Superior Law, The 249
Susannah: A Little Girl with the Mounties (novel) 144
Susannah of the Mounties 17, *68,* 104, 105, 106, 107, 139, 144-145, 265, 275
Swiss Guide, The 248

Talbot, Lyle 234

Tale of the Northwest Mounted, A 250
Tamiroff, Akim *93*, 161, 239
Tangled Trails 256
Tanks are Coming, The 190
Tattoed Stranger, The 176-177
Taylor, Matthew A. *quoted* 81, *quoted* 116
Taylor, Zachary 146
Temple, Shirley 16, 17, 104, 105
Test of Donald Norton, The 261
Texas Rangers 162
Thalberg, Irving 142
That Devil, Bateese 253, 279
Thirteenth Letter, The 85, 268, 279
This is Dynamite 190-191
Thomson, Tom 41 *see also* Group of Seven
Thompson, W. S. 163
Three Brothers 248
Three Secrets 191
Thurston, Carol *158*
Tidden, Fritz *quoted* 84
Tides of Fate 252
Tides of Passion 260
Tiger Rose (1923) *134*, 258-259
Tiger Rose (1929) *33*, 83, 263, 279
Todd, Ann *quoted* 238
Tooker, William *92*
Toronto, Ontario 45
Torrence, Ernest *35*
Tracked in the Snow Country 260
Trade and Commerce, Department
    of 169-191 *passim*
Tragedy of the Northwoods, A 250
Trail of '98, The (novel) 20
Trail of '98, The 128, 227, 262
Trail of the Mounties 267
Trail of the Royal Mounted 270
Trail of the Silver Fox, The 103, 249
Trail of the Upper Yukon, The 250
Trail of the Wild Wolf, The 250
Trail of the Yukon 267
Trail of Vengeance, The 258
Trails of the Wild 264
Trailing North 264
Trans Siberian Railway 41
Translation of a Savage, The (1913) 249
Translation of a Savage, The (1920) *see Behold
    My Wife*
Trap, The 78, 83, 84, 257
Trapped 264
Trapper's Daughter, The 248
Trapper's Revenge, The 97, 250
Treacher, Arthur *quoted* 238
Treasure of the Sierra Madre, The 16
Trevor, Claire 16

Trooper O'Neil 257
Truckee, California 19, 42
Trudeau, Pierre Elliott 139, 204
True to His Trust 104, 248
Tweedsmuir, Lord *157*
20th Century-Fox 32, 45, 79, 139, 144, 172,
    184-185 *see also* Fox Film Company
Two Men 249
Tyrant Fear 53, 124, 253

Ulric, Lenore *134*
Under Northern Lights 51, 255
Under Northern Skies 247
Under Suspicion 263
Union Pacific 16, 18, 208, 209
Universal 31, 46, 51, 171, 189
University of Toronto 188
Unseeing Eyes 103, 258, 281
Unseen Enemy 266
Unselfish Love, An 21-22, 248
Untamed 55, 266, 279
Until They Get Me 114, 116, 120, 252
Up and Going 257

Valley of Doubt, The 75, 255, 277, 287
Valley of Hunted Men, The 267
Valley of Lost Souls, The 258
Valley of Silent Men, The 124-125, 257
Valli, Virginia *196*
Van Dyke, W. S. 16, 108, 137
Van Horne, William Cornelius 209, 210
Vancouver, British Columbia 30, 45, 137,
    138, 276
Vancouver Island, British Columbia 188
Velez, Lupe 15, 83
Victoria, British Columbia 20, 234
Victoria, Queen 108
Vidal, Gore *quoted* 237
Vidor, King 16
Viking, The 263
Virgin's Sacrifice, A 258
Vitagraph Company of America 31, 125,
    203, 273
Vixen 236, 269
Voyager, The 248

Wallace, Edgar 27
Walsh, James Morrow 108, 229
Walsh, Raoul 16
Walter Wanger Productions 188
Walthall, Henry B. 275
Wanderers, The 250
Warner Brothers 76, 113, 115, 143, 226,
    228

Warner, H. B. 15
Washington (State) 275
Way of the Eskimo, The 108, 248
Weakness of Strength, The 252
Wedding Trip from Montreal through Canada to Hong Kong, A 248
Wedman, Les *quoted* 214
Weechume Lake 178
Wellman, William 16
West, Mae 46, 113
When God Wills 250
When the Door Opened 260, 277
Where the North Begins (1923) 82, *94-95*, 258, 279
Where the North Begins (1947) 267
Where the North Holds Sway 261
Whiskey Runners, The 249
White Dawn, The 108, 236, 269
White Hell 83, 103, 258
White Man's Money, the Indian Curse 248
White Mouse, The 250
White Scar, The 251
Whitehorse, Yukon Territory 45
Whittaker, Herbert *quoted* 235
Wild Bunch, The 16
Wild North, The 72, 82, 123, *135, 158,* 178-182, *223,* 226, 268, 278
Wild Sumac 252-253, 280, 287
Wildcat Trooper 122, 265
Wilderness, The 262
Wilderness Mail, The (1914) 250
Wilderness Mail (1935) *222,* 264
Wilderness Trail, The 215, 254, 279
Wilson, Carey 188
Wilson, Clifford *quoted* 101, 147
Wilson, Margery *63*
Winchell, Walter 144
Winds of Chance 219, 260
Winners of the Wilderness 261
Winnipeg, Manitoba 45, 75, 147, 226, 276
Winters, Laska *71*
Winters, Shelley 16, 105, 107
Wise Fool, A 256
Wolf, The (1914) 251, 278
Wolf, The (1919) 254, 279
Wolf Call 265
Wolf Hunters, The (1926) 117-118, 261
Wolf Hunters, The (1949) 267
Wolf Man, The 259
Wolf Pack 258
Wolf Song 262
Wolf's Fangs, The 258
Wolfe, General James 22, 203, 233
Wolfe, or the Conquest of Quebec 251

Wolves of the North (1921) 51, 256
Wolves of the North (1924) 270
Woman Conquers, The 258
Woman Obsessed 79, 269
Woman of Redemption, A 253, 277, 287
Woman's Faith, A 260
Woman's Law 261
Woman's Way, A 77, 82, 247, 273
Women of Tomorrow 176
Wood, Commissioner Samuel Taylor 139, 140, 144, 146, 148-151 *passim,* 163, 164, 180-182, 184
Wood, Zachary Taylor 146
World in His Arms, The 189
Wright, Basil *quoted* 98
Wright, Virginia *quoted* 161-163
Wyler, William 16
Wyman, Jane 76
Wynn, Ed 15
Wyoming (State) 126, 211

Yellowback, The 223, 262
Yellowstone National Park, Wyoming 42, 275
Yosemite National Park, California 32, *33,* 42
Young, Loretta 16, 216
Young, Roly *quoted* 165
Young, Waldemar 127
Yukon Flight 266
Yukon Gold 268
Yukon Manhunt 46, 84, *200,* 268
Yukon River 42, 44, 45, 78, 214
Yukon Territory 41, 45, 46, 48, 78, 79, 118, 142, 207, 211-214 *passim,* 216, 227, 228, 235, 276
Yukon Vengeance 46, 84, 101-102, *158,* 269